ARCHAEOLOGY HOTSPOT GREAT BRITAIN

Archaeology Hotspots: Unearthing the Past for Armchair Archaeologists

Series Editor: Paul G. Bahn, independent archaeologist and author of *The Archaeology of Hollywood* (pgbahn@anlabyrd.karoo.co.uk)

Archaeology Hotspots are countries and regions with particularly deep pasts, stretching from the depths of prehistory to more recent layers of recorded history. Written by archaeological experts for everyday readers, the books in the series offer engaging explorations of one particular country or region as seen through an archaeological lens. Each individual title provides a chronological overview of the area in question, covers the most interesting and significant archaeological finds in that area, and profiles the major personalities involved in those discoveries, both past and present. The authors cover controversies and scandals, current digs and recent insights, contextualizing the material remains of the past within a broad view of the area's present existence. The result is an illuminating look at the history, culture, national heritage, and current events of specific countries and regions—specific hotspots of archaeology.

Archaeology Hotspot Egypt: Unearthing the Past for Armchair Archaeologists, by Julian Heath (2015)

Archaeology Hotspot Great Britain: Unearthing the Past for Armchair Archaeologists, by Donald Henson (2015)

ARCHAEOLOGY HOTSPOT GREAT BRITAIN

Unearthing the Past for Armchair Archaeologists

Donald Henson

ROWMAN & LITTLEFIELD

Lanham • Boulder • New York • London

Published by Rowman & Littlefield
4501 Forbes Boulevard, Suite 200, Lanham, Maryland 20706
www.rowman.com

Unit A, Whitacre Mews, 26-34 Stannary Street, London SE11 4AB, United Kingdom

British Library Cataloguing in Publication Information Available

Library of Congress Cataloging-in-Publication Data Available

ISBN 978-0-7591-2396-0 (cloth : alk. paper) — ISBN 978-0-7591-2397-7 (electronic)

♾TM The paper used in this publication meets the minimum requirements of American National Standard for Information Sciences—Permanence of Paper for Printed Library Materials, ANSI/NISO Z39.48-1992.

Printed in the United States of America

CONTENTS

1

INTRODUCTION

This book is a description of the archaeology of Great Britain. It covers not only some of the major archaeological sites, but also some of its archaeological personalities and debates. Archaeology reveals a great deal about people's lives and about the great changes that have occurred since the island was first settled nearly one million years ago. For those not familiar with British archaeology, there is much that will fascinate. For those who already know something about the island and its past, there will be much that will be new to discover.

We must begin with a word about names. This book covers the archaeology of Great Britain. Strictly speaking, Great Britain does not exist as a nation. It is part of the United Kingdom of Great Britain and Northern Ireland. Northern Ireland is not covered in this book. Its archaeology is shared with the Republic of Ireland and has little in common with that of the rest of the United Kingdom. The three parts of Great Britain are England, Scotland, and Wales, each of which had their own origins in the earlier Medieval period. England conquered the Principality of Wales in 1283, and absorbed it fully within England in 1536. In 1603, King James VI of Scotland succeeded to the Kingdom of England as King James I. His combined kingdoms were informally known as Great Britain, but were not united under one government and parliament until 1707. It ceased to exist as a nation in 1801 when it merged with Ireland into the United Kingdom

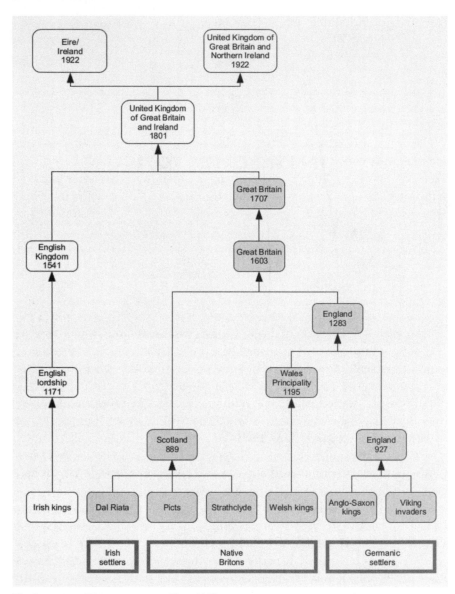

The formation of Britain, courtesy of Donald Henson

(southern Ireland became an independent nation in 1922). Today, both Scotland and Wales have their own parliaments and governments handling internal affairs underneath the parliament of the United Kingdom. England has no parliament of its own. It is governed directly by the government and parliament of the United Kingdom.

Why *Great* Britain? Is this a symptom of pride, or a claim to status? No. The name Great Britain was first used by the ancient Greek geographer Ptolemy in 140 AD to describe the bigger of the two main islands in what were already called the British Isles. Ptolemy described the smaller of the two (Ireland) as Little Britain. Most people now use the simple term Britain as a geographical term to describe the island and reserve Great Britain to describe the political union of England, Scotland, and Wales.

The fact that Great Britain is divided between three governments and parliaments is important for how archaeology is practiced in its three parts. There are now legal differences between how archaeology is carried out and in the laws and organizations governing the heritage of each of the three nations. However, Britain as an island has a long history and prehistory shared between the three nations before their creation in Medieval times.

The most important features that define British history and prehistory are its long-time depth of human settlement, its geography, and the diversity of the ways of life and cultures of its people. Britain has a history of continuous settlement since the last Ice Age, and of sporadic settlement by early hominins long before this (at least 800,000 years). Its landscape is littered with the remains of deep time, with later remains superimposed upon earlier. It takes a skilled eye to be able to disentangle this long history in which a village may contain buildings of the seventeenth to the twentieth centuries and have nineteenth century fields created on top of early Medieval fields and lying below uplands with traces of late Iron Age and Roman period settlements and fields. No part of Britain is free of the imprint of man, even the natural landscapes are not as they appear.

As an island, Britain has a long coastline with many navigable rivers. Most of Britain has easy access to the coast and the movement of people and goods is possible over long distances by ship and boat within easy sailing distance along the Atlantic coast, across the Channel and the North Sea. It is also close to Ireland and was once physically joined to the continent and still lies close to the rest of Europe. Britain has always been open to foreign migration and settlement, able to trade widely with the rest of Europe and absorb foreign influences, albeit sometimes under protest. The English Channel and North Sea also act as a moat effectively defending Britain against all but the most determined of invasions. Compared with most other lands, Britain has been only seldom affected by conquest.

The mainland of Britain is 600 miles long from Land's End in the south to John O'Groats in the north. To the southwest lie the Isles of Scilly and to the north the Orkney and Shetland Islands. Its greatest width is 330 miles from Cornwall in the southwest to Kent in the southeast. The island is cut by major rivers and estuaries. The Clyde and the Forth neatly divide

A multi-period landscape and village at Kettlewell in the Yorkshire Dales, photo courtesy of Donald Henson

Scotland into north and south. The Rivers Tweed, Tyne, and Tees shape the south of Scotland and the northeast of England. The major rivers of Yorkshire feed into the estuary of the River Humber that separates northern England from the south. The River Severn rises in Wales and flows in a long loop into the Severn estuary, separating south Wales from southwest England. The River Thames flows west from London to form the northern border of the ancient kingdom of Wessex.

The geography of Britain is extremely varied in its underlying geology and its landscapes, ranging from flat low-lying wetlands and rolling hills to high bleak moorland and mountain ranges. One thing that archaeologists constantly find frustrating is the designation and management of spaces as "natural." Britain is a much altered and highly managed island. There are hardly any (and some would say no) truly natural wilderness areas in Britain. A fundamental division of Britain throughout its history has been between the highland northwest and the lowland southeast. The soils are more fertile in the southeast, but also dryer and more suitable for growing crops. The northeast is wetter and produces better grazing for animals.

To look at Britain's landscape is to be aware of time. Some settlements have been in the same place going back to Roman times or even beyond. One hillside can bear traces of successive field systems and of exploiting the land over 3,000 years. Some churches have been the site of Christian worship, and graveyards the site of burial, for more than a thousand years. This sense of continuity is deeply reassuring and helps to anchor people with a strong sense of place and identity. Buildings in historic towns and villages may bear the traces of many successive styles of architecture, offering a variety to the built landscape that newly designed estates and suburbs can only envy. Yet the old has never stood in the way of the new. Each generation leaves it mark, and conserving the past while embracing progress is one of the central concerns of modern archaeology in Britain.

The role of archaeology in uncovering this deep progression of time can be illustrated by the Shapwick Project of 1989 to 1999. This was one of the most important archaeological projects of recent years, led by Mick Aston of Bristol University and Chris Gerrard of Durham University. It was an ambitious program of work to explore the settlement history of one whole parish five square miles in size. The project was not limited to professional archaeologists, but was open to anyone who wanted to take part. The local community was fully consulted and involved, and two thousand people were part of the project over the years. Over 250,000 artifacts were recovered, and a range of research methods were used and tested for their effectiveness, such as analyzing the botanical composition of hedgerows. The parish was once owned by Glastonbury Abbey and there is a wealth of documentary evidence to use alongside the archaeology. As well as excavation, a major source of evidence was field-walking, the systematic identification of artifacts on the surface of plowed fields. This was able to produce a picture of how the land was used over time, as well as finding new settlements. The results show a long continuity of activity during prehistory, leading up to as many as ten separate occupation sites during the Roman period. Only half of these survived into the fifth century, and by the early Medieval period there were four farmsteads in the parish. These were deliberately brought together into one village with a separate mill and church, surrounded by planned open fields. This may have been done by the reforming efforts of Dunstan, Abbot of Glastonbury, in the 940s. Similar reorganizations of the land happened elsewhere in England during the early Medieval period and were the origin of the modern English landscape.

Britain's situation off the northwest coast of Europe places it in the path of the Gulf Stream and warm waters from across the Atlantic that today keep its climate mild and well supplied with both rain and sun. This has not always been so. The climate has switched repeatedly since the last Ice Age between long episodes that were warm and dry to ones that were cool and wet. Also, Britain was not always an island and was joined across a dry North Sea to the continent until around 6500 BC. Strong regional differences within Britain become visible after this and continued into historical times. In the Medieval period, we see the origins of England, Scotland, and Wales as separate nations, creating their own specific cultural identities. Even within these, strong regional differences remained and national consciousness often had to struggle against local loyalties (and often still does).

The most prosperous part of Britain today is the southeast, centered on London. This has not always been so. Even recently, the heartlands of the industrial revolution lay to the north and west: in south Wales, the English Midlands, northern England, and the central belt of Scotland. For much of the Medieval period, the east of England was an economic powerhouse with its ability to grow abundant crops and its access across the North Sea to European markets. Two areas far apart became the political centers around which England and Scotland would be created: Wessex in the south and Argyll in the far northwest. It was also Wessex, centered on Stonehenge, in which the most spectacular sites and wealthiest burials of the Early Bronze Age lay (see chapter 8), while spectacular Late Neolithic finds come from Orkney in the north. The importance of the Orkney Islands off the northernmost tip of Britain in the Late Neolithic can only be understood when we see their location as pivotal for maritime contact with both the south of Britain and with Ireland. Likewise, the short-lived Viking Kingdom of York linked Viking Dublin with the homelands in Scandinavia across the Irish Sea and North Sea.

The population of Britain has constantly been topped up by immigration from the rest of Europe. The full picture of migration since the end of the Ice Age is not yet established but it is clear from modern DNA studies that the basic population of Britain was established very early and never replaced, merely added to in varying amounts by later waves of settlers. Some will have arrived peacefully, others through conquest. At some point the Celtic language family was brought to Britain, possibly during the Bronze Age. In the Iron Age, there is evidence for movement at least of kings and aristocrats between Britain and Gaul. The Roman conquest then opened Britain to visitation and settlement from the rest of the Empire. Post-Roman Britain was a major time of migration with Scots coming across from Ireland and Germanic peoples coming from across the North Sea from today's Denmark, north Germany, and the Netherlands. Viking settlers overlaid this some 400 years later and then Frenchmen led a final conquest of England from Normandy in 1066. During the Medieval period there is documentary evidence for settlement by Flemings and French protestant Huguenots among others. In more modern times, the Empire opened Britain to settlement by peoples from the West Indies, China, and the Indian subcontinent. Most recently, Britain's position in the European Union has brought a range of people from the continent to enrich its culture; some temporarily for work, but some to stay. Yet, in spite of this constant flux of peoples, the culture of Britain has a large degree of continuity and distinctiveness. Britain is not a melting pot but has a core which new people cluster around, merge into, and enrich. Discontinuities through conquest or large-scale migration are rare. The creation of Anglo-Saxon culture out of a mix of conquest and migration of Germanic groups and adaptation by native Britons is one of the more obvious discontinuities. Whether the stark change from the Early Bronze Age to the Late Bronze Age around 1500 BC or the adoption of Beaker culture after 2500 BC are other examples is subject to debate. Farther back, the adoption of farming and Neolithic culture around 4000 BC is now looking likely to be a mix of migration and adaptation. None of this alters the evidence for a strong genetic continuity of the British population.

The book is not a history of Britain. It will not be a narrative of events or dates. However, some understanding of the flow of events and major developments is necessary to make sense of its archaeology. Britain's journey through time will be explored in more detail in chapters 2 and 3, which will look at the different periods of Britain's past through the eyes of an archaeologist. This involves looking at technology and material culture, how Britons got their food, their economy, the nature of their society and politics, and the religious practices and beliefs of the people. These have all left archaeological traces for us to find, of different kinds and in different degrees of survival. Chapters 4 and 5 will give a short account of some of the most important or most characteristic sites and finds from prehistoric and then historic times.

This is a deeply personal book by someone who has excavated and surveyed a small part of its archaeological heritage and visited a few of its many sites and monuments. Its archaeological remains are numerous and have many good stories to tell. All that can be done in a book like this is to skim the surface and give a flavor of the riches of Britain's historic environment and the archaeological research that has taken place. A representative sample of different kinds of sites has been chosen from each period, and an attempt made to cover the whole of Britain in roughly equal measure. This is not easy, as various parts of Britain have undergone greater archaeological

Book section	Period	Date BP	Date BC/AD	Characteristics
Industrial advance and the modern world	Modern	190	1760 AD	World Wars, growth and loss of Empire, world power, industrial revolution
Reformation and revolution	Early Modern	429	1521 AD	union of England and Scotland, parliamentary monarchy, Civil Wars, Protestant Reformation
Medieval monarchies	Medieval	1085	865 AD	feudalism, Black Death, English conquest of Wales, creation of England and Scotland
Migrations and kingdoms	Migration	1540	410 AD	Viking attacks, Christianity, Anglo-Saxon and Irish conquests, native British kings
Roman interlude	Roman	1907	43 AD	Roman conquest, villas, pottery industry, growth of towns, roads, standing army
Farms, forts and kings	Iron Age	2750	800 BC	coinage, oppida, emporia, growth of kingdoms, hill forts, increasing population, iron
	Late Bronze Age	3350	1450 BC	hill top sites, flat cemeteries, field boundaries, fortification, bronze widespread
Ritual and hierarchy	Early Bronze Age	4100	2150 BC	rich graves, cremations, upland farming, bronze, fine flintwork, late henges and circles
	Late Neolithic	5150	3200 BC	inhumation burials, copper, Beakers, henges, stone circles, passage graves, Grooved Ware
First farmers	Early Neolithic	6000	4050 BC	farming, tombs, flint mines, stone quarries, pottery, enclosures, new flint tools
Hunter-gather utopia	Late Mesolithic	9850	7900 BC	oak, alder, elm woodland, Britain an island, woodland management, shell middens
	Early Mesolithic	11600	9650 BC	birch, pine, hazel woodland, hunting and gathering, lake and riverside sites, microlithic tools
Ice Age colonisers	Late Upper Palaeolithic	15750	13800 BC	resettlement by hunting groups from across Doggerland following horse and reindeer

Timeline of Britain since the Ice Age, courtesy of Donald Henson

research than others over the last 300 years. There are many monuments which have a historical importance but have been little investigated archaeologically. For example, the site of the Battle of Bannockburn is a key monument to Scotland's successful struggle for independence from England in the fourteenth century. Yet, its archaeology is very poorly known, even

The author excavating in the Yorkshire Dales, photo courtesy of Donald Henson

the exact location of the fighting has still to be found. In contrast, the site of the Battle of Bosworth, which resulted in one English royal dynasty being replaced by another, has received a great deal of archaeological attention, resulting in its accurate identification for the first time, and the recovery of the body of the king who was killed in the battle. I have therefore included Bosworth at the expense of the arguably more significant Bannockburn. All Britain's cultural World Heritage Sites have been included, but there are many more sites just as spectacular and a few additional sites are listed in less detail to round out the coverage. Chapter 6 gives details of the lives and work of some of the key figures of British archaeology. The history of British archaeology cannot be understood only through the lives of its key figures however. Archaeology is often controversial and the history of some of its major controversies is given in chapter 7. Current and recent research is discovering yet more about Britain's past, and pushing the boundaries of our knowledge into new areas and extending what we thought we knew about even familiar sites. Some of this work is covered in chapter 8.

The importance of Britain's landscape and island situation in shaping its human settlement over time means that we cannot understand its history without knowing its geography. Archaeologists in Britain have built their subject on the pioneering work not only of historians but also of historical geographers and British universities treat archaeology as a separate subject in its own right not as part of anthropology. British archaeologists have played a leading role in the development of archaeological theory world-wide. Archaeology within Britain is a thrilling, challenging, and stimulating subject to study and practice, and many who practice it seem to revel in challenging orthodoxy, championing different ways of seeing the past as a virtue in itself.

2

LONG-SETTLED ISLANDS

Britain has a long and varied history. Most of its past is prehistoric; that is, without any written documents and revealed only through archaeology. This archaeological record is rich and full of interesting sites. There are large, fascinating, and mysterious monuments, and beautiful, skillfully made artifacts. New discoveries are still being made, revealing new aspects of prehistoric life and pushing back the date of the earliest settlement of Britain into a very remote past.

Ancestors of modern humans are known as hominins and evolved in Africa and began making stone tools around 2,500,000 years ago. By 1.8 million years ago, hominins had moved out of Africa into Asia and Europe. These early migrants were of the species *Homo erectus*. This evolved through *Homo antecessor* and *Homo heidelbergensis* into *Homo neanderthalensis* in Europe, which became extinct by 32,000 years ago. *Homo sapiens* evolved in Africa around 200,000 years ago and moved into Europe from 46,000 years ago. The earliest hominin settlement of Britain dates back at least 850,000 years. Stone tools and other evidence of that date has been found at Happisburgh (pronounced Hazeborough) in Norfolk. The environment in Britain over these 900,000 years has fluctuated between warm (sometimes warmer than modern times) and very cold (at times with ice sheets spreading south to cover much of Britain). During cold periods, the level of the sea may be low enough for Britain to be joined to the continent. The British Isles would then be a British peninsula and a hominin could walk from Wales eastwards across dry land all the way to Siberia. Only when Britain was warm enough and connected to the continent would hominins be able to settle in Britain. Finds from such times include stone tools from Pakefield in Suffolk from around 700,000 years ago, and a "human" shin-bone along with stone tools and butchered animal bones at Boxgrove in Sussex from 500,000 years ago. The earliest evidence from Britain for our own species, *Homo sapiens*, comes from the earliest deliberate human burial in these islands of a young male at Paviland in south Wales, dated to 33,000 years ago.

ICE AGE COLONIZERS (13,800 TO 9650 BC)

The last full ice age in Britain was at its height from 32,000 to 16,000 years ago. Only the south of Britain was free of ice, but was a cold wasteland, much like northern Siberia today. The reoccupation of Britain could only begin once the climate began to grow warmer, allowing animals to return and humans who hunted the animals. These early hunting groups would have lived in a harsh and still cold environment, following herds of game and living in temporary camps. The ice sheets locked up masses of water, lowering world sea levels. What we now identify as Britain, France, Germany, Denmark, and so forth. were part of one connected landmass across a low-lying plain (now the North Sea).

The return of life to this far northwestern corner of Europe by people of the Magdalenian culture hunting herds of reindeer and horse happened around 15,800 years ago as the climate began to warm. Settlement was not yet permanent. Humans had to retreat from Britain during a return of severe cold conditions before finally coming back for good after around 12,000 years ago. These phases of settlement in Britain are described together as the Late Upper Paleolithic (Paleolithic = Old Stone Age).

Traces of human settlement are easier to find, and better survive, in caves, but a lot of settlement will have been in shelters built out in the open. The earliest evidence of people coming back to Britain as the ice sheets were retreating is from Gough's Cave, at Cheddar Gorge in Somerset. Finds from this site are of butchered animal remains: mostly horse and deer. The most important finds are fragments of human bone. These show signs of cut marks from stone tools. Five human skulls had been purposefully defleshed and shaped to make skull-cups. Why this was done we can only guess. It may be part of cannibalism, of religious practices as part of treating the dead, or simple recycling of valuable raw material.

One important open-air settlement at Hengistbury Head in Dorset lies on a hill top overlooking a river valley, a perfect spot for watching out for herds of game animals. People most likely lived in small family groups, bonded together in larger bands which might come together at certain times of year and then disperse at others. They left behind only their stone and bone or antler tools. Their clothing, leather, birch bark or wooden tools, baskets and so forth. do not survive. What survives tells us that they were part of similar cultures that covered most of northwestern Europe. Britain is used to thinking of itself as somehow apart from the rest of Europe and it is common to refer to finds of this period in Britain as belonging to the Creswellian culture. It is perhaps wiser to use the European labels and admit that Britain was part of wider human activity in northwestern Europe at this time. The three phases of human culture we identify are:

- Phase 1: the Magdalenian culture, 13,800 BC, in which the hunting of herds of horses was a major activity and caves were used as major sites (this is the last period when mammoth is found in Britain);
- Phase 2: the Federmesser culture, 11,470 BC, when people were hunting mostly deer and sea mammals, and open settlements were more important;
- Phase 3: the Ahrensburgian culture, from around 10,130 BC, when horse and reindeer were the major animals being hunted on a seasonal basis by groups who lived mostly to the east.

Late Upper Paleolithic sites are rare in Britain, and mostly survive best in caves.

Paleolithic cave sites at Creswell Crags, photo courtesy of Donald Henson

HUNTER-GATHERER UTOPIA (9650 TO 4050 BC)

Climate change at the end of the Ice Age was rapid. Around 9650 BC, average summer temperature rose by as much as 10° C within one human lifetime. New forests of birch and pine grew and were in turn replaced after 7300 BC by hazel and elm, and then also oak and alder. The people living at this time are described as Mesolithic (Mesolithic = Middle Stone Age). Those of the Early Mesolithic were part of a northern European culture known as the Maglemosian.

The only archaeological finds from this period are stone tools and faint traces of wooden houses. There are no great monuments, no cemeteries, nor villages. On the other hand, climate was at its warmest and it was easy for people to live off a land with abundant animals, plants, and sea food. The traditional view is that people would have come together to live in larger settlements in the lowlands in winter, while splitting into smaller groups for hunting in the uplands during summer. This may be too simple a picture. Some groups may well have settled in small territories by lakes, rivers, and on the coast, or permanently in one place, especially where food could be found all year round.

The flooding of the North Sea plain (now known as Doggerland, see chapter 8) cut Britain off from the rest of the continent about 6500 BC. The climate continued to get warmer to a peak around 6000 BC when temperatures were warmer than today. Evidence has been found recently for one traumatic event at this time: a major tsunami or tidal wave at 6150 BC. The wave was up to twenty feet high and reached far inland, caused by a submarine landslide off the coast of Norway. It flooded 350 miles of coastline in northern Britain and must have severely affected people living in that area.

A few human burials have been found from the period. The most famous and important is a set of human remains from the cave of Aveline's Hole in Somerset. At least twenty-one bodies and possibly more than seventy were buried here between 8350 and 8150 BC, with seashell beads and animal tooth pendants. This is the only known Mesolithic cemetery in Britain. The oldest complete skeleton to be found in Britain is a burial from Gough's Cave, also in Somerset, dating to circa 8350 BC. Various sets of Mesolithic footprints have been found in sands and muds off the modern coastline, at places like Formby (north of Liverpool) and Goldcliff, off the coast of south Wales, which were made at 5500 BC and include the footprints of children.

Early Mesolithic stone tools are mostly triangular shaped blades of flint called microliths. There are also stone axe-heads, scrapers, awls or borers, and engraving tools for working bone and antler. Barbed bone and antler points were used in hunting. We rarely find the wooden tools, nor the baskets, leather, and plant fibers, they must have used as these too easily rot away. One rare find was a dugout canoe excavated at Friarton in Perthshire. Around 7800 BC, the microliths became dramatically smaller and were of a wider variety of geometric shapes. This marks the beginning of the Late Mesolithic, when Britain began to develop its own cultural traditions apart from the continent. Microliths would be slotted into a wooden, bone, or antler haft. The technology was ideally suited to a mobile hunting way of life, being light and easy to make and maintain.

Animals hunted include elk, red deer, roe deer, aurochs, and boar. Fish (from both the sea and rivers), shellfish like whelks, mussels, cockles, limpets, and crabs, and wildfowl were also eaten. Some people think that later Mesolithic people may have herded animals, or at least provided them with food such as ivy. There is evidence for domestic dogs being kept, which could have helped in hunting or herding animals. The commonest plant find is hazelnut, found charred from roasting and in very large quantities. Woodlands may have been managed by burning to create open spaces to attract game animals and promote hazel growth. Settlements seem to have been small with only a few circular houses. The house at Howick was lived in for at least one hundred years and was around twenty feet across in size. Well-made floors have been found on some sites, often of laid stone slabs, or sometimes of birch bark. Coastal settlements are often revealed by their shell middens.

We know little about the religious beliefs or ceremonies of these Mesolithic peoples. There are twenty-one sets of red deer headdresses from Star Carr. These are antlers with a part of the skull attached that had been pierced with two holes for attaching them by leather thongs, presumably to a human head. Their purpose remains a mystery but they could be a hunting disguise, or have been used in rituals or ceremonies. At Culverwell in Dorset, people deposited a flint axe-head, a perforated sea shell, and a round pebble in small pit and then placed a stone on top to seal it. Why, we can only guess. A tantalizing glimpse of religious belief may be seen at the much later site of Stonehenge. Underneath the modern car park at the site, there are four or five Mesolithic pits, three of which seem to have held large upright posts. The purpose of these, and whether they formed part of a larger structure, are unknown. A more recent find is of an alignment of twelve posts at Warren Field at Crathes in northern Britain. It has been suggested that these were used to determine the time of year by using the midwinter sunrise on the horizon and the phases of the moon.

We have to guess at the social and political organization of this time. If Mesolithic people were like more modern hunter-gather groups (and this is an untested assumption that may be more wishful thinking than reality), then they would have lived in small nuclear families, joined together into bands. Families would have been centered on the adult males to enable successful group hunting of larger prey. Loose authority would have been exercised by the elders and by powerful social customs. Religious belief would have been through links with the spirit world. Women would have gathered much of the plant foods and probably contributed most of the food supply on a daily basis in spite of the virile posturing of the male hunters!

FIRST FARMERS (4050 TO 3250 BC)

Farming by planting crops and keeping livestock was the most important development in human history. It developed in the Middle East around 8000 BC. People could now control their environment, produce a surplus of food, and support a more complex society. Farming arrived in Britain around 4000 BC with the Neolithic, a very different culture to that of the Mesolithic.

The Neolithic gave Britain a very rich heritage of different kinds of sites and building on a large scale. There was also a richer set of artifacts with pottery as well as stone and other tools. The Neolithic saw a complete change in technology, economy, society, and religious belief. The Neolithic way of life may have been brought over from the continent by new settlers through the Thames estuary but seems to have been eagerly adopted by most of the native inhabitants in a very short period of time. It had spread to the far north of Britain by 3800 BC.

Bones show that men at this time averaged 5 feet 7 inches in height, and women around 5 feet 3 inches. While they could live well past fifty years of age, many had arthritis and bad teeth. Evidence of broken limbs was not uncommon. It is certain that many more people were living in Neolithic Britain compared to the Mesolithic, but we cannot reliably say how many.

New types of stone tools included leaf-shaped arrowheads, knives, serrated blades, sickles, and stone querns for grinding grain. Axe-heads were now ground smooth. Flint was mined from the soft chalk of the southeast, while outcrops of rock were quarried in the northwest for making stone axe-heads. Trade with the continent is seen in imported jadeite axe-heads from the Alps and other axe-heads from Scandinavia.

Evidence for farming comes from finds of bones of domestic cattle, sheep or goats, and pigs, and remains of wheat, barley, flax, and possibly peas and beans. Marks in the soil left by an ard, a simple kind of plough, have been found. Wild plants such as hazelnuts and crab apples were still gathered, as were shellfish. Wild animals were still also hunted. Some archaeologists think that people in the Early Neolithic may have made temporary clearings in the woodland, farmed them for a short while, and then moved on to a new clearing rather than settling in one place permanently. Others see these early farmers as staying in one place and laying claim to permanent farmland. Houses were mostly rectangular wooden longhouses with a door in at least one short side and usually facing roughly southwest. They can be up to 90 feet by 40 feet in size, and usually occur on their own, but sometimes belong with others inside an enclosure. One such enclosure at Carn Brea in Cornwall was ten acres in size. The largest houses might have held more than thirty people, the smallest perhaps an extended family of less than ten.

Large causewayed enclosures are characteristic of the Early Neolithic, found mostly in the south and east. They usually had from one to four concentric, often incomplete rings of ditches outside banks with timber palisades, surrounding a central area of up to twenty-five acres (exceptionally up to 120 acres at Hambledon Hill). Archaeologists cannot yet agree on what they were. They have been interpreted as places for seasonal feasting and exchange of goods by a tribe, for keeping cattle, as defended settlements, and as places for funerals. Many enclosures have offerings placed in the ditches, including human remains. A large number of arrows at Crickley Hill and two skeletons at Hambledon Hill with arrows embedded in their bodies suggest that some of them were attacked.

While there are some simple burials in pits in open ground, part of the community ended up being commemorated in large, elaborate tombs in a way similar to other peoples on the Atlantic coasts of Europe. There is a great deal of variation in the types of these large tombs across Britain but they all involved a communal effort to bury a group of people rather than individuals, and often after the bodies had been defleshed and reduced to separate bones elsewhere. Some body parts, for example skulls, were often deposited elsewhere rather than the tombs. Among the most important types of tomb are long barrows, long earthen mounds containing either stone or wooden chambers. Similar tombs in stone are called chambered tombs or long cairns. These were up to 400 feet long and 20 feet high, and could contain up to fifty bodies, as stacks of defleshed and disarticulated bones. Feasting and other ceremonies took place outside the tombs. Large round barrows could be built over mortuary houses: wooden chambers where the dead were either cremated or defleshed. Portal dolmens are single chambers under a very large roof slab supported by strong single upright stones. They have more large upright slabs on one side defining an open porch. These are especially common in the west of Britain, and have a lot in common with similar tombs in Ireland.

Perhaps the most enigmatic of all British archaeological sites is the cursus, unique to Britain and Ireland. They are long, linear spaces defined by parallel banks and ditches or post holes along the sides and enclosed at the ends. They vary from 190 yards up to 6 miles long, and 70 to 400 feet wide. Many were aligned northeast to southwest (sunset) or northwest to southeast (sunrise) and could be connected to burial sites. They may have been used for processions associated with burial. One interpretation is that they provided a passageway for the souls of the dead (a suggestion that is impossible to prove). They may have been similar to bank barrows, long barrows without burials which may also have been used for religious or ceremonial processions.

The dead were rarely buried with grave goods. Instead the dead were venerated by feasting and ceremony outside the front of the tomb. Burying the dead in communal tombs was a way of venerating their forebears and claiming their protection. These ancestors would help to lay claim to territory and bind the clan or tribe together and to the land. Warfare between different groups seems to have been common. Analogy with other kinds of simple farming societies is hazardous, but the Early Neolithic may have been a segmentary tribal society, organized by ancestral clans into larger tribal units. In some cases, for example, among the historical Iroquois or Huron of the northeastern woodlands of North America, membership of the clan was inherited through the mother and women assumed a position of some importance. As yet, we have no evidence from Britain to help us understand how families were organized in the Early Neolithic.

RITUAL AND HIERARCHY (3250 TO 1450 BC)

The Late Neolithic began around 3250 BC and has more in common with the Early Bronze Age. Longhouses are no longer built, there are no more long barrows or chambered tombs, causewayed enclosures or cursuses, and the pottery is no longer only simple bowls. Instead, this period is dominated by evidence for religious practice, wealth, and social hierarchy.

The skulls of Neolithic people tend to be narrow, while Early Bronze Age skulls tend to be broader. This may or may not be evidence of new people settling in Britain alongside the native population. Burials on the continent show a change in the population at this time. One study on a British burial near Stonehenge from 2300 BC showed that he had been a child in the northern Alps on the continent.

New types of stone arrowheads, knives, and axe-heads appear, along with battle-axes, axe-hammers, and mace-heads. Gold and copper were used from around 2700 BC. Copper was soon alloyed with arsenic and then tin to make bronze axe-heads, knives, and awls from around 2200 BC. The other new technologies of this period may have been horse riding and wheeled vehicles, certainly available on the continent.

Tools could now be made with great craftsmanship. The finest of all stone tools were made in the Early Bronze Age, especially the beautiful flint daggers. These kinds of tools would signify position in society, as would personal adornment through shale and amber necklaces, hair adornments, earrings, rings, and so forth. Traditional pottery developed into highly decorated Peterborough wares. Grooved ware buckets and tubs began in northern Scotland and later spread south. Beakers were a radically different pottery style, associated with new styles of housing and artifacts across northwestern Europe. They were introduced to Britain around 2500 BC. Other, later styles of pottery were the Collared Urns and elaborate food vessels.

Raw materials for making stone tools were now traded widely across Britain from sites like the flint mines at Grimes Graves or the stone quarries at Great Langdale. The earliest copper axe-heads and most of the gold had

Neolithic stone quarry at Pike of Stickle, Great Langdale, photo courtesy of Donald Henson

come from Ireland, but copper was soon also mined in Britain and tin was available from river deposits in Cornwall. Britain and Ireland both shared passage grave burials and a common art style is found in these graves and on Grooved Ware pots. This first art style in Britain is mostly abstract, made of straight lines, diamonds, chevrons, circles, and spirals. Trade with the continent is revealed by wrecks such as the Dover boat around 1550 BC.

Woodland was increasingly being cleared for farmland after 2500 BC and the uplands were being heavily farmed for the first time. Woolly instead of hairy sheep were bred, allowing woven fabrics to be made. Farmers escorted livestock to upland pastures using standing stones and outcrops of rock art as markers of routeways and claims to land. Salt was being made from seawater after 1850 BC. Salt would keep large herds of cattle healthy and salted beef and fish could be stored for longer. Houses and settlements are still hard to find but sometimes spectacular, such as Skara Brae in Orkney. Late Neolithic houses were not longhouses but were squarish, oval, or roughly circular often around four meters across. Settlements with Beakers were single farmsteads with mostly oval shaped houses.

Late Neolithic burials could be in passage graves, with squarish chambers at the end of a stone passage within rectangular, square, or round mounds. They could hold hundreds of bodies and were tombs for the whole community. In the north of modern England, important people were buried as individuals with grave goods under large round barrows. Elsewhere, people were buried individually in graves or cremated and placed in pits, either in the countryside or at ceremonial, religious sites. Early Bronze Age Beaker burials were made singly in graves, usually placed underneath a low round mound. The bodies would face south with men on their left side and head to the east and women lying on their right side and head to the west. More than 30,000 of these round barrows once existed, in cemeteries of up to forty barrows. Burials had grave goods like fine Beaker pots, European copper axes, knives, awls, and pins, gold ornaments, stone archery wristguards, and native artifacts like flint daggers, stone battle-axes, arrowheads, jet and amber jewelry. Later burials were cremations in pits, bags, or pots in flat cemeteries, with Collared Urns and food vessels. Some burials might have been placed in rivers. In the far north and the southwest, traditional passage graves continued and Beaker culture does not seem to have had much of an impact.

The most characteristic sites of this period are circular or horseshoe arrangements of pits, wooden posts, or large upright stones. Sites surrounded by a circular bank and ditch are known as henges, and may also have these wooden or stone circles inside. Some henges are very large enclosures, marked by a boundary bank and ditch or by a wooden palisade wall. The most spectacular and perhaps the most important was Stonehenge in Wilt-shire, used from 2950 BC until 1520 BC, and aligned for ceremonies at midwinter sunset, and linked to the henge enclosure at Durrington Walls where there were midwinter feasts (see chapter 8 for more about Stone-henge). Avenues marked by banks, posts, or stones would act as proces-sional ways into the henges. Some settings of stones have clear alignments on the rising and setting of the sun at midsummer or midwinter, while other settings seem to have acted as a way of measuring the passage of time, like a large open air calendar. A concern for the ancestors had been replaced by an interest in charting the arrival of the different seasons of the year. A belief in gods and goddesses may be reflected in the rare finding of wooden idols preserved in wet sediments that date from around 2500 BC onwards. However, not all monuments followed the sun. A set of recumbent stone circles in the far northeast near Aberdeen have a flat-lying stone in the southwest of the circle which seems to be aligned on the motion of the moon. These sites date to the period after 2000 BC but reflect Late Neo-lithic traditions in having cup-marks engraved on some of the stones. They may form a local resistance to Beaker culture.

Society was now very unequal, with a strong hierarchy, organized through male-based family networks. Men were buried with weapons, tended to be richer, and were usually the primary burial within a barrow or cemetery. Few burials had metal or large numbers of grave goods. We do not know whether the big-men or chiefs had to establish their status as individuals or whether they could inherit authority from their family. Some henges were centers for communities or "chiefs" to meet from some distance away. The three henges at Thornborough in north Yorkshire had artifacts made of ma-terials from 30 miles to the east, 65 miles to the northwest and 90 miles to the south. Some animals found at Stonehenge seem to have come from the far north, possibly Orkney. The Orkney Islands themselves used art styles and pottery that were also used in Ireland and the south of Britain. The central part of southern Britain, Wessex, had a particularly high concentra-tion of wealthy burials and elaborate sites during this period, with links to the continent.

FARMS, FORTS, AND KINGS (1450 BC TO 43 AD)

The Late Bronze Age marks a major change. We move from a period where we know a lot about how people died and worshiped to one where we know more about field systems and settlements. There were strong links with the continent and Britain was part of a common northwest European culture, although with its own special differences. This was most likely the time when the Celtic languages were first spoken in Britain. Language scholars suggest that the characteristic features of Celtic languages had developed by 1350 BC. Descendants of these languages are still spoken as Modern Welsh in Wales and Cornish in the southwest of Britain. Greek writers in the sixth century BC referred to Britain as *Albión*, possibly meaning "our land" in the Celtic British language. By the second century BC, a different name was being used: *Britannia* in Latin, possibly a description of the natives as the "decorated ones."

Most tools were now made of metal not stone. New weapons appeared such as spears, swords, and body armor, and there were large cauldrons of sheet bronze for cooking over an open fire. Iron was being worked as early as 950 BC, but would not replace most bronze objects until around 600 BC, with new objects such as brooches and better woodworking tools. Small plank-built sailing ships could now be made allowing more adventurous trade across the seas. There is definite evidence for horse riding and wheeled vehicles like wagons or carts and chariots. Lathes were used to make wooden and shale artifacts, and there were rotary querns and iron-tipped ploughshares. Gold and silver were still used, especially for the spectacular neck rings or torcs, made of twisted wire resembling rope. Pottery developed distinctive regional styles, possibly reflecting new tribal identities. However, by the late Iron Age, pottery was mostly made only in the southeast, where potter's wheel had been adopted.

The highest land that had been farmed in the Early Bronze Age was abandoned after 1200 BC as climate worsened and soils became poorer. The uplands in the north and west tended to be wetter with soils more suited to livestock farming where wealth would lie in cattle and horses. The lowlands in the south and east were warmer and drier, more suited to growing wheat and barley (with peas, beans, flax, and hemp) alongside flocks of sheep. New field systems allowed the land to be farmed better, with crop rotations and manuring of fields, and grain was now stored in large quantities. More salt was being produced on the Cheshire Plain, the west midlands, and the southeast coast. Gold coins from Gaul came to Britain from around 150 BC and the Britons in the southeast began to mint their own coins from around 100 BC. These carry inscriptions identifying kings of various southeastern tribes. By the end of the Iron Age, these southeastern elites were in contact with Roman trade networks across the Channel, importing wine, olive oil, and tablewares. Roman writers mention exports from Britain of slaves, corn, cattle, hides, hunting dogs, gold, and silver. Other exports were tin, copper, lead, shale, salt.

The most obvious settlements of the time were the hillforts surrounded by an earthen bank and ditch, and wooden palisade. Some hillforts were large enclosures for protecting livestock, while others were defended villages housing hundreds of people. Most people lived in either smaller defended farmsteads (known as rounds, raths, or duns in the west of Britain) or open farms, hamlets, and small villages. There are also crannogs, lake dwellings with houses built onto platforms and linked to the land by a narrow causeway. In the far north, there are both stone-built wheelhouses, where the inside is divided into chambers like the spokes of a wheel, and late Iron Age brochs, large towers with thick, hollow walls with staircases. Towards the end of the Iron Age, there were large settlements in the southeast known as oppida with zones defined by banks and ditches as centers for trade, for elite residence, and for industrial manufacturing, minting of coins, with wealthy cemeteries, and streets with houses. Most houses in this period were circular roundhouses, up to fifty feet across, with doorways pointing east or southeast to catch the morning sun. The space within the house was often zoned; the northern side for sleeping, the southeast

Recreated Iron Age round house at the Ancient Technology Centre, Cranborne, photo courtesy of Donald Henson

for cooking, and the southwest for working. Some houses had souterrains, underground stone or wooden passages leading to small chambers, which may be for storage of food. More enigmatic are the burnt mounds, elongated heaps of burnt stones, often with a pit or trough. They may be sites of feasting where barbecues were held, or a kind of sauna or sweat lodge.

Late Bronze Age people cremated their dead, placing the ashes in urns in the ground in flat cemeteries. Over time cemeteries were replaced by burying people in rivers, scattering the ashes, or defleshing bodies in the open. Only in a few parts of Britain do formal burials reappear. The eastern Yorkshire Arras tradition after 400 BC placed bodies in graves under a small barrow, surrounded by a square ditch. Some of these were accompanied in the grave by a chariot. In the southeast from 150 BC, the Aylesford tradition placed cremations in graves with grave goods to do with food, drink, and gaming. Both traditions are similar to burials in northern Gaul. A few burials elsewhere are found in graves or stone-lined chambers (cists) and in pits on settlements or under the floors of houses.

Iron Age art belonged to a common style developed across parts of central western Europe that is often called Celtic art, although not made by all the peoples who spoke Celtic languages. This is based on curvilinear abstract designs with some animal or human figures, the use of symmetry, and the placing of blocks of color within the linear designs. It survives best in metalwork with inlay of colored glass or enamel. The biggest art object is surely the Uffington White Horse in Oxfordshire, nearly 350 feet long and carved in the chalk hillside in the Late Bronze Age or early Iron Age.

Religion focused on depositing artifacts in rivers, lakes, and bogs, possibly with cremations. Some tools were made especially for deposition as votive offerings to the gods. A lot of offerings were left in rivers that flowed south or east (roughly flowing toward the rising sun). By around 100 BC, there are square or rectangular shrines with deposits of brooches and coins. Some enclosures surround a sacred grove, pool, or spring which later Roman evidence suggests would be dedicated to a particular goddess. Other evidence of religious beliefs may be the heads that are found on sites of the Iron Age: both stone carved and real.

Power and wealth no longer came from controlling religious practices tied to the seasons. Society was now led by a warrior aristocracy whose wealth came from control of farmland and trade. By the time that Roman writers describe Britain for the first time at the end of the Iron Age, the island was divided into sizable kingdoms or tribal federations. Roman writers, including Julius Caesar, referred to the Britons as using a blue woad body paint, having long hair and moustaches, being tall redheads in the north and dark-haired in the west. We also now know the first named individuals in British history, such as Cassivellaunus who led British tribal resistance to Caesar in 55 BC. Britain was on the verge of becoming part of the historical world we know from classical Roman writers. Britain would never be the same again as it became part of the Roman Empire, its way of life and its culture changed forever, its prehistory forgotten or transformed into myth and legend. Britain's transformation will be outlined in the next chapter.

3

TWO THOUSAND YEARS OF HISTORY

Julius Caesar twice crossed the Channel with his Roman legions in 55 and 54 BC. These only penetrated the southeast of Britain and were an attempt to neutralize British support for opposition to Roman rule in Gaul across the Channel. They introduced Britain directly to the Roman world and left a feeling at Rome of unfinished business. From now onward, we can use both historical documents and archaeological evidence to reveal Britain's story (Britain's past was no longer prehistoric). Where the documents tell us about the lives of the wealthy and powerful, the archaeology can often reveal details of the daily lives of all levels of society. It is also from the last 2,000 years that physical remains begin to survive in large numbers in stone and brick, and often still in use rather than as ruins. Archaeology becomes the study of lived-in historic environments, of landscapes and of buildings as much as of excavated sites.

ROMAN INTERLUDE (43 TO 410 AD)

The Roman conquest of Britain began in 43 AD and Roman rule lasted until 410. The conquest took its time. By 83, the Romans had reached the Gask frontier in modern Scotland. This was not permanent and the frontier would move back to the Antonine Wall, and then finally settle at Hadrian's Wall between the Tyne and Solway. The Romans called their enemies in the north the Picts, those in Ireland they called the Scots, and those from across the North Sea they called Saxons. By the fourth century, the south-eastern coast (the Saxon Shore) was defended by a string of forts, while watchtowers and inland forts defended the north and west against the Picts and Scots. The south and east of Britain were the most heavily Romanized, with towns, villas, and other aspects of Roman civilization. The north and west were more military with the army placed among and recruiting from the local population. Outside Roman Britain, in the far north, traditional Iron Age culture continued.

Roman rule brought a huge increase in the use of metal, glass, and pottery, including oil lamps, the *mortarium*, for grinding herbs and sauces, flagons for pouring wine, and *amphorae* for storing up to twenty gallons of wine, olive oil, or fish sauce. Glossy red Samian Ware imported from Gaul was the commonest tableware, replaced around 230 by British potteries, such as black burnished wares. Orange-red bricks and tiles were used as part of buildings and for roofs.

Bronze was widely used for jewelry and dress fittings, such as the bow brooch, like a big safety pin. Various brooches included enameled flat ones in the shape of people or animals. Iron Age penannular brooches (a pin with a ring attached) lasted into the early Roman period, and were revived again in the fourth century. There were rings and bracelets in bronze, gold, silver, glass, jet, and shale; wire earrings; bronze, bone, and jet pins; and belts with decorated bronze buckles and other fittings. British silverware was particularly fine. There were large-scale iron works in places like the Weald and the Forest of Dean. Britain was also mined and quarried for gold, lead, silver, copper, tin, and iron.

The Romans brought many innovations to the economy, such as growing new crops like grapes and cucumber, and herbs like dill and coriander. There was an increase in cattle at the expense of sheep. New technologies included the water mill, a better design of plough to turn the soil, threshing tools, and corn-drying ovens. Roman coins are abundant finds from the period, used for paying the army and officials, and for taxation. These were usually minted abroad. The only mints in Britain were in Colchester in the 290s and London from 290 to 325.

The Roman army was based at first on the legion, the equivalent of a modern army brigade of around 5,000 men, and one each was based in Caerleon, Chester, and York. Smaller units like cohorts or numeri (about the size of a small battalion) were based in forts elsewhere. Forts of all kinds had a rectangular shape with rounded corners and regular grids of internal buildings such as barracks and storehouses. At first they would be built in wood and later replaced in stone. The army built a major road network, much of which is still the basis for modern major routeways, although transport by river and coastal seas was often quicker and safer. There is one Roman canal, the Foss Dyke, built to connect Lincoln with the River Trent.

Many modern British towns owe their origins to the Roman period, although some were based on existing Iron Age settlements. The provincial capital was at first Colchester and then London. Later, smaller provinces were run from Cirencester, Lincoln, London, York, and possibly Chester. London may have held 30,000 inhabitants. Large towns were laid out on a grid of streets with a forum (town square) of law courts, council chambers, and market. There would be an amphitheater and theater for entertainments and public baths for socializing. Water could be fed to towns by aqueducts. From around 150 AD, towns began to build surrounding walls of earth and later stone as a sign of status or for defense. Smaller market towns had an irregular pattern and no public buildings. Small towns could also form outside forts to supply the needs of the local army garrison.

Villas were farmsteads built in the Roman manner with rectangular buildings with roof tiles and painted wall plaster. Wealthier villas would have mosaic floors, gardens, buildings arranged around a courtyard, window glass, sculptures, and a bath house. Some were built over Iron Age round houses by natives adopting Roman ways, but mostly the natives carried on building in their traditional way. Enclosed farmsteads and small hillforts continued in the far north.

Native peoples continued defleshing bodies, scattering ashes, or burying bodies singly in the landscape. Most Roman burials were of soldiers, officials, and immigrants. These were cremations in an urn in the ground with a box of grave goods, some having inscribed gravestones. By law, burials had to be outside town boundaries and cluster along roads leading out of the towns. Inhumation in a shroud or a coffin began to replace cremation from the late second century. A few wealthy burials were in stone or lead coffins. Children were mostly buried within settlements (a bit like we bury our pets today). By the fourth century, graves were aligned east to west, with the feet at the east, a method used by both Christians and pagans. Christian features from the fourth century are a lack of grave goods and the inclusion of children and babies in cemeteries. Some Roman burial practices are rather hard to understand, such as packing the coffin with plaster or gypsum. Some burials were placed face down in the coffin. Others were beheaded after death and the head may be placed between the knees or by the feet.

Native Iron Age art continued, while Roman art was brought from the Mediterranean, including stone sculpture, architecture, and mosaic floors.

Small statuettes for religious worship were common. Larger stone statues would have been prominent and would have been painted in bright colors, not the plain stone we see today. Mosaic floors were a sign of great wealth. Six schools of mosaic designers have been identified, based in the large towns but serving wide regional areas.

The Romans worshiped their own gods and the deified Emperors, but most people continued to follow the native religion. A few classical Roman temples were built, but most native temples were square or circular shrines within a sacred enclosure, with votive deposits. Sites on or near water remained important, such as the temple at Bath. There were many native gods and goddesses unique to Britain or shared with Gaul, such as Nodens, a god of healing. Religious cults worshiping one particular foreign deity grew during the later Roman period, such as Christianity or the worship of Bacchus or Mithras. Persecutions of Christians took place from 250, until the Imperial promotion of Christianity by Constantine in 313. Emperor Theodosius prohibited pagan worship in 391, ordering pagan temples to be closed. Christian churches and baptisteries, and artifacts and floors with Christian symbols are known from Roman Britain.

MIGRATIONS AND KINGDOMS (410 TO 865 AD)

The later Roman Empire in the west of Europe was beset by invaders from the north and east, as well as rebellion from within. In 407, the bulk of the army in Britain was taken to Gaul by a military usurper trying to win control of the Empire. On his failure in 410, the Empire could no longer send troops or administrators to take back control of Britain and the island was left to be independent, defending itself as best it could.

Britain changed profoundly between 410 and 570. Sustaining Roman-style industries and administration became impossible outside the Empire. As the economy shrank, so did political culture. All the familiar aspects of Roman civilization slowly disappeared. Towns declined, villas were no longer built, forts were no longer occupied by a professional army, commercial potteries ceased, building in stone was rare, and there were no more mosaics, baths, or amphitheaters. There also seems to have been a serious decline in the number of people living in Britain.

At some point, the single Roman administration broke down into smaller kingdoms. Modern England, Scotland, and Wales did not yet exist but their origins lie in this period. The native Britons would rule separate kingdoms in the west and north of Britain. Migrants from Ireland (the Scots) settled

From Roman to Victorian in the City of Bath, photo courtesy of Donald Henson

parts of the west of Britain. They ruled the Kingdoms of Dal Riata (in Argyll) and Dyfed, and there were lesser Irish settlements in Galloway and Cornwall. Angles and Saxons came from northern Germany to settle in the east of Britain, founding a range of Anglo-Saxon kingdoms. They referred to the native Britons as the Welsh (meaning foreigners). The Britons referred to themselves as the *Cymry* (compatriots) and called the Germanic settlers (and still call in Welsh) the *Saeson* (Saxons).

Historical documents or inscriptions before 600 are rare, and it is hard to separate fact from fiction in Medieval tales about this period written more than 500 years after the events. The most famous name from this time is Arthur. Historians and archaeologists are very divided about whether Arthur was a real person. The most positive interpretation is that Arthur (*Artorius* in Latin) was the last "emperor" of a sub-Roman Britain, trying to keep together Britannia as a single entity and that the "empire" collapsed at his death around 520 into smaller kingdoms. The most negative interpretation is that he is a completely mythical character, an invented person within stories developed from the tenth into the twelfth centuries.

Germanic and Irish immigration fundamentally reshaped the geography of Britain. Germanic settlers from across the North Sea did not arrive as hordes of conquerors dispossessing, slaughtering, or subjugating the natives. They were settled by British administrations as family groups (calling themselves Angles and settling in the east) or as hired soldiers (designated by the Britons as Saxons and settling in the south). Only later, between 570 and 660, did the Anglo-Saxons take power and extend their control north and west over the area of modern England and southern Scotland. They broke up the native Britons into separate areas in Strathclyde, Wales, and Cornwall. The leading Anglo-Saxon kingdoms were Northumbria, Mercia, and Wessex. Among the Britons, Gwynedd would emerge as the major power. In the far north, power would be contested between the Picts, Strathclyde, and Irish Dal Riata.

Common artifacts of this period are metal brooches, with different styles seemingly signifying different ethnic groups, such as native British penannular (ring-shaped) and annular, Anglian square-headed and cruciform brooches. A new metalwork style unique to Britain was the quoit brooch style, and may be official issue by British rulers to their officials and Germanic soldiers.

Some late Roman pottery making continued in the west, but most pottery was now handmade and local, while Iron Age pottery had continued in the far north. Pottery and glass were imported from the eastern Mediterranean and Africa to high status sites in the west of Britain, reflecting diplomatic contacts with the Roman Empire at Constantinople up to around 550. Later imported pottery was brought from Gaul.

The heavy wheeled plough pulled by eight oxen in long fields began to be used with a rotation of crops across fields. This helped to increase yields and led to new farming landscapes across much of southern Britain. The economy began to recover in the seventh century, and coins were minted again in Britain, but only by the Anglo-Saxons. Gold coins were minted from the 620s, replaced by silver pennies in the 680s. These are found widely in both towns and rural areas (possibly from seasonal fairs). Anglo-Saxon kings controlled their trade with the near continent through selected coastal towns in the eighth century, such as Hamwic (Southampton) and Ipswich. Similar trading settlements grew up outside the walls of the old Roman towns of London and York.

It is much easier for archaeologists to identify high status sites in the British areas than ordinary settlements, but easier to find ordinary settlements rather than high status sites in the Anglo-Saxon areas. Roman forts in the north continued to be occupied into the fifth century. Hillforts were reoccupied in the British and Pictish areas. New forts were placed on rocky hill tops with an inner citadel and outer ramparts. Coastal forts on promontories and crannogs (settlements built out into lakes) were also used. There were also smaller fortified farmsteads (duns). Rectangular houses had begun to replace the native roundhouses under the Romans, but finally became dominant everywhere during this period. A characteristic type of building on Germanic sites in the south and east is the pit house (known by the German word *Grubenhaus*). These are small rectangular houses dug into the ground leaving a shallow "cellar" under the floor. These were workshops, while people lived in rectangular wooden halls.

Archaeology relies heavily on studies of place-names and language for this period. Place-names in the Anglo-Saxon kingdoms include *-ham* and *-wickham* (an estate), *-burna* (stream), *-dun* (hill), *-eg* (modern -ey, an island), *-feld* (open pasture), *-wella* (spring), *-tun* (modern -ton, a village or parish) and *-leah* (modern -ley, a clearing or wooded area). Names like Bretton, Walton, and Cumberland seem to show the survival of recognizable settlements of the native Britons (Brettas or Walas in Old English and Cymry in Welsh) into the eighth century.

Among the more impressive remains of the period are long linear banks, used as boundaries between kingdoms. A 39-mile boundary in northern Wales, Wat's Dyke, was built, probably by King Æthelbald of Mercia. This was extended between 784 and 796 by King Offa by the addition of the 64-mile-long Offa's Dyke between Anglo-Saxon Mercia and Welsh Powys.

Anglian communities in the east cremated their dead with their grave goods and animal sacrifice, placing the ashes in urns in large cemeteries. In the south of Britain, there are inhumation cemeteries, in which Saxon grave goods show Germanic settlers among the native Britons. Native British cemeteries are known, continuing the late Roman practice of burying inhumations aligned east to west without grave goods. These cemeteries were not associated with churches. Only people of high status, kings and nobles, might give their bodies to be buried in or nearby a church, and then possibly only after the ninth century.

Native Iron Age art styles, especially in metalwork, continued in the north of Britain. One special form of native art developed in the northeast of Britain among the Picts. Their memorial stones were carved with inscriptions, animals, objects, and abstract designs in some kind of meaningful patterns which we have yet to properly decipher. Early Anglo-Saxon metalwork is decorated in the same style as the rest of the Germanic world, based on carving of fragmented human and animal shapes, and from around 550, on interlacing ribbons. The goldwork produced in this style by the Anglo-Saxons is especially skilled and impressive. The influence of the church helped to mix art styles across national and ethnic borders. By the eighth century, a common insular style developed that made use of both Celtic and Germanic, as well as classical Roman styles of artistic motifs. This is seen best in the use of interlacing in the illuminated manuscripts of the seventh and eighth centuries.

Romano-British churches survived in the west of Britain into the Medieval period, while pockets of pagan belief may have still existed, and the Picts to the far north remained pagan. The newly arrived Germanic peoples and Irish would also have been pagan. British Christians were quick to covert the Irish in the mid fifth century. It was the Irish (as the Scots) who then brought Christianity to the far north through the monastery of Iona in Dal Riata, founded in 563. The Britons had little interest in converting the Anglo-Saxons, whose conversion began with missions from Rome to Canterbury in 597 and from Iona to Lindisfarne in 634. The last pagan outpost was the Isle of Wight, converted in 686. The church brought a new form of writing to the Anglo-Saxons and this is seen on sixth century gravestones, alongside their own runic alphabet. The church also brought new forms of building as churches, cathedrals, and monasteries. Most of the early churches were "minsters" with a community of priests serving a large district, and were often founded on royal estates. Stone buildings were rare and good stone masons had to be brought over from the continent. Some Roman stone buildings were still standing and in use, but churches were often small, simple, and narrow and would mostly be built of wood. Monasteries were like enclosed villages with separate houses and workshops and a church within a rectangular or round enclosure. As well as buildings, the church brought stone crosses and sculpture. Memorial stones in the native British areas have inscriptions in Latin, with some also in Irish Ogham script. There are many tall stone crosses, up to twenty feet high, with a cross on a shaft carved with decoration and Biblical scenes, and in different styles in different parts of Britain.

Society was strongly hierarchical. Under the king were his officials and followers, granted estates as landowners over the local commoners. There were strong legal distinctions between nobles, commoners, and slaves. The clergy were a new group in society with their own hierarchy of bishops, priests, and monks. The period was one of various conflicting identities: Christian or pagan, Briton or Irish or Anglo-Saxon. A strong sense of identity among the English as immigrants is reflected (and created) by one of the major scholarly works of Medieval Europe, the *Ecclesiastical History of the English People*, written by the Anglian monk Bede in the monastery of Jarrow in 731. The Welsh had a strong sense of their own identity as the descendants of the native Britons, while the Scots had to create a new identity out of combined Pictish, Irish, Anglian, and British origins looking to the monastery of Iona for its inspiration. As yet these identities were not based in unified kingdoms. That would change with the arrival of the Vikings.

MEDIEVAL MONARCHIES (865 TO 1521 AD)

By the ninth century, the north of Britain formed the Kingdom of Alba, ruled by the Irish immigrant Scots. South of them were the British Kingdom of Strathclyde and the Anglo-Saxon Kingdom of Northumbria. Modern Wales was divided among the major Kingdoms of Gwynedd in the north and Deheubarth in the south, with Gwent and Morgannwg in the southeast. The south of Britain was divided among the Anglo-Saxon Kingdoms of Mercia, East Anglia, and Wessex. In the far southwest was the British Kingdom of Cornwall.

Viking raiders had been attacking Britain since the 790s, but a major Viking invasion arrived in 865 which would fundamentally change the geography of Britain. Strathclyde would be conquered by Alba to create one large Scottish kingdom covering the whole of the north. The Anglo-Saxon kingdoms of Northumbria, Mercia, and East Anglia would be destroyed and taken over by new Viking rulers. Cornwall would be absorbed into

Anglo-Saxon Wessex. Wessex would then subdue the Vikings and absorb all the old Anglo-Saxon kingdoms to create one English kingdom for the first time in 927. The Kingdoms of the English and the Scots dominated Britain, with the native Britons restricted to the Kingdoms of the Welsh. England was then conquered by a new royal house from Normandy in France in 1066, who would later strive for dominance over the rest of Britain. King Edward I annexed Wales in 1283 and took over Scotland in 1296. Wales remained under English rule, but the Scots won their war of independence from 1306 to 1314.

The vast majority of Britain's towns and villages were founded during this period, which was also a time of great technological change and of impressive building in stone. Population seems to have increased until 1300, but the later Medieval period was a time of crisis. Two years of remarkably bad weather in 1315 and 1316 led to the most serious famine of the period, followed by a descent into a little ice age of cold winters and cool summers. Then in 1348 and 1349, Britain was visited by the Black Death (bubonic plague). Around 30 percent of the population died, and more were killed in repeated epidemics after this. By 1450, the population was probably only one third of what it had been 150 years earlier.

The archaeological record once more becomes rich in artifacts. High quality pottery was produced in the English towns from the ninth century, often with the new feature of a yellow or green glaze. Bronze and iron cooking pots were added later and potters concentrated more on jugs and pitchers (and plates and cups from 1450), often decorated with colored designs or applied animal and human figures. Leather, wood and, after around 1300, pewter vessels were also common.

The Medieval period was a time of technological innovation moving far beyond what was possible in the ancient world. Water, tidal, and wind mills became common from the eleventh and twelfth centuries. New inventions from Asia were adapted, such as the horse collar in the ninth century which allowed horses to pull ploughs and wagons. Horses were more efficient than oxen, but also more expensive to keep and so only slowly replaced oxen for ploughing. Nailed-on iron horse shoes came in the tenth century.

Overseas trade became much more important in the Medieval period as shipwrights built new types of ships from the late twelfth century, with a stern rudder and deeper draught able to carry more cargo. And sailing became safer with the use of the compass at the same time. This made it necessary to build better ports with quaysides. New and larger stone buildings were made possible by the use of the pointed arch and of buttresses. Tall spires could be added to major churches. Other innovations included the handgun and the cannon using gunpowder possibly as early as the mid thirteenth century, eyeglasses came in the 1280s, the mechanical clock shortly before 1300, and the practical printing press in 1450.

The classic English village with large open fields with strips of land divided between local families was created by an organized centralization of farms under new manorial landlords from at least the tenth century onward in parts of England. The fields would be ploughed into parallel ridges to give better drainage. Some landowners became major commercial ventures. The new Cistercian monasteries of the twelfth century were important as wool ranchers, turning areas of upland away from arable to sheep pasture, managed by outlying monastic granges. The export of wool and cloth brought great wealth to England from at least the tenth century, when prices were regulated by law.

The economy depended on a supply of good coinage. Anglo-Saxon kings brought coinage under strong royal control, at first as silver pennies. Gold coins began in 1344 with the noble, worth one-third of a pound (80 pence). Scotland minted its own silver pennies from 1136 and gold coins were introduced there in 1357. Scotland was ahead of England in minting copper farthings from 1466. Continuing inflation devalued the coins and a very wide variety of different coin types was minted by the fifteenth century. Markets and fairs became widespread, and towns would often have a central open market space. Industrial activities included stone quarrying and iron working, improved by the use of water-powered trip hammers and bellows. Coal was used as a fuel from the thirteenth century.

Many Medieval buildings still stand and are in use today, not only castles and cathedrals, but also parish churches, town houses, and a few rare rural wooden buildings. There are also many deserted Medieval villages, abandoned from the fourteenth century onward for a variety of reasons, in different parts of Britain. Some parts of Britain had villages, while others had small hamlets of scattered farmsteads.

Fortified towns extended throughout southern England by the tenth century by royal order and Viking takeover, and later grew up around castles and markets. They became prosperous, especially in the east of England, plugged into trading networks across the North Sea. The larger towns would have walls with impressive gateways and later also guildhalls in stone. Winchester was the early capital of England until the twelfth century. The biggest town by a long way was London, followed by York, Norwich, Lincoln, Exeter, and later also Bristol, Newcastle, Boston, Yarmouth, Coventry, and Salisbury. York, Norwich, and Bristol were the major regional centers away from London. Towns in Scotland and Wales began to grow mostly from the twelfth century onward. Britain was criss-crossed by roads, and Medieval people moved around regularly, more than we think. Travel was so important that early Kings insisted landowners build and look after public bridges on the main roads as one of the conditions for holding their land. Early bridges in wood were gradually replaced in stone, especially after the twelfth century.

Early farmhouses included the longhouse with people living in one end with a cattle byre at the other. These were replaced by separate farm buildings around a courtyard, and rural houses were much better built with timber framing from at least the thirteenth century. Only the wealthier houses were built in stone in the towns after the twelfth century. By the thirteenth century, town houses were often built with cellars or with storage on the ground floor and living space on the floor above. Manor houses were based around a common, high-roofed hall, with a sleeping chamber for the lord, but separate chapel, kitchen, stables etc. Manor houses would often be surrounded by a moat and hedge.

Parish churches began to be built in the tenth century in England, the late eleventh century in Wales, and the twelfth century in Scotland. These were often the property of a manorial lord who would jealously develop the church as a source of income. By this period, most churches were usually built in stone, and the cathedrals would be some of the biggest and most advanced buildings of their day. Most churches and cathedrals were rebuilt after the Norman conquest in the new Romanesque style. By the 1170s, a new Early English Gothic style was being used, with pointed arches allowing much stronger doorways and windows capable of carrying heavier and higher walls. From the 1240s, these developed into the Decorated Gothic arch with its elaborate stone tracery and parallel panels of glass, which made the interiors much lighter and airier. When used with new styles of buttress, they allowed for larger and more impressive buildings than any that had been built before. The Romanesque and early Gothic styles were used throughout Europe, but the next style was developed in England and remained a characteristic of the country. This is the Perpendicular Gothic style, used from the 1330s onward, with parallel lines of masonry in wide panels and decorative tracery.

The Norman conquest introduced a new ideal of the warrior aristocracy reflected in their wooden castles. They were created as a way to dominate the English and quell any rebellion. The earliest castles in Wales were likewise built by Norman barons taking over the east and south of Wales from the later eleventh century. The native Welsh kings developed their own castles from the twelfth century. Castles were usually replaced in stone in the twelfth century. By the late fourteenth century, the emphasis was on comfortable occupation rather than defense, although by the fifteenth century blockhouses for housing artillery had also become common.

Romano-British and Anglo-Saxon cemeteries were gradually replaced by the tradition of burial in a churchyard. Burial was a right granted to churches, for which they could charge a fee. Wealthy and ecclesiastical burials were marked by grave markers and a position near or inside the church. There are a few Viking burials of the ninth and tenth centuries, including ship burials in the far north and west, but the Viking settlers quickly adopted Christianity and merged into the resident population. In crowded churchyards, old burials would often be disturbed to make way for new bodies and many had charnel houses for storing the disturbed bones. Large common burial pits have been found associated with outbreaks of the plague.

Medieval arts were sophisticated, intricate, and colorful. Much survives in metalwork, stone carving, and illuminated manuscripts. Something unique to Britain and Ireland are the carved stone hogback memorials. These date from the tenth century in northern England, western Britain, and central Scotland. They were created by the Viking settlers and their descendants and are shaped like houses with bowed sides and pitched roofs. They often have animals, especially bears, holding up the ends. We forget now that Medieval churches were highly painted in bright colors and would contain art on their walls of a type only surviving in illuminated manuscripts. Late Anglo-Saxon art is known as the Winchester style and survives in a few superb books of the tenth and eleventh centuries.

While churches were constantly rebuilt, modified, and extended, it is the monasteries that were a major feature of Medieval Christianity. There were more than 2,000 monasteries in Britain, most in rural locations, although the Dominican and Franciscan friaries were founded in the towns from the thirteenth century. By the twelfth century, most monasteries had a standard plan with a church and cloister (courtyard) at the center of large building complexes for living, looking after the sick, services, storage, and food processing, with fish ponds, mills, and accommodation for guests within a boundary wall. Most of the wealthiest abbeys throughout the Medieval period were of the Benedictine Order. New monastic orders came to Britain at various times, between 1077 and 1283, most importantly the Augustinian canons after 1092 and the Cistercian monks from 1128. It is the Cistercian abbeys that survive today as the most impressive ruins of the period.

England became the largest and wealthiest nation in Britain during the tenth century. Scotland found a new identity after 1306 in opposition to

The ruins of Fountains Abbey, photo courtesy of Donald Henson

England and often in alliance with France. Wales never achieved unity, and was eventually conquered, divided between areas ruled by English baronial lords and the rest as a principality directly under the King of England. Feudal society was full of rules and responsibilities, and intensely hierarchical. Yet it was possible to make a new life in the towns and in the professions of architecture, law, medicine, the church, teaching, administration. Wealth could be made in trade. There was conspicuous consumption by the wealthy in large and impressive buildings and by control of hunting and wild foods, symbolized by dovecotes, fish ponds, deer parks, and rabbit warrens. The Medieval period was a time of learning, scholarship, and growing literacy throughout society. Learning was important to provide the educated professional and administrative class the country needed. Universities were founded at Oxford, probably in the twelfth century, Cambridge in 1209, St. Andrews in 1413, and Glasgow in 1451. From the thirteenth century, the universities were organized around colleges, whose buildings are still impressive monuments of the Medieval age. Inns of Court were founded for training barristers in London by the fourteenth century. These all have important surviving Medieval buildings. Initial education was provided in the grammar schools attached to churches of various kinds since Anglo-Saxon times, such as Westminster School, and growing in number from the thirteenth century. Winchester School was founded as an independent school in 1382, with Eton College following in 1440.

REFORMATION AND REVOLUTION (1521 TO 1760 AD)

It is impossible to give a fixed date for the end of the Medieval period and the beginning of the modern world. The year 1521 is as good as any for Europe. In that year, the Protestant reformer Martin Luther was excommunicated by the Pope and declared an outlaw. There was no turning back for the Protestant reformation. Europe would be divided into ideologically warring camps. Countries would have to decide which side they were on. The reformation came to England in 1534 with the declaration of Henry VIII as the head of a church independent from Rome. The dissolution of the monasteries soon followed. In Scotland, the reformation involved the abolition of papal authority and adoption of Protestant worship in 1560. The monasteries there were dissolved gradually between 1560 and 1587. The wealth that had been bound up in monastic lands and commerce was now dispersed among the secular gentry and aristocracy who soon built themselves grand new country houses to reflect their newfound wealth and status.

Britain achieved political unity during this period. Wales was fully incorporated in England in 1536. In 1603, King James VI of Scotland inherited the throne of England as James I. The two kingdoms kept separate governments and parliaments until they were united as one Kingdom of Great Britain in 1707. A new European superpower was slowly emerging. The English began to settle overseas and create colonies, the earliest being Virginia in 1607, Bermuda in 1609, Masulipatam in India in 1611, and Gambia in 1618. English sea power was based on technological innovation, a long seagoing tradition, good harbors, and a well-administered professional navy. The defeat of the Spanish Armada in 1588 marks the beginning of the modern Royal Navy.

Ideological strife, between Catholic and Protestant in both England and Scotland, and between a new mercantile class and the older landowning nobility boiled over in the Civil Wars that engulfed England and Scotland between 1639 and 1652, and the four military coups in England between 1648 and 1659. These were key events enforcing the ideal of political compromise, a balance between executive and legislative power and constitutional monarchy. Two attempts at Jacobite (Catholic) rebellion in 1715 and

1745 failed to upset the new status quo but dealt the final death blow to the traditional Scottish highland society.

The population increased during this period, almost doubling from over 4 million to nearly 8 million. We know that people were, as they had been for centuries, an average height of 5 feet 7 inches for men and 5 feet 2 inches for women. Their artifacts gradually changed. Green glazed pottery continued to be made, and the brown glazed Cistercian Wares that had begun in the fifteenth century became especially common. Highly decorated colored pots with figures and names appear in the late seventeenth century. It was in the seventeenth century that Staffordshire in the English midlands came to dominate pottery production in Britain with new salt glazed stonewares from the 1670s and highly fired red and white stonewares from the 1720s. Tin glazed earthenwares (Delft wares) were brought over by Dutch potters in 1567, with blue and yellow patterns on white glaze and these would later imitate Chinese willow pattern designs. Finally, porcelain began to be produced in the 1740s. New forms of pottery were needed for the new drinks of the age, coffee, chocolate, and tea, introduced to London in the 1650s.

A major change in the farming of the land was the enclosure of the commonly farmed open fields into separately owned farms, and the division of common uplands into private pastures. This process of land enclosure began in the sixteenth century and was only completed in the early nineteenth century. Farmers would move out of the village into newly built farms in their own set of fields, marked out by hedgerows. New foods were introduced to Britain from the Americas and elsewhere, such as the potato and tomato. The beginnings of livestock breeding improved the size and quality of farm animals and the new farms exploited new technology to increase yields to feed the rising population.

There was a bewildering variety of gold, silver, and copper coins minted in this period, including irregular coins during the Civil War. Machine-made "milled" coins were introduced in Scotland in 1637. England had used milled coins since 1662 based on the golden guinea (worth one pound or 20 shillings, later raised to 21 shillings), the silver crown (5 shillings), the shilling (12 pence) and penny, and the copper halfpenny and farthing. These became the common currency of Great Britain in 1707. Small-scale, local industries began to develop in rural areas taking advantage of water power, such as smelting of iron and mining for lead, copper, and tin. The Cornish tin mines led the way in developing a new form of power. In 1712, Thomas Newcomen developed the first practical steam engine to help remove flood waters from the mines.

The sixteenth century saw a great change in the nature of domestic buildings with the use of chimneys, separate rooms and complete upper floors, and more use of window glass. Wooden houses were generally replaced by buildings in brick or stone from the sixteenth century onward. The open hall was replaced by living in separate rooms on two floors and a kitchen added instead of cooking in a separate building. The Anglo-Scottish border developed a type of fortified stone farmstead, the bastle house, with thick walls, the animals kept on the ground floor, and the people living on the floor above. The moated manor houses of the gentry and the castles of nobility were increasingly replaced by stylish new country houses during the sixteenth century. Wealth was displayed by the laying out of large planned gardens, at first in an artificial French style but from the 1730s in a more naturalistic way, many associated with the great garden designer Lancelot "Capability" Brown from 1739.

Spa towns (such as Bath) developed in the later seventeenth century where the wealthy could holiday and the early steps toward town planning were taken. Medieval building styles were replaced by new Renaissance styles in the mid-sixteenth century, looking back to classical Roman and Greek ideas. The architect Inigo Jones introduced a plain Palladian style in 1619 at the Banqueting House, while Sir Christopher Wren developed a British version of the continental baroque style at St. Paul's Cathedral in 1675. Palladian styles returned with the work of Lord Burlington from 1715. Military architecture was more functional. New styles of defenses were built, beginning with the coastal forts of the 1530s as emplacements for the new artillery to defend against enemy ships. Fortifications continued to develop in complexity with the establishment of a professional army and navy from the seventeenth century. Transport also changed with closed, sprung carriages being used from 1564 and there was a big increase in commercial traffic on the roads. From 1663 an increasing number of turnpike trusts began to levy tolls for their upkeep. Coal and other mines pioneered the use of new wooden wagonways, the forerunner of railways.

New kinds of building were developed in this period. The first purpose-built theater was erected in London in 1576. These were only one form of entertainment. Others included cockfighting in the cockpits and bear baiting in specially built rings. The later sixteenth century saw the founding of a large number of new schools and hospitals, replacing those of the church that had been closed during the Reformation.

Religious life was now dominated by Protestant beliefs. The monasteries had gone and the Reformation removed much of the color and decoration from parish churches and cathedrals. New religious sites were built from the middle of the seventeenth century as nonconformist chapels of the various Protestant sects, plainer and more democratic than the traditional parish churches. Gravestones were rare until the sixteenth century, and were simple in style, with the initials of the dead person and their date of dying. They were either small headstones or flat ledgers placed on the ground above the grave. They became commoner and more finely made from the late seventeenth century, often with symbols of death carved on the stone, such as a skull, bones, hourglass, serpent, coffin, or Father Time. Wealthier or more fashion-conscious families might have a more ornamental baroque style with cherubs as a common motif.

The hierarchies in British society were becoming deeply entrenched. The aristocracy faced a challenge for position and power from merchant wealth. The power of kings gave way to constitutional rule by politicians. Increasing specialization of professions was creating new groups in society, such as architects, scientists, civil servants, and above all professional army and navy officers. Britain was on the threshold of another new era and laying the foundations for a truly groundbreaking role in world history.

INDUSTRIAL ADVANCE AND THE MODERN WORLD (1760 AD TO THE PRESENT)

There is no doubt that the modern world is qualitatively different to what came before, but deciding when the modern world began is not easy. There is no single date that we can use. Two key features of the modern world are the industrial nature of the economy and the widespread use of complex technologies. Industrialization was a long process taking place since Medieval times. However, it was the eighteenth century that saw key new technological developments and a sharp upward increase in economic activity. The accession of King George III in 1760 is a convenient date to use that marks the beginning of a recognizably modern world, but is only a guide, not a hard and fast date at which the world changed. Some key events that happened around that time were:

- the creation of the first modern-style canal, the Sankey Canal, in 1757;
- prices rose above the long-term average of the previous 100 years;
- great military victories in 1759 during the Seven Years' Wars signaled Britain's arrival as a world superpower: Lagos, Quiberon Bay, and Quebec;

- the Wedgwood potteries opened, pioneering new mass pottery of a high quality;
- the British Museum opened its doors placing Britain as the successor of ancient civilizations;
- James Hargreaves developed his spinning jenny to revolutionize the spinning of cotton yarn, helping to develop Britain's major industry for the future in 1764.

Britain acquired a worldwide Empire and rose to the status of a superpower. International influences on material culture, technology, and fashions became much greater than ever before. Great industries arose in the eighteenth century, only declining to be replaced by foreign imports or newer technologies within the last fifty years. Britain became involved in two devastating world wars and lost its Empire from 1947. The archaeology of modern times is very different from that of earlier periods, being concerned with material remains that are still all around us, and often still being used, or that have been reused for different purposes.

Artifacts become better made and much more varied than ever before. Fine, hard porcelain began to be made from 1770, replacing the glazed wares in popularity. Plain earthenware, stoneware, and glazed pots continued to be used in the kitchen and as cheaper fine wares. The dominance of the Wedgwood pottery in Staffordshire began in 1759 where scientific research was applied to pottery production. The Spode factory developed bone China porcelain in 1796. Less expensive pottery included many kinds of glazed earthenwares, especially the white creamwares made in Leeds from the 1780s. Traditional materials like pottery, wood, leather etc. would be added to with new materials such as aluminum, cement, vulcanized rubber, and especially plastic (developed in 1865). New consumer goods were made possible by these new materials, such as household appliances and personal gadgets. New technologies would arise for communications, data processing, energy capture, and transport.

The modern era saw a revolution in sources of power and in technology. Steam took over gradually from water in the late eighteenth and early nineteenth centuries, and newer sources of power arose in the late nineteenth and twentieth centuries: gas, electricity, oil, nuclear, solar, and wind. The archaeology of this time is marked by large reservoirs, huge power stations, a national electricity grid by 1938, and large-scale networks of services in water, gas, and electricity. New technologies would include the telephone, radio, television, the transistor and microchip, computers, and remote controlled devices. The BBC began radio broadcasts in 1922 and television in 1936.

While farming would become ever more efficient with new strains of crops, the use of fertilizers, and new technologies, Britain would become the world's first industrial nation. Increasing wealth and the availability of better and wider varieties of food led to improvements in diet and standards of living, and in stature as the average height of people increased. The farming revolution led to the enclosure of common land in much of England, forcing poorer cottagers and laborers into the cities, and the clearance of the Scottish highlands as land was turned over to sheep farming and local families were forced to move on to small crofts or emigrate abroad or to towns. Migration of people to the new colonies in Canada, Australia, and New Zealand and to the United States increased in the nineteenth century. The twentieth century saw immigration of people from the Empire and its successor the Commonwealth, chiefly from the West Indies, the Indian subcontinent, and Hong Kong in China.

With the growth of factories, the focus of Britain's economy moved outside the southeast to where water power could be harnessed in the Pennines and the midlands of England. Industry then moved again into areas where coal was accessible to power the new steam machinery from 1774, such as the West Midlands, Lancashire, the West Riding of Yorkshire, the valley of the Clyde in Scotland, and the valleys of south Wales. Mills and factories developed as complexes of buildings, often with specially built workers' housing nearby. The key industries were textiles (cotton and woollens), steel, and shipbuilding, connected together by new canals and railways.

A major coinage reform in 1816 brought in the gold sovereign (one pound), but minting of gold coins for circulation ended in 1914, replaced by bank notes. A major change in coinage in 1971 was the replacement of the traditional currency of a pound worth 20 shillings and a shilling worth 12 pence by a decimal system of a pound of 100 pennies.

Styles of architecture have passed through various phases: Neo-Classical from the 1760s, Neo-Gothic from the 1830s, and Modernism in the 1920s to name but a few. New types of towns arose such as coastal holiday resorts, and deliberately planned new towns; suburbs grew along with giant new urban conurbations. New types of urban housing began replacing the slums in the nineteenth century. Council housing and high-rise buildings developed in the twentieth century. New kinds of building developed such as the public house, the hotel, state schools, libraries, museums and galleries, town halls, hospitals, sports stadiums, and cinemas. After 1918, many country houses were no longer economic to run and were demolished or sold, while others ended up being conserved for the nation through the National Trust. Townscapes were revolutionized in the late twentieth century with the growth of retail parks and malls, supermarkets, and out-of-town industrial estates.

Britain's built environment suffered from the effects of aerial bombing on its major cities, with limited damage in 1914–1918 but severe damage in 1939–1945. London was badly hit, but also Birmingham, Liverpool, Plymouth, Bristol, Glasgow, Southampton, Hull, Manchester, and Portsmouth. The historic cities of Bath, Canterbury, Exeter, Norwich, and York were deliberately targeted by German bombing in 1942. Redevelopment of the bombed areas would be slow, not completed until the 1960s, with its legacy of modernist architecture and attempts to improve living conditions by replacing traditional housing by high-rise blocks of flats. Some of these blocks are now controversially listed as being of historic importance.

There were huge changes in transport in this period which have left their mark on the landscape. The eighteenth century saw the development of canals, and also a road network supporting the mail coaches and their coaching inns of the 1780s to the 1840s. These were replaced by steam railways and their railway stations from the 1830s. Steam trains were brought to London with the beginning of the underground in 1863. More durable tarmac roads were built from 1810, and the coming of affordable motor cars to the masses after 1922 eventually led to a new national road network of motorways from 1958. Harbors and ports became major installations with the advent of oceangoing steamships from the 1820s and the development of the Empire. The new technology of the airplane led to the creation of

The 1843 steamship Great Britain in dock at Bristol, photo courtesy of Donald Henson

major airports in the later twentieth century. A new era began in 1994, with the opening of the Channel Tunnel rail link between Britain and the continent. No longer could Britain claim to be an unconnected island off the coast of Europe.

The early twentieth century was a time of industrialized warfare. The need to protect the country from invasion and attack was more important than ever. The first air raid took place in June 1917 on London. Defenses in the Second World War were built all over Britain in brick, concrete, and steel, and many have left traces in the landscape. They include radar stations, gun batteries, searchlights, air raid shelters, antitank blocks, pillboxes (18,000 were built in 1940), and mortar emplacements. The Cold War added its share of new structures, such as the twenty Thor ballistic missile sites of 1959 to 1964 and the underground nuclear bunkers for government.

Until the nineteenth century, graves were often dug in areas already used within the cemetery, disturbing earlier burials. With the rise of permanent stone grave markers and tombs, this became less possible and new cemeteries had to be built or existing graveyards extended. Nonconformist chapels set up private companies to build their own cemeteries after 1819 and private venture cemeteries became common from the 1830s. The Burials Acts of 1852 to 1857 set up local authority cemeteries funded by taxation. Cremations were legalized in the 1880s, and the first publicly funded crematorium opened in 1901. Today, around 70 percent of the dead are cremated. From the mid-eighteenth century, grave headstones became larger and more ornate, while wealthier burials might have a stone rectangular tomb. Simpler Neo-Classical styles were used by Nonconformists while Medieval Gothic was adopted by Anglicans. The use of crosses instead of slabs began around 1850, and in the twentieth century gravestones have become smaller and plainer.

Many historic churches were comprehensively repaired and made to look more Medieval by Victorian "improvers," leading to a backlash against the destruction of genuine Medieval architecture. This led to the Society for the Protection of Ancient Buildings in 1877, the beginning of the modern historic conservation movement. Churches and chapels have now been joined by new religious sites: Jewish synagogues, Islamic mosques, Hindu, Sikh, and Buddhist temples as a feature of Britain from the nineteenth and twentieth centuries onward. What future archaeologists will see is the broadening of religious practices. What they may not see is the contraction of religious belief where the abundance of places of worship masks the decline in overall religious belief among the population.

The modern era has seen more change than in the whole of the previous prehistory and history of Britain. Every aspect of people's lives has been affected by changes in material culture and technology. The landscape of Britain has been transformed and Britain is now one of the most heavily urbanized and densely populated places on earth. Yet there are still large rural spaces, miles of unspoiled coastline, and a landscape that bears the traces of thousands of years of human settlement and use. Britain is modern and ever-changing but it is also very old and deeply attached to its past. It is still very varied from north to south and east to west. It is an archaeologist's paradise for its abundant traces of human activity going back nearly one million years. Selected examples of these traces will be listed in the next two chapters.

4

PREHISTORIC SITES
AND FINDS

The remains of Britain's past are found everywhere throughout the island. The earliest finds are rare but highly prized glimpses of the long journey taken by human ancestors out of Africa. It is only since the last Ice Age that the evidence becomes common and there is then a rich sequence of sites and finds covering the last 15,000 years of settlement in Britain. This sequence reveals a world very different from our own, but one capable of great beauty as well as fascination.

ICE AGE COLONIZERS

Boxgrove (West Sussex)
Gravel quarries that were excavated from 1983 to 1996 revealed sediments from a freshwater pool and stream of around 480,000 years ago. This site has the earliest hominin bone from Britain: a tibia (shin bone) and two teeth, with flint artifacts and butchered horse and rhinoceros bones. The hominin species was *Homo heidelbergensis*, the probable ancestor of the later *Homo neanderthalensis*.

Cheddar Gorge (Somerset)
The three-mile long gorge at Cheddar has various caves. The largest is Gough's Cave, 300 feet deep and 1.3 miles long and containing the largest underground river system in Britain. There are stone tools from the cave

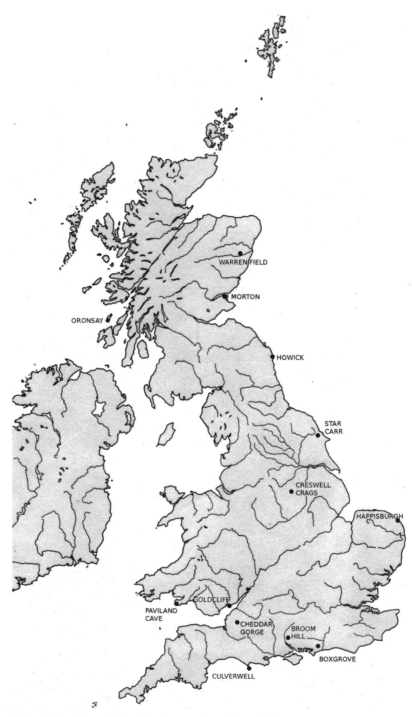

Map of Paleolithic and Mesolithic sites, courtesy of Donald Henson

going back 40,000 years, and bones of five people, dating from 14,700 BP. They had been defleshed and treated in the same ways as the bones of horses that were undoubtedly used for food. Their skulls had been fashioned into bowls. We can only guess whether this was as part of their religious beliefs and treatment of the dead or of the cannibalistic treatment of enemies.

Creswell Crags (Derbyshire and Nottinghamshire), on the UK Tentative List for World Heritage Sites

A limestone gorge, one-third of a mile long, lies either side of the border of two English counties. On both sides of the gorge is a series of caves excavated at various times since the nineteenth century: Dog Hole 1889, Pin Hole 1875, Church Hole 1875, the Arch 1975, Robin Hood Cave 1876, Mother Grundy's Parlour 1876, Yew Tree Shelter 1937, and Boat House Cave in the 1930s. These have been dens and refuges for hyenas and other animals over the last 120,000 years. Stone tools were left behind by Neanderthal hominins between 60,000 and 40,000 years ago, and modern humans began using the caves from around 28,000 years ago. The area was abandoned as the Ice Age reached its greatest severity and humans arrived back in the caves as the ice retreated around 15,000 years ago. Some of the caves were also used after the end of the Ice Age with Mesolithic material being found, for example from Mother Grundy's Parlour. The gorge is famous for having the most northerly Ice Age art in Europe. In 2003, hard-to-see engravings of animals (bison, deer, horse, ibex, and long-necked birds) were found on the walls of Church Hole Cave. These have been dated to older than 12,800 BP. Two of the caves at Creswell Crags had already been famous for their finds of Paleolithic art long before the recognition of carvings on the cave walls in recent times. Found in Robin Hood Cave in 1876 was a section of animal rib with the incised image of a horse. The image shows the horse's head, mane, neck, and forequarters. The whole is elegantly and accurately cut. The date of the rib is probably before 12,500 years ago. In Pin Hole Cave in 1928, a piece of woolly rhino rib was found with a curious carved drawing, a figure around two inches high. The figure has two legs, a body either in two halves or wearing a belt, an obvious and erect penis, one thin arm and an animal head. It looks human apart from the head which has been interpreted as an animal mask. The date of the bone is uncertain. Although it looks similar to finds in France dating to around 14,000 years ago, woolly rhino has not so far been found in Britain after 22,000 years ago.

Happisburgh (Norfolk)

See chapter 8 on recent research.

Paviland Cave (West Glamorgan)

A human skeleton buried with periwinkle shells, ivory rods, and rings was found in 1823 in Paviland Cave (also known as Goat's Hole Cave) in the Gower Peninsula in south Wales. This is one of the earliest human burials known in Europe. The body was laid out without its head in an extended position along the cave wall with its grave goods and smeared with red ocher. The burial may have had limestone blocks placed at the head and feet. There may also have been a mammoth skull laid nearby. Later excavations found at least six episodes of human activity, with flint and bone artifacts, from 35,000 to 13,000 BP. The body was originally identified as a female and known as the Red Lady of Paviland, and only later proven instead to be that of a man. The date of the burial was hard to establish. Early radiocarbon dates suggested he was buried 18,000 years ago, but later investigation produced a date of 26,000. This would have been at the height of the last Ice Age and not far from the limits of the ice sheet covering Britain. Only recently has the true date been shown to be 33,000 years ago, well before the ice sheet had traveled so far south. Tests showed that he had a diet rich in seafood or fish, was 5 feet 8 inches tall, and twenty-five to thirty years of age. He also had DNA that is shared with most modern Europeans.

HUNTER-GATHERER UTOPIA

Aveline's Hole (Somerset)

This may be one of the most frustrating archaeological sites in Britain. Aveline's Hole is a limestone cave in which a whole cemetery of bodies was found in 1797. It is still the only known Mesolithic inhumation cemetery from Britain. It is unclear exactly how many bodies were recovered. More than fifty were taken away by 1805. Twenty-one skeletons were found in excavations after 1914. Two bodies were found in a grave stained with red ocher, and buried with at least one tooth necklace. The rest of the bodies seem to have been laid out on the cave floor, and one had a cache of fossil ammonites by the head, collected from at least twelve miles away. There were also perforated sea shells from the coast among the bones. Unfortunately, most of the bodies were destroyed in a Second World War air raid on Bristol in 1940 (only fragments of nine survive). Dating of what survived showed the bodies were buried between 8400 and 8200 BC. Analysis of the bones shows that they had been born and brought up locally, had not eaten seafood, and were relatively short, perhaps only around five feet tall. There was evidence of iron deficiency in their diet, with episodes of famine while they were growing up.

Cheddar Man (Somerset)

Britain's oldest complete skeleton was found in 1903 in Gough's Cave, Cheddar. The burial is dated to 8300 BC, at the same time as the burials in Aveline's Hole, but unlike them as a single burial in the cave. He was a young adult male, buried in a crouched position after being defleshed, and had no grave goods. A genetic study was able to extract his DNA. The majority of the British population have ancestors who came to Britain in prehistory, and it is not surprising that Cheddar Man would have similar DNA to Britons today. In his case, there was even an exact genetic match with some local residents, who will have shared a maternal ancestor with him. His distant relatives were still living in the local area 10,000 years later!

Howick (Northumberland)

It was often assumed that Mesolithic houses were flimsy, temporary structures used by people moving from one place to another at different seasons during the year. Recent finds have been challenging this assumption. The site at Howick was spotted when Mesolithic flint artifacts were seen eroding out of the coastal cliff. Careful excavation in 2000–2002 revealed a circular hollow, in which had been built a round, sunken-floored house, twenty feet across. The house was built around 7800 BC, using posts over a foot wide. Inside the house were storage and cooking pits and a hearth. Finds included 16,000 stone artifacts (with Late Mesolithic–style microliths), burnt bones of wild boar and grey seal, some shellfish, and roasted hazelnuts. The importance of Howick is that a series of high resolution radiocarbon dates was taken that shows the site was occupied for up to 200 years. The detailed excavation revealed that the house had been rebuilt twice on the same spot during this time. It seems highly likely that the house at Howick was part of a permanent, year-round settlement. Its location would have been ideal for permanent settlement with a wide range of foods available from nearby woodland, the local river, and the sea shore (where flint for making tools was also available). A replica of the house has been built at the location as an experiment to see what kind of structure it could have been. Other sites are also now showing us the possibilities of a more settled Mesolithic than we had previously thought, for example, Lunt Meadows in Merseyside or East Barns in East Lothian.

Morton (Fife)

Possibly the earliest Mesolithic site to be found so far north in Britain is Morton, excavated between 1963 and 1970. The earliest reliable date could be as early as 7300 BC, but most of the dates from site A lie between 6200 and 5140 BC, while site B is dated between 5700 and 3800 BC. The original settlement was on what was then a tidal island. The foods available included whelks, mussels, cockles, crabs, and other seafood, fish such as cod, haddock, turbot, salmon, and sturgeon, seabirds like guillemot, and mammals like red deer, roe deer, wild boar, and aurochs. About 13,500 stone tools were recovered from site A. Various structures were built at Morton, including windbreaks and sleeping-places marked by hearths and stakeholes. It is thought that people repeatedly came back to the site for short spells of time over a long period.

Star Carr (North Yorkshire)

Probably the most famous Mesolithic site in Britain is Star Carr. This settlement is both one of the earliest Mesolithic sites in Britain and one where organic remains have been preserved in peat, giving us glimpses of prehistoric life unavailable at other sites. Star Carr was one of around twenty-five settlements around the shores of the now dried-up Lake Flixton. It has been investigated since 1948. The main early excavator was Sir Grahame Clark, a pioneer of integrating archaeology with environmental evidence and looking at the past as lives once lived rather than assemblages of artifacts. People occupied the lakeside location at Star Carr for around 300 years sometime between 9300 and 8400 BC. The lakeside of reeds and sedges would give way to willow and aspen, and then birch and pine on the higher ground above the lake. Although their plant foods don't survive, the bones reveal they ate and processed the remains of elk, red deer, roe deer, aurochs, wild boar, and various wildfowl. They also kept domestic dogs, possibly for help with hunting. Artifacts found include not only flint tools but bone, antler, wood, amber, and shale items. The wood is claimed to be the earliest evidence for deliberate carpentry in Europe (as opposed to the simple shaping of spear shafts). Wooden platforms and trackways were built by the lakeside and the remains of a building similar to the house at Howick, but a thousand years older, were found on the higher ground away from the lake edge. Among the more spectacular finds are the twenty-one deliberately shaped red deer skulls, which have been worked to leave only the front of the skullcap attached to the antlers and holes inserted, presumably for fastening to someone or something. These are unique in Britain, and are usually interpreted as headdresses to be worn as camouflage in hunting or during religious rituals. Only a small part of the whole site has so far been excavated. Recent work has revealed that the peat deposits covering the site are changing, becoming more acidic and allowing oxygen and bacteria in to destroy the organic remains, which are now disappearing and precious information about Mesolithic life is being lost.

SKARA
BRAE
ORKNEY

CALANAIS

CLAVA

TOWIE

BALBRIDIE

KILMARTIN
GLEN

MOUNT
STUART

ROTTEN
BOTTOM

CASTLERIGG

STREET HOUSE

GREAT
LANGDALE

DUGGLEBY HOWE

YORK

RUDSTON

GREAT
ORME

BIG
MOOR

'SEAHENGE'

MOLD

ARBOR
LOW

MAESMOR

GRIMES
GRAVES

BELAS KNAP

AVEBURY

WEST KENNET

STONEHENGE

CISSBURY

DOVER

TRETHEVY

Map of Neolithic and Early Bronze Age sites, courtesy of Donald Henson

Warren Field, Crathes (Aberdeenshire)

A line of twelve pits was excavated that lay near a wooden rectangular hall eighty feet long which was dated to the Early Neolithic (3800–3700 BC). The pits were originally thought also to be Neolithic, and may have contained wooden posts. The largest of the pits were up to eight feet across. Later analysis has shown the pits to be aligned on the southern horizon at midwinter sunrise, and were designed to allow corrections for the phases of the moon at that time in order to align the lunar and solar calendars. Dating of the pits showed however that they were first cut between 8210 and 7790 BC, therefore in the Mesolithic. They are unique and are now claimed to be the earliest known physical time-measuring device in the world. What is odd, and intriguing, is that some of the pits were recut in the Neolithic, between 3940 and 3650 BC, by the builders of the nearby hall, implying that they were either still visible or in use after 4,000 years. Why would Mesolithic people need to rectify their calendar? Foretelling the timing of migrating herds or the appearance of key plant foods may have been essential for them. Other pit alignments may exist. Does Warren Field shed possible light on the Mesolithic wooden posts that were erected near Stonehenge long before the well-known henge was built?

Other important sites

- Broom Hill, Hampshire: a Mesolithic settlement yielding over 100,000 flint artifacts, with a house dating to 8500 BC
- Culverwell, Dorset: a Mesolithic shell midden underneath an occupation floor of 6200–5900 BC
- Goldcliff, Monmouthshire: human footprints from the Mesolithic, 5600–4800 BC, preserved in the muds of the River Severn

---

FIRST FARMERS

Balbridie house (Aberdeenshire)

Neolithic houses were very poorly known until a substantial wooden house dating to between 3900 and 3500 BC was excavated at Balbridie in 1977–1981. It was 85 feet long by 42 feet wide, rectangular with bowed ends, and was partitioned into separate rooms. The doorway was in the short eastern end. At the end of its life, it was burnt down. Among the finds at the site were 20,000 grains of wheat, barley, and flax, along with some hazelnuts and crab apple. Flint, burnt bone, and pottery were also found. It remains one of the best examples of a house of its period.

Duggleby Howe round barrow (North Yorkshire)

A rare, large Neolithic round barrow, Duggleby Howe is 120 feet wide and 20 feet high. It was excavated in 1890 by one of the last great amateur archaeologist barrow diggers, John Mortimer. The first burial was of a crouched individual in a deep pit in a wooden chamber at the base of the barrow, dated to 3520–3415 BC. A further sixty-seven burials were added to this over the next 1,200 years. Some of the early burials in the mound were unusual for the period in having exquisitely made grave goods. Burial 5 had a finely flaked and polished flint axe-head, with an antler mace-head. Burial 6 had a plaque of flint, usually called a knife but perhaps too fragile to use as such. This is a rectangle of flint, polished down to a thinness of one sixteenth of an inch and less than two-and-a-half inches long. Burial 7 had a collection of six transverse and oblique flint arrowheads, two beaver incisor teeth, twelve boar tusks, and one long bone pin over nine inches long. Grave goods are not common in the Neolithic, and these give a fascinating insight into what was deemed precious in a society without metal.

Folkton chalk drums (North Yorkshire)

Canon William Greenwell was a prolific nineteenth century barrow digger. He excavated his barrow number 245 sometime between 1877 and 1889, and came across the burial of a young child of around five years old. Placed carefully next to the body were three unique objects carved out of the local chalk. These are three cylinders. They range in size from four inches to six inches across and stand around four inches high. Each cylinder has its sides decorated with a carved design, and a raised top, also decorated. The decoration is made of chevron, triangle, and lozenge patterns with a few spirals. Two of the cylinders have what look convincingly like stylized human faces. They look most like copies in chalk of possibly wooden bowls or containers with their lids, although this is a complete guess since no such artifacts have ever been found. They are among the few artifacts that have a "personality" and make us connect with the human being who once owned them. One wonders what the young child might have kept in them that was so precious that it was buried with them after death.

Great Langdale stone quarry (Cumbria)

Evidence of stone working and quarrying at Great Langdale covers forty-seven acres, centered on Pike of Stickle at 2,300 feet. The highly sought-after volcanic ash was used for making polished stone axe-heads. Rough-outs were made on site and taken down to the lowland settlements around ten miles away for finishing into axe-heads. The axe-heads were then traded widely across large parts of Britain. Excavations have shown that the site was exploited mostly between 3710 and 3050 BC. One major trading partner was eastern Yorkshire, some ninety miles to the east. Axe-heads from Great Langdale can be found as far south as the River Thames. Exchange with these and other areas may have taken place at seasonal gatherings between people from different regions.

Maesmor mace-head (Gwynedd)

Some prehistoric artifacts take the breath away with their beauty. One such is the Maesmor mace-head. This was a casual find by a laborer around 1840 when clearing wood on an estate. Its original context is unknown. It is made of a cream-colored flint and is only three inches long. Off center is a very accurately cut perforated shaft hole for the original and long-decayed handle, most likely made of wood. The surface is cut and polished into more than 190 lozenges made of intersecting ridges. We do not know what mace-heads were, but many are finely made and show no signs of wear. They must have been some kind of symbol to be carried by a special person in the community. This symbolism would have been recognized all over Britain as very similar examples are known throughout the island.

Rotten Bottom hunting bow (Dumfries and Galloway)

Finds of prehistoric bows are rare as wood seldom survives in the archaeological record. One was found in peat at Rotten Bottom in the Tweedsmuir Hills in 1990. It was made of a single piece of yew, with a central grip and D-shaped limbs. It had been thrown away after it had broken and originally would have been nearly six feet long, with a draw-weight between 24 and 40 pounds, shooting an arrow 28 inches long. This would have been used as a close-quarters hunting bow. It has been radiocarbon dated to between 4040 and 3640 BC and is the earliest yet found in Britain. Yew did not grow so far north in Britain at the time and the wood, or the bow itself, must have come from farther south, possibly Cumbria.

Rudston ritual complex (East Riding of Yorkshire)

Centered on the village of Rudston is a complex of four cursuses focusing on a giant upright stone monolith now in the local churchyard. The 25-foot-high monolith is the tallest standing stone in Britain, and stands at the bend of the Gypsey Race stream and the Great Wolds Valley where they turn east to the sea. The stone was brought there from ten miles to the north. The four cursuses either skirt the monolith or run up towards it. Each cursus varies from one to two-and-a-half miles long and 60 to 100 yards wide. They head south, west, southwest, and north from the monolith. Such a concentration of cursuses is very rare. Rudston is also a major center of concentration for the stone axe-heads from Great Langdale. To the north, farther along the valley is the later monument of Maiden's Grave Henge at Burton Fleming, where the valley turns westwards onto the high

Wolds. The Duggleby Howe barrow lies at the western end of the valley, on the highest point of the Wolds. This valley seems to have been a major ceremonial center during the Neolithic.

West Kennet long barrow (Wiltshire), part of the Avebury World Heritage Site

The West Kennet long barrow is 328 feet long, with a wide, stone-faced eastern end and a narrower plain end at the west. A 30-foot-long stone passage leads from the eastern face to an end chamber and four side chambers. Within the chambers were the remains of forty-six bodies, mostly disarticulated, of both adults and children. Others may have been robbed in the seventeenth century by a local doctor for human bones to grind up into medical potions! Some of the skulls and long bones are missing and there is evidence that the bodies had been exposed and de-fleshed elsewhere before some of the bones were collected for burial. The last body to be buried was an adult male laid whole and probably killed by an arrow lodged in his throat. Most of the bones had been tidied into heaps. Each chamber may have been for particular classes of person, for example, children in the southwest chamber. Grave goods included many pots, beads, animal bones, and stone tools. The tomb was built between 3670 and 3635 BC and bodies placed there until 3640–3610. The stone façade is ten feet high and has large stones blocking the passage, which seem to have been placed to seal off the tomb from further use some time after 2500 BC.

Windmill Hill causewayed enclosure (Wiltshire), part of Avebury World Heritage Site

Windmill Hill was the first causewayed enclosure to be identified and investigated. The site was built between 3700 and 3600 BC, and has three concentric rings of discontinuous ditches, dug as the quarries for material to build banks on the inside. The outer bank survives to over three feet high. The ditches enclose an area of twenty-one acres. There is some evidence for earlier rectangular buildings before the ditches were dug. Finds include stone artifacts, pottery, animal bones, and chalk cups found in rubbish pits. Waste from feasting was deposited within the ditches and the site seems to have been a place for seasonal meetings or festivals for people from a wide region (pots were found from Somerset and the western end of Cornwall). There are also stone axes from all over southern and western Britain. A similar enclosure excavated in modern times at Etton in Cambridgeshire yielded evidence of a fence dividing the enclosure into an eastern half for dealing with the dead and carrying out religious activity, and a western half where livestock were kept and feasting took place.

York hoard (North Yorkshire)

In 1868, some building workers stumbled across a pit underneath a layer of gravel. Inside this pit was a remarkable hoard of flint tools. Unfortunately, the hoard has not been fully preserved and kept together as a unit. We do know that there were at least seven axe-heads, nine large leaf-shaped items that may have been intended for further working into spearheads or knives, three arrowheads, three scrapers, two points or awls, and eleven blades. The number of axe-heads may originally have been up to twenty. Among the axe-heads are the very fine Seamer type, with a polished blade and a narrow waist. The artifacts are finely made but are working implements, intended to be used, perhaps the work of one knapper and maybe his store of pre-made tools to be drawn upon when needed. Flint was the basic raw material without which people in the Neolithic could not survive. Hoards like this would have been highly valued.

Other important sites

- Belas Knap, Gloucestershire: an Early Neolithic chambered tomb, 3800 BC, 180 feet long, with a false façade and three side chambers
- Cissbury, Sussex: Neolithic flint mines, 270 shafts up to 40 feet deep, with carvings on the walls and human burials
- Street House, North Yorkshire: an Early Neolithic mortuary house and burial cairn used for cremations from 3750 BC
- Trethevy Quoit, Cornwall: an Early Neolithic portal dolmen, a stone burial chamber 9 feet high with a 10-ton capstone

---

RITUAL AND HIERARCHY

Avebury (Wiltshire), World Heritage Site

Avebury is a key site in the development of archaeology in Britain. It was visited by John Aubrey, whose thoughts on the site, written down much later in 1663, are the earliest consideration of British prehistory and mark the beginnings of archaeological thinking about the past. The false interpretation of William Stukeley in 1743 that the site was connected with the ancient druids has bedeviled popular images of stone circles ever since. The site is a circle henge: a bank and internal ditch were built between 3070 and 2780 BC, with four entrances surrounding a circle of 98 stones. The ditch encloses an area 380 yards across or more than 28 acres, and the modern village of Avebury lies partly inside the monument. The ditch itself is 70 feet wide and up to 30 feet deep, and the outer bank is 100 feet wide and was up to 18 feet high. The entrances were at the NNW, SSE, ENE, and WSW, and the tallest stones (19 feet high) seem to have been at the NNW and SSE entrances. Inside the site were two smaller stone circles: a northern concentric double circle of twenty-seven stones in the outer circle with a central cove (an open chamber aligned to face midsummer sunrise) and a southern single circle of twenty-nine stones with a single 21-foot high stone (since demolished) in the middle. Both inner circles are aligned NNW to SSE and are around 340 feet in diameter. Other settings of stones existed elsewhere inside the henge. Outside it, the now demolished Beckhampton stone avenue ran from the WSW entrance, while the West Kennet stone avenue led from the SSE over 1.5 miles towards the site of the Sanctuary (a succession of timber buildings and stone circles). The avenue had around 100 pairs of stones, with tall stone pillars alternating with squat lozenge-shaped stones, and was around 80 feet wide. Early Bronze Age burials have been found laid by some of the stones. The northern circle's cove may be aligned on the midsummer sunrise, while it has been suggested that the southern circle has alignments to the midwinter and midsummer positions of the moon. Attempts to remove the stones were being made early on. A body was found crushed underneath one of the stones of the outer circle that had fallen on him around 1320 AD.

Balnuaran of Clava burial cairns (Highland)

The Balnuaran cairns are five stone mounds along a ridge, built around 1910 BC. The three surviving cairns are 50 feet across, built as a single act of burial. The middle cairn has an open space surrounded by a circle of stones. The two on either side are small round passage graves, with a burial chamber linked to the outside by a short stone passage. All three have an outer stone kerb, a low platform, and a stone circle surrounding the cairn. Ridges of stones radiate like rays out from the middle through the cairn towards individual stones of the surrounding circle. The highest stones in the circles are at the southwest and lowest at the northeast. The two passages also face to the southwest. Both passage graves have 48 stones in the kerb, 13 in the passage, and 12 in the circle. Tall stones and cup-marked stones tend to occur on the left-hand side of entrances and chambers. Lighter stones, especially white quartz, tend to occur toward the northeastern side of the cairns, while red sandstone tends to be in the southwest or facing the southwest. The cairn at the southwest of the line of three also has more red sandstone than the cairn at the northeast. It is clear that white has an association with the midsummer sunrise, while red is associated with the important alignment of the passages towards midwinter sunset. Both passage graves allow the midwinter sunset to light up the back of their chambers. Seen from the northeastern cairn, the sun sets directly over the southwestern cairn. The cairns show the complexity of people's religious beliefs. People seem to have believed the dead journeyed toward rebirth or successful passage to a land of the dead.

Callanais stone circle (also known as Callanish, Western Isles)

The site of Callanais has thirteen stones in a circle, 43 feet across, built around 2750 BC. Callanais shows well the role of stone circles in working out the calendar based on observations of the heavens. This is a complicated site. Three short rows of stones radiating from the circle were added by 1600 BC. One pointed east for 17 yards aligned on the rising of the Pleiades constellation, another south for 30 yards aligned on the night sky meridian line that runs through the north pole star, and the third to the west for 13 yards aligned on sunset at the equinox. A 90-yard long avenue leading north was added 400 years later aligned on a setting of the moon. The effect is to form a rough cross shape. The stones are up to 16 feet high. A small burial chamber lies inside the circle, but this was added at a late date.

Dover boat (Kent)

The Dover boat was found during the building works in 1992. It is claimed as the world's oldest surviving fragment of a seagoing boat, dating to 1520 BC. What survives is over 30 feet of wooden planking. There are two bottom planks and four side planks. One end of the boat did not survive but it may have originally been nearly 40 feet long and taken a crew of twenty rowers or paddlers with over three tons of cargo. The planks are made of oak and are elaborately carved to fit together using oak wedges and yew stitches. It was waterproofed with moss and beeswax. An experimental replica was made in 1996 which showed how technically sophisticated was the design. An example of the kind of cargo carried across the Channel during the Bronze Age was found on an underwater wreck in Langdon Bay, Dorset, where more than 350 bronze axes and other artifacts being brought over from France were recovered by archaeologists in 1979.

Great Orme copper mines (Gwynedd)

Soft, easily dug limestone near Llandudno contains large amounts of copper ore. Archaeologists have found mine workings there from 1880 to 600 BC, and mining has continued into modern times. There are four miles of tunnels covering 60 acres and going as deep as 220 feet underground. Ore yielding 2,000 tons of copper was extracted. The chalcopyrite ore weathers to malachite and azurite, both easier to smelt and the preferred ore in ancient times. So far, over 1,000 hammerstones, also stone mortars, pestles, and anvils for processing the ores have been found. There is also animal bone waste from food, and bones used as chisels, gouges, scrapers, and levers. Fires were also lit against the rock face and then doused with water, weakening the rock and making it easier to dig away. This is a prehistoric industrial site showing that the sophistication of the Early Bronze Age rested on the hard graft of ancient miners.

Grimes Graves flint mines (Norfolk)

First excavated in 1852, and then by William Greenwell in 1868–1870, Grimes Graves is the largest flint mine in Britain. There are 433 shafts and pits in an area of nineteen acres. Some thirty-five shafts have been fully excavated between 1868 and 1976. The biggest shafts are over 25 feet wide and 40 feet deep. At one shaft, the estimated yield was fifty tons of flint. The shafts were dug using antler picks, and access would have been by wooden platforms and ladders. The main period of mining was 2100 to 1800 BC, with some shallow open cast quarrying up to 1650 BC, and the site is therefore an Early Bronze Age flint mine when flint was competing with bronze as a high status raw material. The extracted flint was worked on site, most likely into prestige flint tools: axe-heads, arrowheads, discoidal and other knives, sickles, etc. There are various horizontal, vertical, and diagonal lines scratched on the walls of some galleries, possibly as tally marks for the amount of flint extracted. A theory that the mines were Paleolithic in date was put forward in 1912, to be comprehensively disproved in 1933. There is strong suspicion that an otherwise excellent archaeologist, Leslie Armstrong, planted forged art in excavations in 1916–1921 in order to "prove" a Paleolithic date. In 1939, he was leading an excavation at the site, at which a carved chalk goddess and incised phallus were found. This was almost certainly a hoax some of the excavators played on the site director. After shafts were emptied of flint, they were used as pits for disposing rubbish, and even human burials. Visitors to the site today can climb down into the 30-foot-deep pit 1, and pass through the three seams of flint (the top, wall, and floorstones), and view the seven galleries leading away from the base.

Mold gold cape (Flintshire)

The Mold cape is a unique and astonishing artifact, found in 1833 on the upper part of a skeleton in an Early Bronze Age grave. The cape is 18 inches wide and is made of sheet gold hammered into shape and riveted onto a cloth and bronze base. It covered the shoulders and upper body, including the arms. The whole cape is decorated with horizontal bands of ridges, lozenges, circles, and squares. When found, there were over 200 amber beads of a necklace in the grave, most of which have since been lost. There is no proof, but it has the appearance of being a golden version of a woven cloth cape. The sex of the body is unknown but is assumed to be female. The cape would have pinned the wearer's arms to their sides and was not a practical garment, and therefore perhaps used only on special, or ceremonial occasions.

Mold gold cape from Flintshire in North Wales; Bronze Age, circa 1900–1600 BC, © 2005 David Monniaux

Mount Stuart jet necklace (Isle of Bute)

Jet necklaces are quite common in prehistoric Britain (other materials were also used, including amber). The one at Mount Stuart was found on the skeleton of a young woman buried crouched on her side in a stone cist under a round barrow. She was also buried with a pot (known as a food vessel), a corroded bronze object in her hands, and two bronze pins. The necklace was made of 100 beads, six flat plates, and a toggle for fastening, all of jet. The plates are all decorated. Around the neck of the woman, and over a woven tunic, this would have shone with the highly polished black jet. The desire for jewelry and "bling" goes back a very long way in human history. It may also have signaled her status in society, perhaps age, marital status, or social standing. We are unlikely ever to know.

Orkney: Barnhouse settlement (Orkney)

Discovered in 1984, Barnhouse is a settlement of late Neolithic stone houses, associated with Grooved Ware pottery. The site lies north of the Stones of Stenness. There is a large oval building 46 by 36 feet with at least six houses built around it. Another seven were later added to the settlement. To the south a 23-foot-square house was built with walls ten feet thick and an entrance facing the midsummer sunset inside an 85-foot-wide walled enclosure. In the open courtyard there were several hearths for cooking. The Barnhouse Stone is a separate site, a 10-foot-tall standing stone, almost half a mile from the passage grave at Maes Howe and aligned with it along the midwinter sunset.

Orkney: Maes Howe passage grave (Orkney), part of the Orkney World Heritage Site

The round mound of Maes Howe in Orkney was excavated in 1861. It was finely built of stone using impressive masonry skills and is 115 feet across and 24 feet high. It is surrounded by an enclosure 295 feet wide marked by a ditch 45 feet wide and up to 6 feet deep. It was erected sometime before 2700 BC. Within the mound, a 37-foot-long low stone passage leads to a central 15-foot-square chamber under a high corbeled roof, with three side chambers. The side chambers seem originally to have been sealed off and are assumed to have been for burials. The passage was aligned to the southwest allowing the midwinter sunset to shine directly down the passage and light up the end of the chamber. The burials at Maes Howe no longer survive, being robbed at a later period. This was probably by the Norsemen in the twelfth century, who left twenty-four runic inscriptions and drawings as graffiti scratched on the walls of the chamber.

Orkney: Ness of Brodgar (Orkney)

See current research (chapter 8).

Orkney: Ring of Brodgar stone circle (Orkney), part of Orkney World Heritage Site

On the western promontory only a mile away from the Stones of Stenness, the Ring of Brodgar is a stone circle 340 feet across inside a ditch cut up to 10 feet deep into the bedrock, 466 feet in diameter. There are twenty-seven surviving stones out of a possible original sixty, each quarried from a different part of Orkney. It truly was a communal monument for the whole island. Two entrances faced the northwest and southeast.

Orkney: Skara Brae settlement (Orkney), part of the Orkney World Heritage Site

Covered in sand until a storm in 1850, Skara Brae is a settlement first occupied around 3100 BC, modified 300 years later to the form we see now, and abandoned around 2500 BC. It is the best preserved and most evocative prehistoric settlement in Britain. Major excavations took place in the 1920s and 1970s. It was a small community of no more than fifty people living in six to eight houses at any one time. Each house was nearly 400 square feet in size and made of a single large room. Some of the stones on the internal walls were scratched with designs and may well have been painted. The houses were built off a covered passageway, and built into a midden of weathered refuse brought to the site to give extra strength and windproofing to the walls. Stone cupboards and alcoves were built into the walls, and each

Neolithic house at Skara Brae, Orkney, photo courtesy of Donald Henson

house seems to have had its own toilet also in the wall with an underfloor drain. There was a hearth in the middle of the house, a bed for the man (and his wife?) to the right of the door, and a bed for the woman or children to the left of the door. Opposite the door on the other side of the hearth is a stone dresser or storage space. The stone hearths were aligned on the midsummer and midwinter sunrise and sunset. Similar alignments exist at Barnhouse and at Maes Howe. Finds from the site included stone, bone, and wooden tools, bone necklaces, beads, pendants, and pins, and enigmatic carved stone objects about whose use or symbolism we can only guess.

Orkney: Stones of Stenness stone circle (Orkney), part of the Orkney World Heritage Site

On the eastern promontory of the entrance to Loch Harray is the stone circle of Stenness, placed within a bank and ditch 144 feet across with an entrance facing the settlement at Barnhouse to the north and less than a mile away from Maes Howe. Only four stones survive of the original twelve in the circle. A square stone setting in the middle contained cremated bone. A further stone setting was found elsewhere in the circle. The site may have been built between 3012 and 2864 BC, and activity continued until at least 2100.

Silbury Hill (Wiltshire), part of the Avebury World Heritage Site

One of the most impressive ancient sites in Britain is Silbury Hill. This is a gigantic conical mound (the largest man-made mound in Europe) that was begun around 2400 BC. It is now 160 yards across and 102 feet high. It was originally more than 130 feet high. The first recorded excavations in 1776 found a burial on the summit of unknown date, possibly Medieval. The first mound was covered in turf and was 120 feet across and 3 feet high. This was then enlarged to 50 feet high and 350 feet across by piling new material up against it and encircling it with a ditch with an internal bank. This was then further enlarged up to 130 feet high with a sophisticated system of chalk walls and steps to create a very stable slope underneath the smooth outer sides. It would have taken 700 men up to ten years to build and contains 12.5 million cubic feet of chalk and soil. The flat top may date from Medieval times when some kind of structure was built on the summit. An excavation of the site was televised in 1968 and 1969. No burials have ever been found inside the mound and its purpose remains a mystery, although only a very small proportion of it has been investigated.

Stonehenge (Wiltshire), World Heritage Site

See current research (chapter 8).

Towie stone ball (Aberdeenshire)

Some prehistoric objects are enigmatic, unlike anything we know of and with a purpose or meaning we can only guess at. Found in the mid-nineteenth century during the digging of a drain, the Towie stone ball is a superb example of various similar balls found in Britain. It is three inches across and made of a hard igneous rock, picrite. The stone has been ground down into shape and then incised with decoration. The are four circular faces to the ball. One is plain, one has four interlinking spirals on its surface, one has a central spiral surrounded by curved lines and pits, and the fourth has lobed concentric circles with three dots in the middle. All the designs are very elaborate, very finely cut, and may have been made with a copper or bronze tool. They resemble the designs used on the walls of some Late Neolithic passage graves, especially those in Ireland, and on the surface of Grooved Ware pottery of the same period. Various other stone balls are found, mostly in the northeast of Britain in modern Aberdeenshire. They are mostly the size of a tennis ball, and vary greatly in shape and design. Suggested uses for the stones include as weapons, weights for fishing nets, for telling the future, for attaching hides in leather-working, or as "ball-bearings" to help in moving stones for stone circles.

Other important sites

- Arbor Low, Derbyshire: a well preserved Late Neolithic henge with internal stone circle
- Big Moor, Derbyshire: a settlement with its fields and burial/ceremonial sites on either side of a stream on the high moors
- Castlerigg, Cumbria: a Late Neolithic stone circle 100 feet wide, sited on flat ground surrounded by the high fells
- Kilmartin Glen, Argyll: a landscape with 150 Neolithic to Early Bronze Age burial cairns, circles, henges, standing stones, avenues, and rock art

Map of Late Bronze and Iron Age sites, courtesy of Donald Henson

FARMS, FORTS, AND KINGS

Birdlip mirror (Gloucestershire)

One of the finest items of Iron Age art in Britain is the Birdlip mirror, found in 1879 by a workman digging for road stone. What was found were three Iron Age burials, two men and a woman, either in one or, more likely, in separate stone cists. The men were buried without any grave goods; not so the woman. She was buried with a silver gilt brooch and two bronze bowls, bracelets, tweezers, a knife handle shaped as the head of a bull, and a necklace of amber beads. The artifacts are of late styles, dating her burial to some time before 50 AD. The most impressive is the bronze-handled mirror. The round mirror is 11 inches across and has a 4 inch long handle all in bronze. One face would have been highly polished to be the face of the mirror. The handle is in the form of linked loops decorated with red enamel dots. The back of the mirror is decorated with typical late Iron Age swirling patterns. The mirror shows the taste of high status women at the time as well as the sophistication of native British society before the arrival of the Romans. The high status given to women at the time is recorded in historical documents at the time of the Roman conquest.

Camulodunum oppidum (Essex)

The site at Camulodunum was a major Iron Age center for the tribe of the Catuvellauni, although it may have been originally Trinovantian only to be taken over later by the Catuvellauni. The site covers 15 square miles, defended by a complex system of linear dykes (banks with ditches up to 13 feet deep). Excavations have been taking place within the oppidum since 1929, and have found two main concentrations of occupation. Gosbecks in the south was the main agricultural center, while Sheepen in the north was the center for manufacturing and trade. Sheepen was particularly rich in finds, with forty tons of artifacts being recovered in excavations from 1930 to 1939. The third major site within the oppidum was the Lexden cemetery, containing more than 600 burials. A separate Stanway cemetery seems to have been a high status burial area, with five enclosures each containing a wooden burial chamber. The dating of the site is still not certain, but the Gosbecks farmstead was most likely the earliest part of the oppidum, sometime around 50 BC. The northern settlement was then added, followed by the deposition of the earliest burials at Lexden around 25 BC. This seems to have coincided with the arrival of Addedomaros as King, making the site his capital. Camulodunum later became the capital of Cunobelinus, the most powerful king of southeastern Britain and an ally of Rome. The Roman conquest of Britain was signaled by the arrival of the Emperor Claudius at

Camulodunum in 43 AD, with the Legio XX Valeria. The legion was moved elsewhere in 49 AD but retired soldiers were settled in a new town on the site of the fortress, which also served as the first capital of the new Roman province of Britannia. This was destroyed by the Britons during the revolt of Boudicca in 61 AD, leaving a layer of burnt debris to be found by archaeologists. Although the capital was moved to London, the town was rebuilt. The earlier oppidum had a religious focus at a sacred enclosure and this was continued as a Roman temple and theater. Colchester's surviving Roman remains are among the most extensive in Britain, and have been under almost continuous archaeological investigation since 1929. The only known *circus*, Roman racing track, in Britain was found during recent excavations. Parts of the Roman city walls survive and include a large gateway. Archaeological work has been directed since 1963 by the Colchester Excavation Committee, an early forerunner of the modern archaeological field units.

Capel Garmon firedog (Conwy)

Cutting of peat for fuel has often led to the finding of ancient remains that were originally placed as offerings in wet, boggy places. One such offering was found by a farmworker in 1852 and is one of the best pieces of ornamental ironwork to be found in Britain. This was a firedog, a part of a hearth designed to contain and hold up logs of wood to help them burn. This particular firedog is 41 inches long by 30 inches high and consists of a metal bar near the ground joining two uprights at each end. The uprights are elaborately made with an ornamented shaft and a head at the top that combines features of a horse's head and that of a bull. It was made out of eighty-five separately shaped pieces and shows high skill on the part of the blacksmith. As part of the central hearth in a round house, it would have been an impressive and elegant centerpiece. A comparison with other firedogs in Britain suggests it was made between 50 BC and 50 AD.

Danebury hill fort (Hampshire)

The 12-acre site of Danebury is one of the best excavated hill forts in Europe, being dug from 1969 to 1988. The first hill fort on the site was built around 550 BC, with one line of vertically faced defenses and an external ditch with entrances in the southwest and east. The south of the fort was the residential area with round houses, while the north of the site was dominated by granaries and storage pits. The ditch was later enlarged to 20 feet deep and 39 feet wide, and the rampart behind was increased to over 30 feet high. By its end, there were shrines in the center and the houses were built along the insides of the ramparts with storage pits filling the rest of the inside. It may have housed up to 350 people. The gateways were defended by complex outworks, and a new area of thirteen acres was incorporated into the hill fort by building further defenses, possibly for guarding livestock. Much of the grain stored in the fort seems to have come from the surrounding farms. The fort was attacked and taken around 100 BC. Around 100 dead bodies were buried in pits and the fort was then abandoned.

Dartmoor settlements and field systems (Devon)

Dartmoor is an amazing relict landscape of the Late Bronze Age, underneath the open and exposed moorland that most people think is natural wilderness. Two major categories of site belong to this period: settlements and field systems. Grimspound is a settlement in a stone-walled enclosure, 500 feet across with 5-foot-high walls. It covers four acres and contains at least twenty-four houses and buildings. The buildings are circular and up to 15 feet across and with 3-foot-thick walls. The site was built around a stream and has a paved entrance facing uphill. The houses had low stone walls and high conical thatched or turfed roofs. Finds from the site show it was occupied during the Late Bronze Age, after 1200 BC. Holne Moor is a good place to see the Dartmeet reave system of Bronze Age fields. This is one of the best preserved and excavated sections of the moor. There are at least twenty-seven parallel reaves. A reave is a long land boundary that began as a fence and hedge, later replaced by a stone wall. Smaller cross-walls divided the land into farmsteads and fields. There are at least fifty-eight stone round houses, each up to 32 feet across. Traces of earlier wooden houses have been found in excavations. The reave system with its smaller fields and farms was laid out around 1500 BC, covering the whole of Dartmoor (around 40 square miles). This seems to have been an attempt to maintain heavy grazing of the uplands by livestock from approximately 1480 to 1080 BC.

Flag Fen settlement and field system (Cambridgeshire)

Flag Fen is a low-lying basin within the large embayment in eastern England known as the Fens. These are now drained and fertile farmland, but originally were wet marsh and fenland. Modern archaeological investigations at the site began in 1971. The high ground around the fen had fields and paddocks marked by banks and ditches, separated by droveways for livestock leading down to summer grazing at the water edge. A platform in the middle of the fen was connected to farms on either side by wooden causeways across the wet ground. Within the fen basin some 300 weapons, helmets, ornaments, and tools have been found, along with animal bones and pots. These were deposited in the shallow water of the fen between 1363 and 967 BC. The site is famous for its preservation of wooden artifacts that do not survive on dryland sites. There are even Bronze Age footprints preserved in the sediments. Occupation on the edges of the fen basin continued up to around 400 BC. The site is currently at the forefront of managing excavations through modern digital means of crowd-funding and crowd-sourcing for money and labor.

Hasholme boat (East Riding of Yorkshire)

Various logboats have been found in Britain over the years. One of the finest was found at Hasholme in 1984, preserved in the waterlogged bank of the River Foulness. It was made around 300 BC out of one oak tree and was 42 feet long and four-and-a-half feet wide. The stern was an upright, flat transom while the bow was shaped with extra timbers. The boat could have carried a full crew of twenty, poling or paddling it along the inland waterways, or had fewer crew and a cargo of five tons of goods. When found, it was carrying meat and timber. Wooden artifacts rapidly decay if left to themselves after excavation. A special tank was built to house the boat in the Hull and East Riding Museum, where it was sprayed with special chemicals for nearly twenty years before being allowed to dry out naturally in the air. Its condition needs constant monitoring and treatment. The boat is a reminder of the importance of Britain's waterways, and of what we miss on most land sites where wood and organic materials are not preserved.

Jarlshof settlement (Shetland), on the UK Tentative List for World Heritage Sites

Jarlshof was settled from the Neolithic period right through to the seventeenth century AD, with later houses being built on top of earlier ones. Coastal erosion has destroyed part of the site, including half the broch, a fortified stone tower with dry-stone walls approximately 5m thick. The earliest houses were oval-shaped, but by the end of the Bronze Age, around 800 BC, these were replaced by a group of roughly circular and, in some cases, interconnecting houses. One was used as a smithy; the style of bronze mold suggests that he might have been Irish. Souterrains, underground storage chambers, first appeared at this time. This settlement was replaced in the Iron Age by a broch and had a defensive courtyard. Once the need for such massive defences passed, the upper part of the broch was dismantled and reused to build large roundhouses, and the interior of the broch was remodelled. These were subsequently replaced by wheelhouses which had a central hearth surrounded by corbelled cells. It is the almost intact survival of these cells which earns Jarlshof its international standing. In due course, the Vikings settled and there are several longhouses visible. The earliest appears to be 70 feet long, but in fact represents an amalgam of several phases of alterations. Eventually the Viking village evolved into a medieval farm and a late 16th century prestigious house.

Old Scatness was equally long-lived by its remarkable preservation of the broch and surrounding Iron Age village. Excavated in recent times with modern techniques, it has rewritten what we know about the Iron Age in Northern Europe, re-dating the site (400-200 BC) and helping to interpret Jarlshof. The impressive two-story roundhouses were single skinned, but had diameters greater than that of the brochs, a remarkable feat of Iron Age engineering. There are wheelhouses at Scatness, too; one of which had the totem of a bear carved onto one of the upright piers at the end of the cell opposite the doorway. Today, replica buildings help the visitor to appreciate what Iron Age life might have been like.

Lindow Man (Cheshire)

Peat cutting often reveals the remains of human bodies, with their skin preserved by the peat. Found in 1984, Lindow Man turned out to be particularly interesting. One interpretation of his remains is that he had been killed by garroting, having his throat cut and being hit on the head, and was therefore some kind of religious sacrifice. Others dispute this and think he was simply murdered by a blow to the head. He was then buried face down in the bog. This happened sometime between 2 BC and 119 AD, so either late in the Iron Age or early in the Roman period. The man was in his mid-twenties, around 5 feet 7 inches tall, with a well-trimmed mustache and manicured fingernails, and therefore may have been from the well-to-do aristocracy. A year earlier, the head of a woman dating to around 210 AD was found in the same area. This was at first thought to be a modern murder victim and the discovery of the head prompted a confession to the murder from her husband who assumed the head was that of his wife! Parts of another body were found in 1987, and further parts of Lindow Man in 1988.

Little Woodbury settlement (Wiltshire)

The site of Little Woodbury is important in the development of British archaeology. New, more refined techniques of excavation were brought to Britain by the excavator of the site, Gerhard Bersu. He was a German archaeologist who had left Nazi Germany as a refugee and brought with him continental methods of excavation. He dug at the site in 1938 and 1939, only to be halted by the outbreak of war, and the internment of Bersu as a potential enemy alien. He never returned to the site and it remained only partially excavated. The site had first been identified by aerial photography. Bersu was able recognize the remains of wooden postholes which made possible the excavation of prehistoric settlements and the identification of round houses. He also recovered animal bones and cereal grains, allowing the examination of ancient farming. Until this dig, British archaeologists had assumed that prehistoric people lived in holes dug into the ground, so-called pit dwellings. These were revealed by Bersu to be storage pits, while people lived in well-built wooden round houses.

Llyn Cerrig Bach (Anglesey/Ynys Môn)

Lakes and wet places were often sites of votive deposition of offerings to the gods in later prehistory. In 1942, Llyn Cerrig Bach (Llyn means lake in Welsh) yielded evidence of more than 150 bronze and iron objects being offered over 400 years between 300 BC and 100 AD. The site has not yet been properly excavated, the finds being made accidentally during the building of an airfield. Some of the objects are related to warfare such as swords, spearheads, shields, iron tires for wagon or chariot wheels, horse gear, and a trumpet. Others are more related to daily life: blacksmith's tools, a sickle, cauldrons, animal bones, and iron bars for trading. There were also two sets of gang chains. These are neck shackles joined by links of chain, used to control a line of five people as prisoners. They may be evidence of the slave trade, since Roman writers tell us that Britons exported slaves to the continent in the late Iron Age. They may also simply have been used to control prisoners in battle being taken for sacrifice or execution. They are though among the most evocative of archaeological finds from Britain.

Maiden Castle hill fort (Dorset)

A Neolithic causewayed enclosure was the first site on the hill top of Maiden Castle, and a later bank barrow some 20 yards wide and 600 yards long was the next use of the hilltop. These were eclipsed many centuries later by one of the largest Iron Age hill forts in Europe. The first phase was built around 600 BC and was a 16-acre fort defended by one wooden-faced rampart and ditch. The ditch was later deepened to 23 feet and the gateway strengthened. The fort was extended to 47 acres around 450 BC. This larger fort was defended with a 9-foot-high bank, which was then enlarged with three ramparts added to the north side and four to the south. The entrances were made even more complex. Inside were round houses, stone laid streets, and storage pits, replaced by above-ground granaries in the later phase. The fort was attacked and taken by the Roman army during its conquest of Britain. A cemetery of fifty-two bodies was originally interpreted as a war grave after this attack. It is now thought to include some bodies from the attack (fourteen had signs of a violent death, one with a Roman catapult bolt in its back) but was probably the fort's normal cemetery, in use for some time before the fort's capture. By the time it was taken, the settlement seems to have shrunk and the eastern part of the fort was used for iron working. People continued living at the site for another generation but the site was abandoned sometime before 100 AD. A late Roman temple and a single Anglo-Saxon burial are the only signs the hill top was ever used again.

Mam Tor hill fort (Derbyshire)

Sited on the junction between the limestone of the White Peak and the gritstone moors of the Dark Peak is an impressive high hill overlooking the valley below. This is Mam Tor, the site of a 16-acre hill fort. It is not particularly large, nor are the defenses especially complex or grand. The first defense was a timber palisade, later replaced by a single line of stone-revetted ramparts. Inside this were house platforms, level terraces dug into the slope of the hill, some 23 feet across. A spring provided fresh water inside the fort. There were two entrances at either end of the hill with in-turned passages into the fort. What makes the site special are the dates of occupation, between 1541 and 1209 BC. These are Late Bronze Age dates, and it had been assumed that hill tops were only occupied in this way during the Iron Age. The early date is backed up by the finding of a socketed bronze axe-head on site. The defenses are assumed to have been added later, during the Iron Age. Mam Tor symbolizes the beginning of a new age in British prehistory, when new types of site dominated the landscape. The hill consists of soft shales and part of the face of the hill has eroded away and is still subject to landslides, slowly taking part of the hill fort with it.

Mousa broch (Shetland), on the UK Tentative List for World Heritage Sites

Built around 400-200 BC, Mousa has one of the narrowest footprints (just under 50 feet as measured so far) and is the best preserved broch anywhere, standing over 42 feet high. The walls are almost 15 feet wide, with a narrow entrance and three corbelled cells built into the ground floor. The staircase inside the double-skinned walls and the upper walkway still survive. Originally there were two timber stories, but like Jarlshof it was subsequently remodelled as a wheelhouse; perhaps uniquely, the original tower was left intact. The broch was used as a refuge in the Viking period.

Peelhill hoard (South Lanarkshire)

Ancient hoards were not always of precious metal. The Peelhill bronze hoard, found in 1961, consists of twenty-nine spearheads with their shafts preserved as fragments of burnt and unburnt wood, an axe-head, a sword, three rings, and a ferrule. They were deposited in a bog towards the end of the Late Bronze Age, around 950 to 750 BC. This action would normally be interpreted as a votive offering. However, many of the objects have been broken or are bent or partially melted. They look very much like a scrap metal hoard awaiting melting down for recycling. Interpretation is never easy in archaeology. Of course, there is no reason why both could not be accurate and that a smith made an offering of some of his surplus scrap to the gods.

Roos Carr figurines (East Riding of Yorkshire)

Among the more mysterious prehistoric finds from Britain are the wooden figures found at Roos Carr in 1836. There were originally eight figures, probably in two groups of four, each group standing on a wooden boat. Only five of the figures and one boat now survive and are in the Hull and East Riding Museum. They were carved out of yew, are between 14 and 16 inches tall, and have eyes inset with pieces of white quartzite. They also each have a detachable penis, and there are also shields and paddles. The figures were carved between 606 and 508 BC and are a votive offering made in a bog. We can only guess the reason for the offering. Where they gods, or ancestors, or living warriors wanting a blessing on a forthcoming venture? They are not unique—other wooden figures are known from the Early Bronze Age to the Iron Age—but they are one of the most well known and most intriguing.

Snettisham hoards (Norfolk)

In 1948, a farmer ploughing his field in Snettisham turned up a yellow metal object he identified as part of a brass bedstead. Other objects soon turned up and it was realized the bedstead was in fact an Iron Age golden torc (metal neck ring). Between 1948 and 1973, a total of five hoards of torcs were ploughed up in the field. A metal detectorist, Charles Hodder, returned to the field in 1990 and turned up more. He promptly reported his find and an excavation was mounted by the British Museum over the next two years. In all, eleven hoards have been found, and Snettisham is the largest group of gold and silver from one location in Iron Age Europe. There are 175 torcs or fragments of torcs, more than 100 ingot rings or bracelets, 234 coins and other pieces of metal. Most of the torcs are made of twisted gold or silver wires, resembling rope, while a few are golden tubes. The artwork and craftsmanship is of the highest order and still awe the viewer today. The hoards were deposited around 70 BC, perhaps as offerings, but perhaps as the material of a metalworker deposited for safekeeping. Around 150 years after their deposition, in the late first century AD, a 20-acre enclosure ditch was dug around the site. There is no indication of any structures or other deposits. The site remains a mystery. A separate hoard, the Jeweller's hoard, has been found in a different part of Snettisham, deposited around 155 AD. This was a pot containing 110 coins, 117 carnelian gemstones, rings, chains, necklace-clasps and pendants, bracelets, scrap silver and gold, and a quartz burnishing tool: the store of a jewelry maker.

Uffington White Horse (Oxfordshire)

On a chalk hill in the Berkshire Downs is the 374-foot-long figure of a horse carved into the chalk. The white horse gleams against the green

Golden torc from the Snettisham Hoard, photo courtesy of Andrea Offdenkamp Kendrick

grassy background. The figure is very stylized and resembles designs found in Iron Age art. Scientific dating shows it to have been carved sometime between 1200 and 800 BC and it is therefore Late Bronze Age. It may possibly be a tribal symbol.

Witham shield (Lincolnshire)

Among the many votive offerings in rivers in Britain is the Witham shield, found in 1826. Dating from the fourth century BC, this is the bronze covering of what would have been a wooden shield. It was deposited not far from the Fiskerton causeway. The wood has now vanished, leaving only the bronze cover. It was made of two long sheets of bronze beaten until wafer thin. The central boss has two long ridges covering the join of the two sheets, each ending in a circular design. The shield also originally had the large figure of a boar attached to the surface, possibly made of leather. The whole shield is over three-and-a-half feet long. The decoration on the ridge, boss, and roundels is a superb example of the La Tène art style found in Britain and western Europe at the time. The central boss has inlay of red coral that most likely comes from the Mediterranean. The shield cover is a rare find, not only in Britain but also in prehistoric Europe.

Other important sites

- Castell Henllys, Pembrokeshire: an excavated Iron Age hill fort, open as a visitor center with reconstructed round houses
- Eildon Hill, Scottish Borders: the largest Iron Age hill fort in northern Britain, covering 40 acres with at least 300 houses, occupied from 1000 BC into the Roman period
- Fiskerton, Lincolnshire: an Iron Age wooden causeway 175 feet long, used for making offerings into marshland, rebuilt at midwinter lunar eclipses every eighteen years from 457 to 339 BC
- Gurness, Orkney: an Iron Age broch occupied from 200 BC to 100 AD, 65 feet across with an outer settlement for up to forty families
- Hengistbury Head, Dorset: an Iron Age promontory fort with evidence for manufacturing and trade with Gaul, Italy, and Spain
- Oakbank Crannog, Perthshire: an Iron Age dwelling built out in a platform jutting out into Loch Tay, the basis for the reconstruction at the Scottish Crannog Centre

Iron Age Broch of Gurness, Orkney, photo courtesy of Donald Henson

5

HISTORIC SITES AND FINDS

Historic sites reveal the growing sophistication of British life and how the modern landscape has developed. Many of the sites that help to tell this story are still standing and in use. They include sites of international importance, exhibiting not only beauty but also technical ingenuity. Britain pioneered the modern industrial world, but built that world on secure medieval and earlier foundations. There is much to see and admire that still survives in Britain's urban and rural landscapes.

ROMAN INTERLUDE

Antonine Wall frontier (Central Scotland), World Heritage Site
After abandoning the attempt to take the northern highlands of Britain in 142 AD, the Romans marked the most northerly frontier of their Empire by building a wall linking the estuaries of the Forth and Clyde, the narrowest part of northern Britain. The wall was a 37-mile-long earthen rampart on stone foundations. It was 14 feet wide and at least 10 feet high fronted by a deep ditch. Soldiers were based in forts at intervals of every two miles along the wall and linked along the wall by a road. There are ornate stone inscriptions, the Distance Slabs, which record the building of sections of the wall by the detachments of the three legions then in Britain (II Augusta, VI Victrix and XX Valeria Victrix). The wall itself was garrisoned mostly by

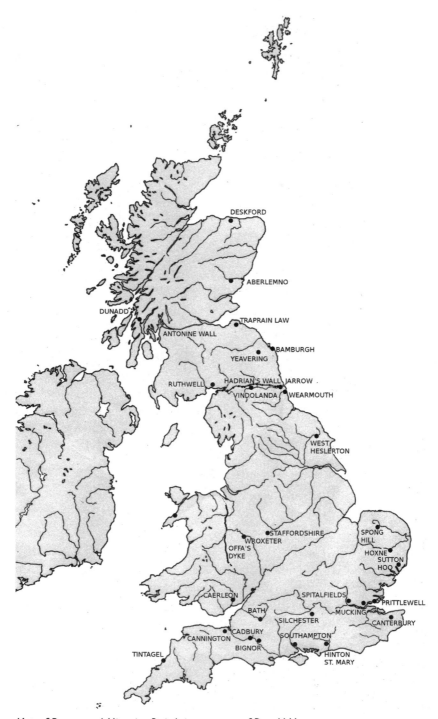

Map of Roman and Migration Period sites, courtesy of Donald Henson

auxiliary units. Twenty-five miles of the wall survive to the present day. The best places to see the wall itself are at Croy Hill and Seabegs, while buildings survive at Bar Hill, Rough Castle, and Bearsden. The frontier was short-lived, abandoned in 158 AD when the Roman frontier was moved farther southward back to the earlier Hadrian's Wall boundary line.

Bath temple complex (Somerset), World Heritage Site

A temple and baths complex dedicated to the goddess Sulis, equated with Roman Minerva, was built in the 60s around a hot water spring. This spring rises from a geological fault and produces 240,000 gallons of water a day at a temperature of 115° F. At first, the spring opened within the temple courtyard, but was later enclosed within a roofed stone shrine. The temple to the goddess was built in classical Roman style containing a statue of Sulis, the gilt bronze head of which survives. Much of the temple has survived later destruction and rebuilding. The Roman drains at the site are still largely in use. Attached to the temple was a public baths suite with a large bathing pool and smaller bathing, sauna, and changing rooms. Around 12,600 coins and 1,500 votive curse tablets of lead or pewter have been found deposited in the spring. From around 350 AD, the temple was not kept in a good state of repair and began to decline, to be finally demolished sometime between 450 and 500 AD. The site was reused from around 1100 AD when new baths were built around the spring, and has been in use ever since.

Bignor Roman villa (West Sussex)

Villas are farmsteads built in a Roman manner with long ranges of rectangular rooms connected together, roofed in tiles with plastered walls and often with mosaic floors. This is different from the round house tradition of the native Iron Age. They can be quite simple farmsteads or grand "manor houses," even "palaces." One of the earliest villas to be excavated was Bignor, discovered in 1811, and soon becoming a major tourist attraction. It has some of the finest mosaics yet discovered in Roman Britain. A late first century native farmhouse was replaced by a rectangular farmhouse by 250 AD. Side wings were added to this by 300, with a bath suite and barn added around the courtyard. A fourth range then enclosed the courtyard and a perimeter wall was added. The whole villa then comprised sixty-five rooms. Rather fine classical mosaic floors were added to the north wing. One of the mosaics still survives for a length of 80 feet. The farm may have been at the center of a 2,000-acre estate. What became of the villa at the end of the Roman period is still a mystery.

Caerleon fort and amphitheater (Newport)

Caerleon is the best surviving legionary fortress in Britain. Known to the Romans as *Isca*, it now takes its name from the Welsh for city of the legion

(*Caerllion*), founded around 75 AD as the headquarters of the Legio II Augusta. The fort itself covers 50 acres, and has associated baths, amphitheater and quayside on the River Usk. The barracks and amphitheater were designed to house 6,000 soldiers. There is a sixth century tradition that early Christian martyrs Julius and Aaron were executed there. Recent excavations have uncovered a large storeroom with supplies of soldiers' armor. An early administrative suburb abandoned after 200 AD lies just outside the fort. The legion may have moved to the southeast coast of Britain after 296 AD and the fort was abandoned, although the amphitheater seems to have been still used.

Deskford carnyx (Aberdeenshire)

A carnyx is a form of elongated trumpet or horn, having a long upright stem and an animal's head at the top. They were used throughout Europe to accompany armies in battle and are known as early as 300 BC. The carnyx found at Deskford in 1816 is the only one so far found in Britain. It was found in a peat bog and was probably deposited there as a votive offering. Pottery and animal bones have been found at the same spot, the remains of other offerings. Only the head of the carnyx was found. This was made of sheets of bronze and brass, and made to resemble the head of a boar, a notably fierce animal connected with bravery and aggression. The presence of brass shows that it was made from recycled Roman objects, and probably dates to between 80 and 200 AD, while the Iron Age continued in northern Britain at the same time that the south was under Roman rule. A reconstruction was made in 1993 and has helped to bring the sounds of the past alive, and has been played as part of modern musical composition. Sadly, we don't know how the carnyx would have sounded in its original time.

Hadrian's Wall frontier (northern England), World Heritage Site

Emperor Hadrian accepted that the Romans would not conquer the whole of Britain, and in 122 AD decreed a 73-mile-long fortified frontier be built along the line of a military road, the Stanegate which connected the west coast at the Solway estuary with the east coast at the River Tyne. The wall would not only defend the province but would allow control of movement in and out of it, and so enable the Romans to levy taxes and customs on people passing through it. Hadrian's Wall was constructed with fifteen major forts placed at regular intervals, with milecastles in between every one Roman mile (0.92 of a statute mile) and towers every third of a mile between them. The fortified frontier was continued twenty miles southward along the line of the west coast as far as Maryport. The wall was part of a system involving supply depots behind the wall and outpost forts to the north. The western half of the wall was first built of turf and later rebuilt in stone while the eastern half was stone from the beginning and was up to 10 feet thick. The wall itself would be up to 20 feet high in places. The frontier was moved northward to the Antonine Wall by 142 AD, only to move back permanently to Hadrian's Wall after 158 AD. The size of the army garrisons was reduced around 275 AD, and the villages that had grown up around the forts seem to have been abandoned. The later history of the Wall is very poorly known. Continuity into the migration period is known from some forts, but is hard to identify without very careful modern excavation. The main forts on the frontier, with their associated civil settlements (*vici*) that have been excavated and open to the public are:

- Birdoswald (Cumbria), *Banna*, where excavations have revealed the site was not abandoned until around 520;
- Chesterholm (Northumberland), *Vindolanda*, the site of long-term excavations in waterlogged ground revealing rare organic evidence of life in Roman times (see chapter 8);
- Chesters (Northumberland), *Cilurnum*, with a well-preserved bath house;
- Corbridge (Northumberland), *Corioritum*, two-and-a-half miles south of the Wall;
- Housesteads (Northumberland), *Vercovicium*, one of the best surviving examples of a fort from Britain.

The latrine block at Housesteads Roman fort, photo courtesy of Donald Henson

Hinton St. Mary mosaic (Dorset)

The excavation of a Roman villa in 1963 revealed what may be the earliest known depiction of Christ. The floor was in two halves. One half is classical, showing Bellerophon slaying the monster Chimera. This may simply be an example of classical mythology, or it may represent the triumph of good over evil. Elsewhere, the floor has various hunting scenes and other images. The main feature is in the middle of the other half of the floor. This is a figure inside a circle, facing the viewer and with the Christian symbol of the Chi-Rho behind his head and flanked by two pomegranates (images of eternal life). The face is clean shaven with short hair and typical of early portrayals of Christ. It has been suggested that this image was adapted from a coin minted in 352 that had Christian symbolism, and the image is an adapted version of the Emperor Magnentius used to represent Christ. It is the only known portrayal of Christ in a mosaic floor from anywhere in the Roman Empire. Mosaics of Christ become common in the later Roman Byzantine Empire.

Hoxne hoard (Suffolk)

Discovered in 1992, the Hoxne hoard is one of the biggest ever found in Britain. There are 14,780 gold, silver, and bronze coins. The gold jewelry includes eighteen bangles, one armlet, six necklaces, three finger rings, and one chain. The other objects are of silver: seventy-eight spoons, twenty ladles, nine toothpicks, ear cleaners and cosmetic brush handles, five vases, four pepper pots, three wine strainers, one other strainer and funnel, two vases, and one handle. The latest coins are of the British usurping Emperor Constantinus III who reigned after 407 AD. The hoard must have been placed in the ground sometime after this. After Britain left Roman rule in 410, few Roman coins came into the island. Many of the silver coins have been clipped by having their edges trimmed to collect silver. This silver was then used to mint new coins as copies of Roman originals (usually termed forgeries), some of which are found in the hoard. Various names are inscribed on some of the items. Aurelius Ursicinus was inscribed on ten of the spoons, Peregrinus, Faustinus, and Silvicola occur on others, and one bracelet has an inscription to the lady Juliana. The artistic quality of the objects is very high. The handle is an impressive prancing tiger, while the pepper pots are in the shape of a bust of a woman, a statuette of Hercules, a goat, and a hound and hare. Some of the objects had Christian symbols on them, crosses or the Chi-Rho symbol and an inscription (*vivas in deo*, may you live in God). The hoard was found by a metal detectorist, Eric Lawes, who immediately reported the find without trying to dig it all out of the ground himself so that it could be excavated properly.

Spitalfields woman (Greater London)

A stone sarcophagus excavated in 1999 turned out to have a lead coffin inside with the remains of a wealthy young woman who died in fourth century Roman London. The excavations were of a large Medieval priory and hospital cemetery, which happened to lie above a much earlier and smaller Roman cemetery. The woman was in her early twenties and 5 feet 4 inches tall. She was laid with her head lying on a pillow of bay leaves. Her lead coffin was decorated with scallop shells and inside the sarcophagus were two delicate glass phials and jet artifacts, possibly for applying makeup. Isotope analysis of her remains shows that she had been brought up in Rome, and probably came to Britain after childhood. It is likely that she was part of the family of Roman officials posted to far-away Britannia. That the family was wealthy is not in doubt. Traces of textile were preserved under her body, including gold thread and silk (from China) as well as wool. The whole find is one of the most spectacular Roman burials to be found in Britain. A reconstruction of her face was made for the television series *Meet the Ancestors*.

Tre'r Ceiri hill fort (Gwynedd)

This is a very well-preserved hill fort with its house foundations, intact gateways, and its stone ramparts surviving almost to their full height of more than eleven feet with its parapet walk still existing in places. Trackways lead up to two separate entrances with passageways into the interior. A second wall was added to the west and north. Stone stock enclosures lie outside the fort defenses. There are around 150 houses inside the fort which show that stone-built round houses were succeeded over time by ones of rectangular shape. Although beginning in the Iron Age, most of the finds in the fort were from the Roman period and show the site was still in use through the Roman occupation. Roman-style settlement was rare on the western edge of the Empire.

MIGRATIONS AND KINGDOMS

Aberlemno Pictish stone (Angus)

The churchyard at Aberlemno contains three carved Pictish standing stones. The most elaborate of them is a cross-slab standing nearly eight feet high. As well as being one of the most artistically impressive of the Pictish stones in northern Britain, it also has great historical importance. It has a triangular top and widens towards the base. One side has a high relief cross, intricately decorated with geometric interlaced and spiral designs standing above the flat background decorated with intertwining animals. The back of the slab has two Pictish symbols at the top—the notched rectangle and Z-rod—above a depiction of a battle between foot soldiers and men on horseback. Reading from the top, the battle shows bare-headed warriors defeated a force of helmeted enemies. Early interpretations of the stone were that this depiction was a commemoration of the Battle of Dunnichen on 20 May 685, where a Pictish army decisively defeated a major invasion from Anglian Northumbria: clearly an event worth celebrating in stone. More recent scholars have preferred to date the stone to the ninth century, leaving the identity of the warriors and the battle uncertain.

Cadbury Castle fort (Somerset)

The site of Cadbury Castle is also known as South Cadbury (not to be confused with Cadbury-Congresbury). It is not a castle at all but a prominent 20-acre hill fort. Excavations have revealed Neolithic settlement of around 3500 BC, also Late Bronze Age and Iron Age settlement. Roman conquest led to it being abandoned. There was some occupation in the fourth century, and then again from the 470s to the 580s. A wooden hall 63 by 34 feet was built. The excavations found pottery from the eastern Mediterranean, imported by the high status British ruler based at the site. A tradition was recorded in the sixteenth century of the site being the Medieval Camelot. This was a false assumption based on the name of the nearby village of Camel and has no historical basis.

Canterbury St. Martin's Church (Kent), World Heritage Site

St. Martin's is possibly a church founded in Roman times. It lies just outside the city walls and was given by King Ethelbert to his Christian Frankish wife Bertha around 580. The western half of the chancel, just 14 feet wide and 18 feet long, is built out of Roman brick. The nave is 38 feet long and 24 feet wide, and was built in the seventh century. The eastern half was extended in the twelfth and thirteenth centuries, and a tower added in the fourteenth century. It has been in continuous use as a church for nearly 1,500 years.

Dunadd fort (Argyll and Bute)

Argyll was a part of northern Britain settled by Irish kings and their followers (the Scots) in the fifth century, creating the Kingdom of Dal Riata. Dunadd was their capital until the ninth century. The site they chose was an earlier Iron Age hill fort built around 300 BC. Fortifications were added in the fifth century and extended at times into the ninth century to make an enclosure on the top of the hill, approached through the outer defenses below. The fort included a major metalworking workshop of the seventh century using gold, silver, copper alloys, lead, and iron, especially making penannular brooches and other objects. There were large amounts of pottery and glass, imported from Gaul, and other objects from the Mediterranean. One intriguing part of the site is a flat outcrop of rock with a carved footprint, and a carved Pictish boar and Ogham inscription. The footprint is most likely part of the inauguration ritual of the kings of Dal Riata. Dunadd declined after the Kings took over the Pictish kingdom to the east and moved their center of power to the Pictish heartland on Tayside.

Mucking settlement and cemetery (Essex)

A long-term excavation at Mucking between 1965 and 1978 involved the full recovery of a 45-acre settlement and its cemetery. A Roman settlement and cemetery here were abandoned in the fourth century before early fifth century Saxon settlers moved in. The settlement slowly moved northwards over the next 200 years. There were two main types of buildings: 203 small sunken-floored workshops or storerooms and up to 53 larger rectangular dwellings. Some of these were large halls up to 50 feet long by 25 feet wide. As well as pottery and brooches, there were also early fifth century military belt fittings of Roman origin which may show the origin of the settlement as that of Saxon soldiers brought over to serve native British authorities. The cemetery was used up to the mid-seventh century when burials were moved elsewhere, presumably to a new Christian site. There were 399 inhumations and 468 cremations in two separate cemeteries. At any one time, there were perhaps 100 people living in several farmsteads on the site.

Offa's Dyke (Clawdd Offa in Welsh, on the English/Welsh border)

Offa's Dyke is one of the most impressive monuments of the period. It is a long linear bank with a ditch 7 feet deep and 23 feet wide, that runs north-south along the Welsh Marches (crossing and recrossing the modern border between England and Wales). The bank mostly faces to the west and still survives up to 23 feet high in places. There are no obvious gaps or gateways through the dyke, nor are there any forts attached to it. One research project, that ran for thirty-one years, defined the dyke as a 64-mile-long border built by the Anglo-Saxon King Offa of Mercia (757–796) to defend his kingdom against attacks from the Welsh Kingdom of Powys. Other scholars disagree and extend the line of the dyke to a total of 80 miles, running all the way southward to the Severn estuary. They see the dyke as the result of a treaty between Mercia and various Welsh kingdoms.

Southampton town (Hampshire)

Key excavations took place at Southampton in the 1960s and 1970s which revealed evidence for occupation from around 650 AD, and there is documentary evidence that by 721 it was already an important port and market for the Kingdom of Wessex. Its name in Old English varied between *Hamwic* and *Hamtun*, meaning the settlement on the *hamm*, the promontory between the Rivers Itchen and Test. The town was carefully planned with proper roads, laid-out streets, and areas of industrial activity including metalworking, textile production, bone and antler working, and glass working.

The deliberate planning was most likely the result of its founding by royal authority to serve their capital of Winchester a few miles to the north. The town covered around 100 acres and may have held up to 3,000 inhabitants, a large size for the period. Many coins from the continent were found in the excavations, along with quernstones from the Rhineland, glass and pottery from northern France, the Rhineland, and the Low Countries. The main focus of settlement moved southwestward to the area of the modern city from around 850. The excavations at Southampton revealed for the first time evidence of a flourishing economy in a period that had hitherto been thought to be a primitive society with little economic activity. It was a milestone in enlarging our understanding of the seventh and eighth centuries.

Sutton Hoo cemetery (Suffolk)

Sutton Hoo is a cemetery of eighteen early Anglo-Saxon round barrows (thirteen of which are still standing). A spectacularly rich burial was excavated in 1939, completed just two weeks before the outbreak of the Second World War. The mound covered a ship 90 feet long and 15 feet wide. All that was left of the ship were the outline of the planks and the iron rivets, as the wood had long since rotted away. Inside the ship was a burial chamber 18 feet long by 15 feet wide. The bones of the body had long since been eroded away by the acidic sandy soils of the area. However, there were spectacularly rich gold and silver grave goods, amongst the most beautiful and technically skilled gold and silver work ever found in Britain or even Europe. Some were clearly imported. There was a silver bowl from the Byzantine Empire in the eastern Mediterranean, coins and a belt buckle from the Frankish kingdom in modern-day France and Germany, and the elaborate iron helmet and shield are similar to others found in Sweden. There were also hanging bowls that had come from the native Britons to the west. Other objects included a sword, several spears, an axe and a coat of chain mail, a standard and scepter. Gaming pieces, bowls, dishes, drinking horns, a ladle, a cup, and a lyre show an expectation of feasting in the afterlife. The Frankish gold belt buckle is of extremely high quality, but is eclipsed by the gold and garnet shoulder clasps and purse lid, showing a spectacular level of craftsmanship as well as stunning beauty. The burial may have been that of King Rædwald of East Anglia who died in 626. The burial itself is pagan, but the goods do include two silver Christian spoons and we know that Rædwald had dabbled with Christianity while still being pagan. Later excavations at the site have uncovered more burials, including thirty-nine from the eighth to eleventh centuries of people executed by hanging or beheading. The skeletons had decayed in the sand leaving only a dark crusty stain that needed very careful excavation. One very strange, puzzling execution burial was of a man laid out in a running position and buried with what might have been a simple plough.

Traprain Law treasure (East Lothian)

The hill fort of Traprain Law (also known as Dunpender) was occupied on and off since the Late Bronze Age. It lay in the lands of the *Votadini*, or in its later Welsh form *Gododdin*. Excavations revealed that the inhabitants had imported a lot of items from Roman Britain to the south. A major find in 1919 was a hoard of Roman silver. It was deposited sometime after 410–425, after Roman rule had ended. There were fragments of 150 objects weighing more than fifty-three pounds, including tableware, items from a church or domestic chapel, a lady's dressing items, coins, and fittings from military uniforms. The objects had been cut into pieces and many were folded flat. This was either loot from raiding the south of Britain or perhaps a payment by rulers in the south to an ally to help defend them against Picts to the north.

Wearmouth-Jarrow monastery (Tyne and Wear), on the UK Tentative List for World Heritage Sites

A monastery was founded at Wearmouth by Benedict Biscop in 674 and linked as a joint monastery with another site at Jarrow in 682. Benedict imported masons and builders from Gaul to build the monasteries in a Roman style using stone rather than timber. The two sites would become a major center of learning and craftsmanship in western Europe. What survives at Wearmouth is the west end and tower of one of the three churches in the monastery. At Jarrow, the chancel and part of the tower survive from the church which was dedicated in 685. This dedication was recorded on a stone laid into the wall of the church and still survives. Both monasteries were later attacked and burnt by Vikings, and were renovated and restored in 1075, becoming cells of Durham Cathedral in 1083. They were abandoned after the dissolution of monasteries in 1539. The sites are historically important as the home of Bede who joined Wearmouth aged just seven and moved to Jarrow at the age of ten. Bede was one of Europe's greatest scholars, writing many works on theology and a key historical work, the *Historia Ecclesiastica Gentis Anglorum* (Ecclesiastical History of the English People) in 731. This is the founding narrative of English history and did much to shape the identity of the English in the early Medieval period. He wrote in the scholarly language of the time, in Latin. His history, along with other works, was translated into Old English in the late ninth century as part of the creation of the cultural identity of the new Kingdom of England.

West Heslerton settlement and cemetery (North Yorkshire)

An Anglo-Saxon cemetery with 201 burials was excavated in 1977 to 1986 as part of the total archaeological investigation of the parish of Heslerton. The cemetery was placed about 300 yards north of the settlement, and had around 500 bodies dating from 450 to 650 AD. Some of the grave goods indicate links with southern Scandinavia. Chemical analysis of the bones has provided evidence both for immigration from the continent, and for some settlers arriving from the west of Britain, showing that the migration period was more complex than we thought. The nearby settlement was excavated in 1986–1995. This was a very large and detailed excavation, yielding over 130,000 artifacts. The first settlement had been founded in the Iron Age, but around 450 the people moved to a new site about three-quarters of a mile to the south on higher ground next to a freshwater stream coming from a spring which had been the focus for a Roman shrine since the fourth century. The new village eventually covered 32 acres, with homes in the east, craft production and agricultural processing in the west. There was a possible high status farm at the south. There were 130 sunken-floored workshops and stores, and more than 90 wooden domestic buildings. Many of the sunken-floored buildings seem to have been used for storing grain and other items. The settlement shrank after 650 to a smaller area.

Wroxeter town (Shropshire)

The excavations at Wroxeter from 1955 to 1990 were one of the country's most important and innovative field research projects. The town began as *Viroconium*, a temporary Roman fortress. When the army left in 90 AD, the town became the civilian capital of the Cornovii tribal area. The buildings were mostly of timber, and only a few were rebuilt in stone. It was prosperous with industries in bronze, iron, glass, leather, bone, and pottery, and imported whetstones from Kent, pottery from Gaul, and glass vessels from Cologne. The town's temples were destroyed by Imperial order late in the fourth century, and there is evidence for a church being built near the center of the town. The baths complex had a large meeting hall, hot and cold rooms, latrines, two taverns serving food and drink, and an outdoor plunge pool that only lasted for sixty years in the cold British climate before being filled in. There was also a market hall built next door. Finds from the excavations included more than one-and-a-half tons of pottery and one ton of animal bones, as well as 11,000 other artifacts. A small part of the wall of the baths survives, 60 feet long and 23 feet high. The high standard of excavation was rare in archaeology at the time and revealed a long history of the site into the post-Roman period, very unusual in Britain. A stone tombstone was found with an inscription in Irish to a man named Cunorix, who died between 450 and 475, an Irish migrant to Britain. The town center was redeveloped in the middle of the fifth century with various large timber-framed buildings of a classical Roman style. It may have been a high class residence for a powerful ruler, the "palace" of the local bishop, or a complex of shops for public use. The whole block was dismantled and replaced by two smaller buildings, possibly around 550. The town and surrounding area were taken over in the seventh century by the Anglo-Saxon kingdom of Mercia, possibly in 642 or 658. After this, it dwindled to become a small village, as it still is today.

Yeavering (Northumberland)

Just below Yeavering Bell Iron Age hill fort, is a site discovered by aerial photography in 1949. Excavations from 1953 to 1962 found late sixth century buildings and an enclosure for livestock (either cattle or horses). Structures include a unique wooden grandstand of six, later extended to nine, rows of seats. There was a large timber hall with various smaller outbuildings around it. A building near the cemetery was full of ox skulls from pagan sacrifice. Yeavering was built by the Angles who were conquering the Kingdom of Bernicia in Northumbria in the sixth century and seems to have been one of the royal centers of the kingdom. The presence of a Frankish belt buckle of 575–635 and a copy of a Frankish *coin* minted circa 625/35, both probably from Kent, may reflect the marriage of King Edwin to a Kentish princess, Æthelburh. There is evidence of destruction of some of the buildings by burning, perhaps during the many wars that afflicted Northumbria during its turbulent political history at the time. The burials from the cemetery are in both Anglo-Saxon and native British traditions, a sign of the mixed origins of the kingdom. The excavator of the site, Brian Hope-Taylor, had his briefcase stolen at Hamburg railway station in 1960, which contained the only copy of his first excavation report. He had to rewrite the whole again from scratch.

Other important sites and artifacts

- Cannington, Somerset: a second to ninth century cemetery showing the change from pagan to Christian burials and the arrival of Anglo-Saxon culture among the native Britons
- Franks Casket (British Museum): an eighth century bone casket decorated with scenes from Christian, Roman, and Germanic mythology, with inscriptions in Latin and Old English
- Lindisfarne Gospels (British Library): a masterpiece of human creativity and one of the greatest of all European illuminated manuscripts, a version of the Christian gospels, made at the monastery of Lindisfarne possibly before 698 or around 715. An Old English translation was added to the gospels in the late tenth century
- Ruthwell Cross, Dumfries: an eighth century stone cross shaft with carvings of scenes from the Bible and an inscription of Old English poetry
- Spong Hill, Norfolk: the biggest Anglo-Saxon cemetery yet excavated, with 2,384 cremations and 57 inhumations of Germanic immigrants of the fifth century
- Tintagel fort, Cornwall: foundations of 100 stone buildings at a native British trading site importing goods from the central and eastern Mediterranean in the fifth to the seventh centuries

ISLE OF LEWIS

DURHAM

GOSFORTH
CROSS

FOUNTAINS
ABBEY
VALE
WHARRAM PERCY
TOWTON
YORK
SANDAL
CASTLE
BARTON

BEAUMARIS

CAERNARFON
CONWY
CHESTER
GOLTHO

HARLECH
REPTON
BOSWORTH

LONDON
WESTMINSTER

Map of Medieval Period sites, courtesy of Donald Henson

MEDIEVAL MONARCHIES

Alfred jewel (Ashmolean Museum, Oxford)

The Anglo-Saxons were expert craftsmen in jewelry. One of the finest surviving examples is the Alfred jewel, from around 890. This was most likely the ornamented end of an *æstel*, a wooden or ivory pointer used to guide the eye when reading a text. The jewel is an open gold fretwork mount in the shape of animal's head, containing a large piece of crystal, behind which is a portrait of a figure holding symbols of kingship. The figure may be of Christ. An inscription around the side tells us, in Old English, *Ælfred mec heht gewyrcean*, which in modern English is "Alfred ordered me to be made." This was undoubtedly King Alfred the Great and it was probably made and given as part of his program of translating key works into English for use in teaching in the cathedral and palace schools. It is thus a symbol of the origins of English kingship.

Canterbury Cathedral (Kent), World Heritage Site

Canterbury Cathedral is the home of English Christianity and the seat of the metropolitan Archbishop of Canterbury, the symbolic head of the worldwide Anglican communion. The first cathedral was built between 598 and 602 and was remodeled on a bigger scale from the ninth century onwards. The Anglo-Saxon cathedral was burnt down in 1067 and was rebuilt in a Romanesque style in 1070–1077. Another fire in 1174 led to another rebuilding of the cathedral choir in 1184. The nave and transepts were rebuilt in the Perpendicular style in the fifteenth century. Two of the three towers were added in the fifteenth century, the third in the 1830s. Inside was the shrine of the murdered Archbishop Thomas Becket, a major object of pilgrimage. The cathedral became a monastic chapter in the tenth century and remained monastic until 1540. The monks' cloister was built on the northern side of the church, which is unusual, but this was the side farthest away from the busy city streets. It has a separate lavatory, which was where the monks washed before going in for their meals (it did not have today's meaning of the toilets!). Some of the monastic buildings survive, such as the brewhouse and bakehouse. Monasteries were leading the architectural technologies of their day, and were renowned for their water supplies. Canterbury cathedral brought its water through a set of filter beds outside the city walls.

Canterbury St. Augustine's Abbey (Kent), World Heritage Site

The abbey of St. Augustine's in Canterbury was the earliest monastery to be created among the Anglo-Saxons. It was founded in 598 on land outside the old Roman city walls. Augustine was the leader of the Christian mission from Pope Gregory to the Anglo-Saxons, and the first Archbishop of Canterbury. The monastery was extensively remodeled after 1000, and again from the 1070s in a more modern Romanesque style. A new cloister was built in 1276, and many of the outer buildings were rebuilt in the fourteenth century. There was even some repair work needed after Canterbury was struck by an earthquake in 1382. The monastery was dissolved in 1538 and some of the outbuildings were refurbished as a royal palace for King Henry VIII, while the church was demolished and sold for building materials. The palace was sold to private owners after 1547. Since the eighteenth century, parts of the site have been a brewery, a prison, a hospital, and a college. The King's School and its playing fields now occupy part of the site in buildings of the 1840s.

Chester Rows (Cheshire)

The rows of Chester are a unique Medieval townscape. Each row is a covered walkway on the floor above the ground-floor shop fronts. This allowed access to an upper story of shops, with space for display of goods in the open. They developed during the thirteenth century, along the four main streets that run north-south and east-west through the middle of Chester. The ground floor of each shop was originally the undercroft, for storage of goods. The first floor above would be the shop front. The buildings above, behind, and below the rows have been continually redeveloped and altered since the sixteenth century, yet the rows remain and the Medieval character has been largely preserved by later architecture being built in a Medieval style.

Durham Castle (Durham), World Heritage Site

The castle at Durham was built in 1072 for the Earls of Northumbria and passed to the Bishop of Durham in 1075. It guards the neck of the peninsula in which the cathedral sits. The Bishop of Durham gave the castle to the new University of Durham in 1838, and it has been much modified. Parts of the original structure remain, including the Constable's Hall that was built in 1170 and the Great Hall that was built in 1290. A chapel was added in 1540. The keep was rebuilt by the university to create student accommodation.

Durham Cathedral (Durham), World Heritage Site

The Bishopric of Durham has its origins in the early Bishopric of Lindisfarne, sited on an island off the coast. This was vulnerable to Viking attacks and the bishop moved inland, first to Chester-le-Street in 883 and then to Durham in 995. The relics of St. Cuthbert were also brought, and became the focus of pilgrimage at the new cathedral. The Anglo-Saxon cathedral was replaced by the current Romanesque building between 1093 and 1140.

By this time, the Bishops of Durham had been granted wide powers and governed what would become the County of Durham as representatives of the King (the Bishops were often known as the Prince-Bishops of Durham). Their cathedral is one of the best examples of Romanesque architecture that still survives, apart from the eastern end and the towers which date from the thirteenth century. The cloisters and some of the buildings of the cathedral monastery still survive, including the original monks' dormitory. There was a separate polygonal kitchen behind the refectory. There was even a small cell known as the prison for disobedient monks.

Fountains Abbey (North Yorkshire), World Heritage Site

Fountains Abbey is one of the best, and most extensive, monastic ruins in Britain. The abbey was founded by a group of dissident monks from the Benedictine St. Mary's Abbey in York in 1132. The monks joined the new Cistercian order, which believed in a purer, less elaborate form of Christian observation. Their buildings were plainer, less decorative. The 350-foot-long church and other buildings began to be built in the Romanesque style, but were refurbished and finished in the newer Early English Gothic with pointed arches and narrow windows in the early thirteenth century. The cloister has the typical Cistercian plan of the refectory at right angles to it instead of parallel. Other parts of the abbey included an infirmary, guesthouses, domestic blocks for the monks and lay brothers, kitchens, bakehouse, malthouse, and mill. The only major changes to the buildings were the insertion of Perpendicular-style windows and the addition of a new 170-foot-high tower in the later fifteenth century. The abbey (with only thirty-two monks) was dissolved in 1539 and stripped of its furnishings, but most of the walls of the buildings still survive, including the 300-foot-long vaulted cellars in the west range of the cloister. The site passed into the hands of the Aislabie family in 1768 who owned the next-door Studley Royal estate.

Goltho aristocratic residence (Lincolnshire)

Excavated from 1971 to 1974, Goltho yielded rare evidence of an Anglo-Saxon aristocratic residence under a later Norman castle within a deserted Medieval village. Native British and Roman period farms on the site had been abandoned around 400 and the site left empty until two Anglo-Saxon farms were built in 800. These in turn were replaced around 850 by an aristocratic fortified residence. The defensive rampart and ditch enclosed an area of 160 feet square and contained a long hall and outbuildings such as a bower (bedchamber), kitchen, weaving sheds, and latrine. New buildings replaced these around 950 within the existing defenses. Then around 1000, the whole site was enlarged with new fortifications enclosing an area

325 feet long and 270 feet wide within formidable thick ramparts. Inside was at least one hall, 38 feet long and 24 feet wide. After the Norman Conquest, the site was given to new conquering lords and a motte (mound) and bailey (courtyard) castle was built over the site around 1080. The motte had a wooden tower on top (the keep). The small 60-foot-long bailey was the main living space. Finally, around 1150, the whole castle was rebuilt as a defensive ringwork. The hall within the defenses was large, 65 feet long and 41 feet wide, but otherwise the site had returned to something that more resembled its Anglo-Saxon ancestor. The site seems to have been abandoned shortly afterwards, possibly between 1158 and 1161.

Lewis chessmen (British Museum and Museum of Scotland)

A group of seventy-eight twelfth-century chess pieces, mostly made of walrus ivory, was discovered on the Isle of Lewis in 1831. The Western Isles were part of the Medieval Kingdom of Norway and the chess pieces were probably made in Norway. Traces of coloring show that the two sides in a game would have been red and white. The pieces are sharply carved and the representations of human figures are very individual, such as knights biting their shields. The British Museum hold sixty-seven of the pieces, the other eleven being held in the Museum of Scotland in Edinburgh.

London, the Tower, World Heritage Site

The Tower of London was built around 1080 by King William I to secure control of London after his conquest of England in 1066. It was built into the southeastern corner of the old Roman city wall, on the shore of the River Thames. In style, it was a classic Norman rectangular keep, 90 feet high with walls that were up to 15 feet thick. The great hall was on the third, top story of the keep. An outer bailey was added in 1097. This in turn was surrounded by an outer wall in 1190, to form a new and larger outer bailey. This was rebuilt in the thirteenth century and then a further, new outer bailey was added around 1300, with a wide, deep moat. The main gate in the southwest corner was guarded by an outer gate and barbican, and a water gate controlled access from the River Thames. The whole castle remained as a symbol of royal power into modern times.

Repton church and Viking burials (Derbyshire)

The abbey of Repton lay in the heartland of the Anglo-Saxon kingdom of Mercia, and two of its kings were buried there: Æthelbald in 757 and Wiglaf in 840. An invading Viking army made its winter quarters there in 874, building a fortification between the church and the River Trent. The abbey church was restored in the 960s as a parish church, with additions and replacements from the thirteenth to fifteenth centuries. The only remnant of the earlier Anglo-Saxon abbey is the eighth century crypt (15 feet square and 9 feet high), accidentally rediscovered in 1779. Excavations of a mound in the vicarage garden (42 feet long and 36 feet wide) uncovered a stone mausoleum of two burial chambers. In the eastern chamber were heaps of disarticulated bones of 216 men and 49 women surrounding a single burial in a stone coffin of a Viking who had been violently killed and dating to 874. This was most likely the Viking leader King Ivar the Boneless. It has been assumed that the other bodies are of Viking warriors and their Anglo-Saxon women camp followers, although none of the bodies shows signs of death by violence. The bones are more likely to be earlier burials moved to make way for the dead leader. Other burials, laid out normally, were found in the grounds of the church which do seem to be of Vikings buried with their weapons. One of these was an adult male, killed by a sword blow and buried with a pendant of the pagan Viking god Thor.

Sandal Castle (West Yorkshire)

Britain is dotted with numerous castles. Sandal Castle, south of Wakefield, is one of the very few to have been completely excavated, between 1964 and 1973, and shows what careful excavation can reveal about the life of its residents. It began in the 1120s as a typical wooden motte and bailey castle, with the keep on a 34-foot-high mound, separated from the lower bailey by a 26-foot-deep inner moat. The whole was surrounded by a 71-foot-wide outer moat. By 1270, it had been rebuilt in stone into a small but formidable fortress. The bailey buildings eventually included an outer barbican (defended inner gate to the keep), a bakehouse, kitchen, larder, ovens, living chambers, a hall, and lodgings for the constable. It was owned by three nationally important families: the Earls of Surrey, Earls of Lancaster, and Dukes of York before passing to the King in 1460. It was given to private hands in 1566. Castles are thought of as military installations, but they were also administrative headquarters and homes. Excavations found 2,000 metal objects, 18,000 pot sherds, and 39,000 animal bones. As well as local pots, there were pots from the south of England, Spain, and Germany. Just to the north of the castle was fought the Battle of Wakefield in the Wars of the Roses where the Duke of York was defeated and killed by a royal army in 1460. During the Civil War, the castle was held for the King and besieged three times by Parliamentary forces in 1645. The surviving garrison of twelve officers and eighty-eight men finally surrendered and the castle was then demolished. Finds showed how the soldiers had manned the castle in teams of eight, each with their own cup but sharing a container of beer and placed in watches around the defenses. Nine Civil War graves were found inside the castle, three of the bodies killed by artillery shrapnel. Among the Civil War finds on site was a baby's bone dummy, an unexpectedly evocative artifact not at all related to warfare.

Towton battlefield (North Yorkshire)

The Battle of Towton was fought on 29 March 1461 between forces loyal to King Henry VI of the House of Lancaster and an army led by a new claimant to the crown, Edward IV of the House of York. It was always reputed to be the largest, longest, and bloodiest battle ever fought on English soil, although the exact figures of 40,000 soldiers on each side and of 28,000 dead have often been doubted. The battle was fought in a snowstorm that blinded the Lancastrian forces and allowed the Yorkist archers an advantage. Yorkist victory was ensured after reinforcements arrived midway through the action. Henry VI retreated to exile in Scotland and Edward IV secured the throne. Various burial mounds and pits in the area have been associated with the battle. Excavations under Towton Hall in 1996 found forty-three bodies buried in a pit 20 feet long and 7 feet wide. Many of the bodies were powerfully built with particular injuries and muscle development that showed them to be experienced soldiers, aged between 17 and 50. They had been killed by repeated blows to the head and face from pole-axes and other weapons. The lack of injuries on the arms or body suggest they may have been massacred after capture or surrender. Medieval warfare was no different from that of modern times, being brutal and vicious. Some of the skulls had evidence that noses and ears may have been cut off, possibly as souvenirs. The battlefield itself has yielded the first ever find of parts of a handgun and bullet on a European battlefield, while the locations of arrowheads, spurs, belt buckles, and strap ends have shown where the armies actually stood and fought.

Welsh castles and towns of Edward I (North Wales), World Heritage Site

The conquest of the Principality of Wales, at the time centered on the ancient state of Gwynedd in north Wales, by Edward I of England in 1282–1283 was cemented by the building of a string of castles to house English garrisons. Four of these are part of the World Heritage Site and represent the height of military architecture of their day, and a real advance in the design of Medieval castles. Beaumaris (Anglesey) and Harlech (Gwynedd) consist of two concentric lines of wall surrounding an inner and outer bailey. The defense was concentrated on the massive gatehouses, each with three portcullises and an inner and outer door. Caernarfon (Gwynedd) and Conwy (Conwy) had two baileys side by side, surrounded by a single strong wall with towers and gateways. The main gateway was defended by a barbican (outer wall or passage). At Caernarfon this had four portcullises and two doors, and an inner passage with a further two portcullises and another two doors. Beaumaris and Caernarfon had a defended dock where the castle could be supplied by ship.

Westminster Abbey (London), World Heritage Site

Westminster Abbey was founded as a monastery in 959, the first of the Benedictine-style Medieval monasteries in England. It was rebuilt in the new Romanesque style from 1045 by King Edward the Confessor, and has been the coronation site for English Kings since 1066. It is also the burial place of most Kings from Henry III in 1272 to George II in 1760. Other important figures in national culture and politics are also buried in the abbey, such as the poet Geoffrey Chaucer (1400), musician Henry Purcell (1695), scientist Sir Isaac Newton (1727), novelist Charles Dickens (1870), scientist Charles Darwin (1882), politician William Gladstone (1898), and actor Lord Olivier (1989). It is also the site of the Burial of the Unknown Warrior in 1920, an unidentified soldier killed in the First World War. The undercroft dates from the 1070s, but the eastern half of the abbey church was rebuilt in the Decorated Gothic style from 1245 to 1269 by King Henry III, and the western half was rebuilt from 1375 onward. The two western towers were added in 1722 to 1745 in a Medieval style. Henry III built a shrine in the abbey to King Edward the Confessor, now a saint and still a focus for pilgrimage and veneration by both Anglicans and Roman Catholics. In front of the high altar is an intricate 25-foot-square mosaic floor, the Cosmati pavement, made with 80,000 colored stone and glass tiles and symbolizing the universe from its beginning to its end. The abbey was dissolved and the church taken into the King's direct control in 1539, and is now the national church of the monarchy and people of Britain. Nearby is Saint Margaret's Church, the twelfth century local parish church, rebuilt by 1523 in the Perpendicular style and now the parish church for members of the House of Commons.

Westminster Palace (London), World Heritage Site

By the side of Westminster Abbey lay one of the many palaces of the Kings of England from the time of Cnut (1016–1035) to Henry VIII (1509–1547). This housed the main government offices from the thirteenth century, and parliament made Westminster its permanent home in 1547, although it had often met in the Palace or at the Abbey since its origin in 1258. The surviving Great Hall was built in 1097 as a large ceremonial space, remodeled in 1394–1399 and provided with the largest Medieval open roof in England at 240 feet long and 68 feet wide. Most of the palace was destroyed by fire in 1834. It was rebuilt to a design by Sir Charles Barry and Augustus Pugin in a Tudor period style. The result is one of the most outstanding examples of nineteenth century Neo-Gothic architecture, and the inspiration for the Victorian Gothic revival. Its long side lies along the bank of the River Thames and is a façade 870 feet long. The 315-foot-high northern tower is the Elizabeth Tower, completed in 1858 and housing the clock with its bell, known as Big Ben. The tower and the chimes of Big Ben have become icons of British identity.

Wharram Percy deserted Medieval village (North Yorkshire)

The township of Wharram Percy covers 1,500 acres and once had a 30-acre village at its heart. It is one of many deserted Medieval villages in Britain. Unlike most others, it is one that has come back from the dead, due to more than forty years of investigation from 1948 to 1990. Excavations found evidence of Roman period farmsteads and occupation continuing into the Medieval period, making use of the old Roman field boundaries. The separate farms were brought together under two manors with commonly ploughed open fields in the late Anglo-Saxon period. When these manors were united in 1254, the village took on a more unified and planned appearance. Traces of the homesteads and manor houses survive as low earthworks, on narrow plots of land (tofts), where they were frequently rebuilt. At the back were the crofts where they grew their own garden crops. Each manor had its own watermill and mill-pond. The village church served as the parish church for Wharram and four other townships. It stopped being used regularly in 1870 and was allowed to fall into ruin after 1950. It began as a small eighth century wooden church, rebuilt in stone by the eleventh century and later enlarged before a declining population led to it being reduced in size from the fifteenth century. Studies of nearly 700 skeletons in the graveyard shed light on Medieval health and nutrition. Poor diet meant that a fourteen-year-old at Wharram was only the same stature as a modern ten-year-old. On the other hand, about 40 percent of burials were aged over fifty. Fish were a significant part of the diet, and infectious diseases were less common at Wharram than in the overcrowded towns such as York, although the villagers were prone to tuberculosis. By 1488, there were only four families left in the village, and these had all moved or been evicted by 1506, to allow landlords to graze sheep. Wool and cloth were at that time England's main export.

York city (North Yorkshire)

Known to the Romans as Eboracum, York was founded as a legionary fortress in 71 AD on the northeastern bank of the River Ouse. A civilian settlement soon grew on the opposite side of the river. The city was taken over by the Anglo-Saxons in the late sixth century, and short periods of Viking rule between 875 and 954 were followed by the city being taken over by the new Kingdom of England, first in 927, and finally in 954. York was capital of England as the site of the King's court and parliament at various times between 1298 and 1337, and the headquarters of the King's Council in the North from 1482 to 1641 (whose building now houses the University's archaeology department). There are many buildings and remains of the Medieval period surviving inside its almost complete circuit of Medieval city walls, including the impressive York Minster, cathedral of the Archbishops of York. Heritage now forms an important part of York's identity, with its long-established yearly Viking Festival, its Centre for Early Music, occasional revivals of the Medieval street theater Mystery Plays, the rebuilt fifteenth century town house of Barley Hall, and its various museums. There have been many archaeological excavations within the city. Among the most important are those at Coppergate which exposed part of the tenth century town with remarkable preservation of wood and other organic materials, displayed in the Jorvik Viking Centre. Excavations at Jewbury recovered parts of a Jewish cemetery of 1230–1290, and recent work at Hungate has uncovered a long history from the Roman period up to the nineteenth century.

York Minster, seat of the Archbishops of York, and the site of the largest Medieval stained glass window in the world, photo courtesy of Donald Henson

Other important sites and artifacts

- Æthelwold's Benedictional (British Library): a manuscript of blessings, one of the high points of Medieval English art in sumptuous color and gold, made between 971 and 985
- Barton-upon-Humber, Lincolnshire: a typical English parish church, begun in the tenth century and continually remodeled from then into the twentieth century
- Gosforth cross, Lancashire: a 14-foot-high stone cross, decorated with scenes of the crucifixion and Norse pagan mythology
- London Medieval waterfront: repeatedly rebuilt stone and wooden embankments moving out into the River Thames from the tenth to the fifteenth century yielding many rare artifacts in the waterlogged deposits
- Luttrell Psalter (British Library): a book of psalms made for Sir Geoffrey Luttrell 1320/40, with abundant drawn and painted images of daily life on a Medieval estate
- St. Cuthbert's vestments (Durham Cathedral): a gift by King Athelstan to Durham cathedral of a bishop's ceremonial clothing made in 909/916
- Vale of York hoard, North Yorkshire: a small hoard of coins and other silver deposited between 927 and 929, at the time of the unification of England in 927

REFORMATION AND REVOLUTION

Berwick-upon-Tweed fortifications (Northumberland)

The town of Berwick lies on the northern side of the River Tweed. Part of Scotland since the late tenth century, it was captured by England in 1296 and then changed hands up to fourteen times before at last falling to England in 1482. The town was naturally heavily fortified. Little remains of the Medieval walls. However, King Henry VIII began the upgrading of the defenses to make them proof against artillery and the sixteenth century fortifications are remarkably complete. The Medieval walls were modernized by 1569 into low, very thick ramparts with sloping earthen sides, and gun platforms on angled bastions that can defend outwards and along the line of the ramparts. Modifications were made in 1639–1655 during the Civil Wars. The Ravensdowne Barracks was added in 1717–1721, which were the first purpose-built army barracks in Britain since the Roman period. The defenses were effectively demilitarized after 1815, although guns were still placed there to defend the coast in the World Wars of the twentieth century. The castle had been partly

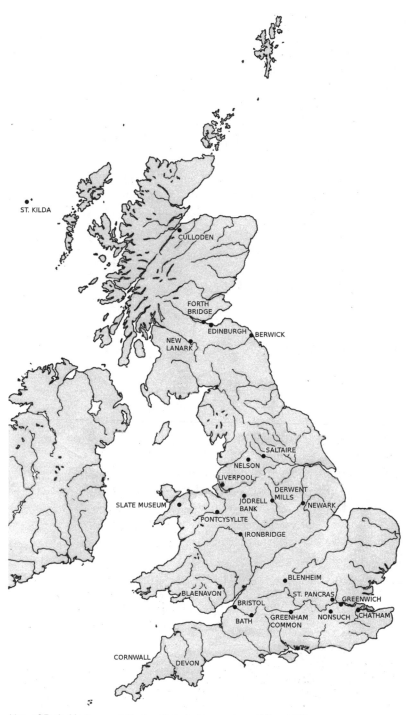

Map of Early Modern and Modern Period sites, courtesy of Donald Henson

demolished to provide stone for the barracks, and was fully demolished in 1847, when the railway station was built in its place.

Blenheim Palace (Oxfordshire), World Heritage Site

Blenheim Palace was built from 1705 to 1722 as a gift from Queen Anne and the nation to the First Duke of Marlborough for military success on the continent against the French, most notably the Battle of Blenheim in 1704. It was designed by Sir John Vanburgh and Nicholas Hawksmoor in the continental baroque style, which only had short-lived favor in Britain. The site of the palace was the royal manor of Woodstock, and remains of the Medieval royal lodge were demolished to make way for the new building. The design was on a huge scale and was meant to impress and overawe, with a sense of theater using optical effects such as perspective. The chapel within the palace is the mausoleum where the first and later Dukes are buried. Outside, the gardens are an artificially created natural landscape, designed by the great garden designer Lancelot Brown in 1764. Formal gardens nearer the palace were created in the late nineteenth century. The Palace is also noteworthy as the birthplace of Sir Winston Churchill, grandson of the Seventh Duke, in 1874.

Cornish and West Devon mines (Cornwall and Devon), World Heritage Site

Cornwall has long been an important source of tin, copper, and arsenic. Cornish tin from surface streams became important during the Bronze Age (bronze being an alloy of copper and tin). The ancient Greeks certainly knew of, and had contact with, tin producers in Britain during the Iron Age. They may even have referred to Britain as the Cassiterides, the tin islands. From the late seventeenth century, it was copper that was the main product of the mines. Two-thirds of the world supply of copper in the early nineteenth century came from Cornwall and west Devon. By the end of the nineteenth century, Cornish mining again focused on tin, and later also on arsenic. The last Cornish mine closed in 1998. The Cornish mines pioneered the new steam technology that made possible the industrial revolution. The World Heritage Site covers ten separate geographical areas of mining. The main remains to be seen are the old engine houses, their chimneys, and spoil heaps. Within the Tregonning and Trewavas area is Wheal Vor, whose name means the great mine in the Cornish language. The mine began in the fifteenth century and covered four square miles by the mid-nineteenth century, when it was the largest of all the Cornish tin mines. Shortly after 1698, it was using an early steam engine to pump water out of the mine workings. This is probably the earliest industrial use of steam power in the world, replaced by a more advanced Newcomen steam engine around 1710. It remained a leading center of mining technology and innovation into the nineteenth century. Production declined after 1866 and it closed in 1910.

Crossbones Graveyard (London)

An unconsecrated burial ground at Redcross Way in Southwark (west of Greenwich and south of St. Pancras) was mentioned by John Stow in 1598 as a graveyard for local prostitutes. By 1769, it was mentioned as a paupers' graveyard. Lack of room for any more burials led to its end as a cemetery in 1853. It is known as Crossbones graveyard, although the site is now a concrete space behind large iron gates with no graves to be seen. Attempts to develop the land have been resisted as it is a site of burial that should not be disturbed. Part of the site with 148 nineteenth century burials was excavated in 1992. Southwark prostitutes had been licensed by the Bishop of Winchester, and were known as the Winchester geese. A play written in 1996 about the life of these women led to the creation of a yearly Halloween festival from 1998 to commemorate their lives. The Friends of Crossbones hold a monthly candlelit vigil at the site. The gates at the site are festooned with plaques and offerings commemorating women and prostitutes. Too often, heritage sites and archaeology celebrate the rich, the powerful, or the spectacular. Crossbones offers a way of remembering the silent lives of the past, and often forgotten members of the population, as well as the lives of one half of the population (women) at all times in the past.

Culloden battlefield (Highland)

The last invasion of Britain happened during the war with France from 1739 to 1748. The opportunity came from events sixty years earlier when the Catholic Stuart dynasty of King James II was ousted by a Protestant regime. The Protestant crown eventually passed to the House of Hanover in 1714, leaving the Stuarts as rival claimants in France. The rivalry was not only religious. The Hanoverian crown ruled through a permanent Parliament, while the Stuarts believed in a more continental-style dominant monarchy. Stuart supporters were known as Jacobites (after the Latin form of James, *Jacobus*). The French enabled a Jacobite invasion in 1745 through northern Scotland where Jacobite support was strongest. The Jacobite army reached as far south as Derby, only 125 miles from London, before retreating into Scotland. Eventually, a loyal Hanoverian army under the Duke of Cumberland at Aberdeen faced the Jacobite army under Prince Charles Stuart at Inverness. Each army consisted of Scots, English, and foreign troops (Hanoverian German and Jacobite French and Irish). They met in battle at Culloden on 16 April 1746. The Jacobite army fled after an hour's hard fighting and heavy slaughter. Not all the highland clans were Jacobite, but to make sure there could be no repeat, the government dismantled the highland clan society and culture. Ironically, highland regiments would in future become an honored and respected mainstay of the British army. The battlefield has a modern visitor center and battle and grave memorials erected in 1881. Archaeological analysis of the battlefield since 2001 has done much to illuminate important details of the battle.

Edinburgh Old Town, World Heritage Site

The Medieval town of Edinburgh grew in the twelfth century along the road connecting the castle with the abbey of Holyrood. The road occupied a spine of land that fell away steeply from the ridge. Buildings on the high street would be built into tall tenement blocks separated by narrow lanes (called closes or wynds). The High Kirk of St. Giles is one of the few surviving Medieval buildings, mostly of the fourteenth century. The royal palace at Holyrood began in 1498 and the nobility would build their own residences near the palace along the lower part of the High Street, such as Moray House and Queensberry House from the early seventeenth century. Much of the present streetscape belongs to the sixteenth century onwards. Gladstone's Land is a six-story tenement block of the 1620s. Various closes were built over in the eighteenth century, such as Mary King's Close, named after a local businesswoman of the 1630s, which can be visited today and is a warren of underground rooms and streets, hidden and unused since they were built over.

Greenwich Hospital (Greater London), World Heritage Site

Queen Mary II gave an old royal residence at Greenwich to found a hospital for wounded sailors. The new buildings were designed by Sir Christopher Wren and other key architects of the time and are masterpieces of the English baroque. Parts of the earlier palace were kept, such as the Queen's House of 1635 (designed by Inigo Jones) and King Charles' Block of 1665. The hospital itself was built between 1696 and 1742 with the expertise of Sir John Vanburgh and Nicholas Hawksmoor. This includes the magnificent Painted Hall of 1708–1727. The chapel had to be rebuilt after a fire in 1779, in a neo-classical style. The hospital moved to other premises in 1869 and the buildings were the home of the Royal Naval College from 1873 to 1998. Much of the site is now used by the University of Greenwich. The site presents a magnificent vista from the river. Within the Park is also the Royal Observatory built in 1675, and since 1884 the zero meridian for the world's time zones and navigational longitude. Greenwich Mean Time begins here.

Mary Rose warship (Portsmouth)

Naval warfare underwent a revolution in the sixteenth century and one ship symbolizes this more than any other, the Mary Rose, launched in 1511.

She became a major warship in King Henry VIII's fleet before sinking in action against the French at Portsmouth in 1545. Only twenty-five survived out of her crew of over 400 men. She was one of a new type of warship, with an armament of cannons facing outwards through gunports in the hull: the basic warship design from then until the late nineteenth century. The site of the ship was discovered in 1971 and became the object of meticulous and groundbreaking maritime archaeological survey and excavation. The 20,000 artifacts recovered shed light on sixteenth century fashion, games, tools, and weapons. The raising of the surviving section of the hull from the seabed in 1982 was televised around the world. The remains of the ship have been the object of careful conservation and the whole Mary Rose project has been hugely influential in the field of maritime archaeology.

Newark fortifications (Nottinghamshire)

The town of Newark was loyal to King Charles I during the Civil War, and was besieged by Parliamentary forces three times between 1644 and 1646. The last siege began in November 1645, and the town only surrendered when ordered to do so by the King on 6 May 1646 at the end of the first phase of the war. Very few Civil War fortifications have survived to the present, but Newark has the greatest concentration of those that do. The Royalist garrison minted its own lozenge-shaped emergency coinage in silver during the siege. They also built a new defensive perimeter to the town with outlying forts. One of these forts survives, the Queen's Sconce. This is a star-shaped fort with four large angled bastions and covers three acres. Its ditches are up to 15 feet deep and 70 feet wide, and the ramparts are 23 feet high. Outside the defenses were various Parliamentary siege works. Surviving examples include the Edinburgh fort, Sandhills Sconce, and Stoke Lodge. Various parts of the defenses and siege works have been excavated, such as Colonel Gray's Sconce, dug in 1958.

Nonsuch Palace (Surrey)

Begun in 1538 for King Henry VIII, Nonsuch Palace was based on the new, elaborate style of architecture in France and Italy, inspired by classical Rome. This was the Renaissance given physical form. It was built from scratch as a completely new building, and was probably the most magnificent of his palaces. It was given up by the crown in 1670, and demolished in 1682. There are no surviving ruins and even its location was lost until the site was excavated in 1959–1960. This was a truly public excavation, carried out by more than 500 volunteers led by Martin Biddle, and funded entirely by donations and guidebook sales from more than 75,000 public visitors to the site. The inner court was reputed to be the largest timber framed building in England, while the outer court was built in stone. The whole building was extravagantly decorated with stucco figure sculptures and was a sight-seeing wonder of its age. Biddle's research of over fifty years integrating excavations with historical documents and engravings was used in 2011 to create a physical scale model of the palace (7 feet by 3.5 feet). Excavation of post-Medieval sites was very rare in 1959 and the dig marked an important beginning of post-Medieval archaeology in Britain.

Rose and Globe Theatres (Greater London)

The reign of Elizabeth I (1558–1603) saw the establishment of the modern theater in Britain. By 1576, new purpose-built open air theaters were being erected in imitation of the open courtyards of inns where plays had earlier been performed. Theaters were often built outside the limits of the City of London, to escape the anti-theatrical City Corporation. The borough south of the river opposite London is Southwark and its riverside area known as Bankside. Here the Rose Theatre was built in 1587 by Philip Henslowe, as the first of four in the area. The others were the Swan in 1595, the Globe in 1599, and the Hope in 1614. We know that the plays of Christopher Marlowe were performed at the Rose, as were Shakespeare's *Henry VI* and *Titus Andronicus*. Shakespeare may well have also acted there. The Rose Theatre was closed in 1603 and soon demolished. Excavations have found that the theater began as a 14-sided building 72 feet wide. It was timber framed with tiers of seats in galleries around an open courtyard holding

The reconstructed Globe Theatre in Southwark, Greater London, photo courtesy of Donald Henson

around 400 standing people paying a penny each, while seats in the galleries cost two pennies (tuppence) or three pennies (threepence). The stage was on the northern side of the yard, 37 feet wide at the back tapering to 27 feet at the front and 16 feet deep. The Globe Theatre was less than 100 yards to the east, on the other side of the road, built by Richard Burbage, and the home of Shakespeare's acting company, seeing the performances of many of his later plays. It too has been partly excavated and now lies half under a car park and half under an eighteenth century tenement block. American actor Sam Wanamaker led a long campaign to build a replica of the Globe, finally completed in 1997. The reconstructed Globe is only 250 yards from the original site, and is a live theater with educational facilities. It is also a useful piece of experimental archaeology incorporating information from the archaeological excavations.

Studley Royal Park (North Yorkshire), World Heritage Site

Studley Royal Park is a union of two estates. After the dissolution of Fountains Abbey (see previous entry), some of its stone was used by its new owners to build Fountains Hall from 1598 to 1604 with its typical formal garden. This was taken over by the Aislabie family who created the modern Park. Their home was Studley Royal House, rebuilt in Palladian style in 1716 and remodeled through the eighteenth century. The house was destroyed by fire in 1946 and only the stable block of 1732 survives. Excavations have revealed evidence of the house's Medieval predecessor and village. The gardens of the house still survive largely unaltered although partially tidied and cleared in the nineteenth century, and are one of the finest surviving eighteenth century stately gardens. They were created in 1718 1781, based on lakes, canals, bridges, temples, statues, cascades, and follies with lawns and formal walks, all designed to catch the eye. The ruins of Fountains Abbey were included as an integral part of the gardens from 1768. The Park also contains an especially fine Victorian Gothic church of 1871–1878, one of the high points of Victorian church architecture.

INDUSTRIAL ADVANCE AND THE MODERN WORLD

Arthur's Seat coffins (Edinburgh)

Recent artifacts are not always well known or understood. In 1836, seventeen miniature wooden coffins (each less than four inches long) with clothed bodies inside were found in a cave on the hill of Arthur's Seat in Edinburgh. These are unique finds and what they represent is unknown.

One theory is that they may be a mock burial to commemorate the victims of William Burke and William Hare who murdered sixteen people in Edinburgh in 1827–1828 to sell their bodies for anatomy dissections. Could the seventeenth body represent Burke who was hanged for the crime?

Bath (Somerset), World Heritage Site

The city of Bath is famous not only for its Roman remains (see previous entry). Its modern fortunes were made in 1676 when a local doctor published a work praising the medicinal benefits of its hot spring. The wealthy then made Bath into a spa resort, as reflected in the novels of Jane Austen, who lived in the city from 1801 to 1806 (and apparently did not like it much). The new wealth of the town was shown in its rebuilding in the eighteenth century. Bath became a showcase for Palladian architecture, achieving a unity of design and beauty in its buildings, views, and landscape, rarely matched elsewhere. From the beginning of Queen Square in 1728 to the building of The Corridor shopping arcade in 1825, Bath acquired a series of architectural gems, such as the Royal Crescent in 1767–1774, the Assembly Rooms in 1769–1771, and the Grand Pump Room in 1789–1799. The inspiration of Palladian architecture in Bath came mostly from classical Rome. The influence of Venice inspired the Pulteney Bridge, one of the few surviving bridges in the world to have shops on either side across its whole span. Much of the Georgian splendor survives unaltered, although some had to be restored after German bombing in the Second World War.

Blaenavon (Welsh Blaenafon) Industrial Landscape (Torfaen), World Heritage Site

The hills at Blaenavon had long been a source of iron ore, but the first modern ironworks was built there in 1788 using the new steam engines to run powerful blast furnaces. The area became a network of mines, quarries, canals, railways, and workers' housing surrounding the ironworks. The railway included the world's first railway viaduct built in 1790, whose location was recovered by archaeological excavation in 2001. A new steelworks was added in the 1860s, which pioneered new methods of exploiting phosphorous-rich iron ores. Coal was also obtained from the mines, especially from Big Pit (sunk in 1860), and became the main export from the site in the twentieth century. Steel production ended in 1938 and coal mining ended in 1980. Blaenavon contains all the elements of South Welsh industry in one location and is a rare survival of a complete industrial revolution landscape. Big Pit is now an internationally renowned museum where visitors can go 300 feet underground. The ironworks is its own separate museum.

Chatham Dockyard (Kent), on the UK Tentative List for World Heritage Sites

Covering 400 acres and employing 10,000 people, Chatham dockyard in the Thames estuary was a major industrial complex. A royal dockyard opened at Chatham in 1567 and moved to its present site in 1622, fitting out and building ships for the Royal Navy. The dockyard closed in 1984. The site contains important buildings of the eighteenth and nineteenth centuries. These include the oldest surviving naval storehouse in Britain (1723), and various timber seasoning and manufacturing sheds, workshops, offices, and guardhouses. One of the few buildings still in its original use is the 1811 ropery, over 1,100 feet long for making maritime cables. The eighteenth century part of the dockyard complex is now open to visitors as a heritage site. Associated with the dockyard are other important parts of the overall naval and military complex at Chatham, including barracks, houses of dockyard workers, and various forts. Renovation work at the Wheelwrights' workshop in 1995 revealed that the building had been refurbished in 1834, using timbers from a broken up wooden warship. Careful archaeological detective work identified this as HMS *Namur*, a 90-gun warship launched in 1807 and broken up in 1833.

Derwent Valley Mills (Derbyshire), World Heritage Site

The modern factory system that was the bedrock of industrial production began in Derbyshire. Richard Arkwright was the pioneer who put new machines for spinning cotton into large buildings for mass use, powered by waterwheels. His first water-mill was built at Cromford in 1771–1772. Cromford lies in a 15-mile-long stretch of the River Derwent which contains a remarkable collection of early mills and associated housing. A larger mill was added at Matlock Bath in 1783, the Masson Mill. This mill was 143 feet long by 27 feet wide and five stories high. Its design was the template for many other later mills elsewhere. Other settlements in the valley had their own mills, including ones for paper, corn, leather, and two mills for crushing flint as an ingredient for making porcelain. The last of the mills to be active was Masson Mill, which closed in 1992. Other important sites in the valley include the Cromford canal, which linked the mills with their markets, and the specially built workers' housing that survives best at Milford.

Forth Bridge (Edinburgh and Fife), on the UK Tentative List for World Heritage Sites

The world's longest cantilever bridge, the Forth Bridge opened in 1890 for rail passengers and freight across the Firth of Forth. The central cantilever section spans 570 yards within the overall length of 1.6 miles. Built in steel, and far ahead of its time in design, the bridge remains a technological triumph but is also admired for the beauty of its design. Its originality and scale marked a significant shift in engineering towards new methods of construction. The central cantilever towers are 330 feet high, carrying the railway 150 feet above the high tide of the river.

Greenham Common protest site (Berkshire)

A Royal Air Force (RAF) base was established at Greenham Common in 1942 and closed in 1993. For most of its life, it was leased to the United States as one of its overseas airbases. A decision was taken to base 96 nuclear cruise missiles there in 1980, and a women's peace camp was established outside the base in 1981 to protest the presence of nuclear weapons. Attempts to evict the protesters repeatedly failed. Their protests included 50,000 women linking hands to surround the airbase in 1983. Many protesters stayed after the missiles left in 1991, finally leaving in 2000. The former protesters maintain a peace garden at the site, while the former missile bunker is now a protected scheduled monument. The sites of four of the camps have been surveyed and recorded by archaeologists. This has yielded surprising results, such as milk bottles being found at one of the sub-camps that was supposed to be only lived in by vegans. The archaeological work provides missing details and refinements to the oral and written histories. Yet the archaeologists found it hard to get funding for an archaeological study of such a recent past. The project did much to highlight the importance of archaeology as the study of human material culture of all periods, not only the distant past.

Ironbridge Gorge (Shropshire), World Heritage Site

A three-mile stretch of the River Severn can lay claim to being one of the birthplaces of the industrial revolution. Within this are various important industrial remains such as mines, foundries, factories, workshops, warehouses, canals, railways, and workers' housing. As early as 1709, Abraham Darby began the use of coke to smelt iron, kick-starting the production of iron on a commercial scale at Coalbrookdale. His grandson, also Abraham Darby, built the world's first iron bridge across the Severn gorge in 1779–1781. This area soon became known as Ironbridge and is now the symbolic heart of the area. South of this were the Blists Hill furnace, brick, and tile works. This is now the open-air museum that celebrates the industrial heritage of the gorge, including the coal mine at Jackfield, porcelain factory and second iron bridge at Coalport, and the Coalport canal.

Liverpool (Merseyside), World Heritage Site

Liverpool in Lancashire was one of the greatest ports in the world. It was given its charter by King John in 1207 but it was not until the eighteenth century that it became a major port with the building of the world's first commercial wet dock in 1715. The city has several important buildings: the Royal Liver Building of 1908–1911 (the most recognizable symbol of the city), the Cunard Building of 1914–1917, and the Port of Liverpool Building of 1904–1907. Also important are its warehouses, dock facilities, shipping, exchange, and financial offices, merchants' houses, and various civic buildings. The Town Hall of 1749–1754 is an especially fine example of neo-classical building, as is the much later St. George's Hall built in 1841–1854. More modern in design is Oriel Chambers, the world's first metal-framed building and a probable inspiration for later skyscraper designs. Its dock facilities and warehouses were at the cutting edge of harbor design, especially the Albert Dock of 1846. The first modern canal, the Sankey Canal, was built in 1757 to link the estuary with the St. Helen's coalfield and the major Liverpool-to-Leeds canal was built in 1770 to 1816. The world's first regular passenger railway was built to connect Liverpool with Manchester in 1830. Emigrants from all over Europe left Liverpool on their way to North America. The world's first oceangoing steamship left from Liverpool in 1833. The harbor's fortunes declined dramatically in the late twentieth century and it is now a major cultural and museum center.

St. Pancras railway station (London)

The Midland Railway from Sheffield to London built its grand terminus in London at St. Pancras in 1868. The train shed was the largest single-span covered open space in the world at 245 feet wide and 100 feet high. The front of the station opened as a hotel in 1869 and was designed by Sir George Gilbert Scott, a high priest of the Victorian revival of Medieval architecture. Plans to demolish the front were put forward in 1966 and provoked a public outcry over the redevelopment of London causing the loss of so many historic buildings. Led by the poet Sir John Betjeman, the campaign was successful and the station was given legal protection in 1967. This marked a turning point in modern conservation. A similar campaign in 1961 had failed to halt the demolition of the entrance to the nearby Euston railway station, the Euston Arch (built in 1837 to a neo-classical design). The hotel reopened after a major refurbishment in 2011 and the station is now the terminus for the Eurostar trains linking Britain to the rest of Europe and a symbol of modernity. The past does not have to be lost in the creation of a vibrant future. History can even be repeated. Building the new Eurostar terminus uncovered a burial ground from 1792 to 1854 with more than 1,300 burials. This echoes the disturbance of 7,000 bodies from the same burial ground by the building of the first railway in 1860. Both disturbances of the burials led to public outcries. The modern excavation was done to a high standard in difficult working conditions, and a sample of bodies has been analyzed to give great insight into the population of this part of London in the early nineteenth century.

Whitefield, Nelson housing estate (Lancashire)

Pendle Council proposed the demolition in 2000 of 400 houses in the town of Nelson for redevelopment. This was immediately resisted by residents who formed the Whitefield Conservation Action Group. Nelson had been a typical Lancashire cotton mill town. The housing in Whitefield had been built as workers' housing from 1864 to a planned design of terraced streets. It is one of the few urban landscapes of the late nineteenth century in Lancashire that remains largely unaltered. The local council claimed that the area was deprived and in need of improvement. However, a majority of the local residents are of immigrant origin from the Indian subcontinent with strong family structures. They were used to living close together and would often amalgamate houses into bigger living spaces. They lived harmoniously with local white residents and together they won two public inquiries into the plans, which led to the area being granted conservation area status in 2004. Their homes would be renovated rather than demolished. The residents were helped by both English Heritage and the Council for British Archaeology. English Heritage pointed out that the long-term maintenance costs of a Victorian terraced house would be cheaper than for more modern houses. The involvement of the Council for British Archaeology (CBA) showed that archaeology is as much concerned with the material culture of the recent past and of living communities as it is with the distant past. The fight against demolition also showed how local people of whatever origin could take a pride in the heritage of their local place.

Other important sites

- Edinburgh New Town, World Heritage Site: town planning between 1767 and 1820 in a neo-classical architectural style
- SS *Great Britain*, Bristol: designed by Isambard Brunel and launched in 1843, the first all-iron-hulled screw propeller steamship and largest ship in the world at 320 feet long
- Jodrell Bank Observatory, Cheshire: on the UK Tentative List for World Heritage Sites, established in 1945 and for a while the largest radio telescope in the world, an icon of modern science and an object of archaeological study

- Kew Royal Botanic Gardens, Greater London, World Heritage Site: created in 1759 and a major center for world botany with many historic buildings, including Kew Palace
- New Lanark, South Lanarkshire, World Heritage Site: one of the largest cotton mill complexes in the world, built in 1785 and famous for its exemplary workers' housing and amenities associated with the social pioneer Robert Owen
- Pontcysyllte aqueduct and canal, Wrexham, World Heritage Site: a 1,100-yard-long and 126-foot-high aqueduct carrying a canal across the River Dee, built 1795 to 1805
- St. Kilda, Highland, World Heritage Site: a group of four islands 40 miles northwest of the Hebrides in the Atlantic, abandoned in 1930, with traces of human settlement from at least 1850 BC as well as surviving prehistoric breeds of sheep
- Saltaire, West Yorkshire, World Heritage Site: an industrial village built by a philanthropic industrialist Sir Titus Salt from 1851 to 1876
- HMS *Victory*, Portsmouth, Hampshire: the most famous warship in the Royal Navy, launched in 1765, on which Admiral Nelson was killed in 1805, still commissioned in the Royal Navy as flagship of the First Sea Lord, the operational head of the navy
- Welsh slate industry, on the UK Tentative List for World Heritage Sites: nineteenth-century remains of the largest roofing slate producer in the world, with quarries, harbor, railways, and workers' housing

6

MAJOR PERSONALITIES
IN ARCHAEOLOGY

What follows is a selection of the major archaeologists of Britain. They have been influential in the history of archaeology, the development of archaeological methods, and in uncovering spectacular remains of the past. Some have had a big impact on archaeology overseas, and those listed here have had an importance that lies beyond the excavation of one site or the discovery of one particular find.

THE PIONEERS

Archaeology arose out of antiquarian inquiries into the past in the sixteenth and seventeenth centuries. The first public museum, the Ark, was set up some time after 1610, at first in London and later moved to the Ashmolean Museum in Oxford. The antiquarians were concerned with recording the past through whatever memorials it had left behind, chiefly documents and remains that could be easily understood such as tombs or churches. It would be in the seventeenth and eighteenth centuries that some of these antiquarians would develop a greater interest in ruins, earthworks, and less easily understood monuments like stone circles. They would develop new ways of looking at the past and methods of recording or investigating it. Archaeology was being born.

Sir William Dugdale 1605–1686

It is hard to pick only one among the early antiquarians as a pioneering archaeologist. Their range of interests spread widely across ancient monuments, historical documents, folklore, and so forth. However, if there is one whose practices were more archaeological than the rest it would be Sir William Dugdale. Like many early antiquarians, he held an official position as a herald in the College of Arms. Also like many, his sympathies during the Civil War were on the side of the King as he understood that the Puritan Parliamentarians and army were hostile to both aristocracy and the historical traditions of the church. He was keen to follow in the footsteps of previous antiquarians tracing the origins of the noble and gentry families of England, and nostalgically looking back on the religious heritage of the nation that had been lost with the Reformation and the dissolution of the monasteries.

Dugdale began his studies in the 1630s, and these really took off when he came into contact with national scholars like Sir Henry Spelman and Sir Christopher Hatton. He spent much of his time documenting a past that was under threat and so based his work on a scrupulous concern for the accurate recording of evidence: charters, tombs, stained glass, inscriptions held in family or state archives, castles, churches, cathedrals, and monastic ruins. He was one of the earliest practitioners of the modern archaeological practice of preservation by record. While he wanted to conserve the past, he also understood that an awareness of the past expands our experience of the world, and allows us to learn from the lives of the past. He also saw that the present itself would become part of a future past. After the Battle of Edgehill in 1642, he spent time making a record of where the armies had been on the battlefield, and where the dead had been buried. This shows a rare understanding of the importance of heritage. Although he was not directly interested in ancient architecture, nor in field survey (apart from Edgehill), he did appreciate the need for accurate recording of remains. His books would contain many illustrations as a record of what he observed, and he included also a surveyed plan of Kenilworth Castle, the first of its kind. He was also the first person in Britain to publicly accept the human origins of stone tools (first accepted in Italy in 1570). His career shows the importance of belonging to a network of scholars, sharing ideas and contributing to each other's work through the informal society the Students of Antiquity founded in 1638. Dugdale would be a good example to later scholars by making sure his researches were published and so made available to others. Lack of publication is the original sin in archaeology, and still regrettably common. His major works were:

- *Monasticon Anglicanum* (with Roger Dodsworth), 1654–1673 (three volumes), a history of the monasteries up to their dissolution;
- *The Antiquities of Warwickshire Illustrated*, 1656, one of the best of the traditional county antiquarian studies done to a high methodological standard;
- *The History of St. Paul's Cathedral in London*, 1658, a key source for the cathedral that was destroyed by fire in 1666;
- *The History of Imbanking and Drayning of Divers Fenns and Marshes*, 1662, a rare work dealing with the development of a landscape based on field observation;
- *Origines Juridicales*, 1666, the history of the law and the Inns of Court;
- *The Baronage of England*, 1675–1676 (two volumes).

John Aubrey 1626–1697

The first person whom we can call an archaeologist rather than an antiquarian is John Aubrey. Like Dugdale, he was born into the gentry. There the similarity ends. Aubrey knew Dugdale and was inspired by him, but they were very different characters. Where Dugdale was methodical and rigorous, Aubrey was disordered and imaginative. Dugdale disagreed with his speculative approach and his interest in field recording of monuments of unknown nature and origin, feeling that this went beyond an objective recording of the past. Aubrey was a Fellow of the Royal Society and a friend of many of the leading scientists of the day, absorbing their attitude to experiment and demonstration.

Aubrey only published one small work, leaving a mass of research in his private papers. What makes Aubrey important is that he was interested in the whole of the past, not only the past of the nobility, the gentry, or the church. His was a past filled with people who lived ordinary lives. He wanted to know that past in all its details and, for example, how people in the past were affected by differences in soil and climate. For Aubrey, studying the remains of the past was a way of getting close to the lives of past people. But, like Dugdale, he saw the destruction wrought by the Civil War and the attitudes of the Puritan regime to the past. He was acutely conscious of the need to conserve both the monuments and intangible traditions from destruction and loss. Aubrey was an innovative thinker and pioneer of new methods. He was the first person to carry out proper surveys of monuments, using the surveyor's plane table for accuracy and observing earthworks and crop marks. He insisted on a comparative method where his field observations of remains would be compared with each other, treating classes of monument instead of individual sites. Monuments would also be analyzed within their landscape setting and their relationships to other nearby sites. To understand the monuments as the remains of real people, he would use comparative ethnography, assuming that prehistoric people had a similar way of life to such peoples as Native Americans. He was happy to accept a relative chronology for monuments, where they could be dated before or after each other even if they could not be given a true calendar date. In this way he could push back the notion of time and he was the first person in Britain to accept a deep, non-Biblical, prehistoric chronology. That monuments could be studied in their own right, and not only through documents, is a truly archaeological point of view. His method also enabled him to be the first to develop a typology of architectural styles for the Medieval period, and he attempted the same for costume and handwriting styles. Aubrey made his first visit to the henge and stone circles at Avebury in 1649, and it was there and at Stonehenge that he first applied his principles, presenting a paper to the Royal Society in 1663 (probably the first true archaeological presentation in Britain). He was the first to accept them as prehistoric in date. However, as the only prehistoric people he knew of, he naturally but falsely attributed their building to the Druids. Aubrey's only published work was *Miscellanies*, in 1695, a treatise on supernatural phenomena. Like many archaeologists, he could never decide when to stop perfecting his work instead of completing it for publication. His unpublished works were studied by others before they were published, long after his time, and included among others:

- *Naturall Historie of Wiltshire*, 1656–1691, partly published in 1847;
- *Hypomnemata Antiquaria*, 1656–1671, partly published in 1862, a study of the antiquities of Wiltshire;
- *Monumenta Britannica*, 1663–1693, partly published in 1980–1982, his main archaeological work;
- *Natural History of Surrey*, 1673–1692, partly published in 1718–1719;
- *Brief Lives*, 1680–1693, a series of short biographies of leading people of his day, partly published in 1813;
- *Remaines of Gentilisme and Judaisme*, 1687–1689, partly published in 1881, a study of folklore.

William Stukeley 1687–1765

One who was inspired by Aubrey was William Stukeley who did much to perfect the approach of Aubrey to the past. Stukeley was a physician and clergyman, and a fellow of both of the chief learned societies of the day, the Royal Society and the Society of Antiquaries (and a friend of Sir Isaac

Newton). His approach to fieldwork, undertaken from 1718, was to record as accurately as possible and place sites in their landscape setting. Stukeley observed that burial mounds would often be sited on the crest of hills so as to be seen from the valley below. He completed Aubrey's plan of Avebury, discovered two stone avenues leading to Stonehenge, and added the technique of excavation to his archaeological field investigations. From at least 1722, he excavated various burial mounds, observing their stratigraphy and publishing the earliest British archaeological site section. Stukeley understood that the remains of the past were fragile and that his own investigation would be part of their future history, and so left dated coins in the backfill of his excavations to help any future excavators recognize his own actions at a site. Stukeley was very firm about the need for conservation of ancient remains. He wrote against "improvers" seeking to modernize Medieval churches, and against farmers raiding prehistoric sites for building stone. His own recordings of monuments were a way of preserving knowledge of what was being lost. Stukeley even tried applying science as a way of dating sites. Assuming that Stonehenge had been built to align on magnetic north and knowing that the location of magnetic north changed over time, he deduced that the monument had been built in 460 BC. This is entirely false, but is a commendable attempt to base archaeological interpretation on scientific principles.

Unfortunately, the weakness of Stukeley was his religious faith. He sought to explain ancient stone circles and barrows as remnants of an ancient religion that connected with Christianity. To do this, he used Aubrey's connection of such sites with the Druids and developed a theory of the prehistoric settlers of Britain coming from the Middle East after the Biblical flood and bringing with them their Jewish faith which then decayed into Druidism. He erected a complex Druidic explanation for prehistory based entirely on his imagination rather than his field observations. In later life, his lack of critical awareness would lead him to be taken in by historical frauds. How to interpret the past without an undue exercise of the imagination is still a key problem for modern archaeology. Stukeley saw scholarly endeavor as a social activity and was always searching for, or founding, societies of like-minded people, hence, his membership in the Freemasons in 1720. His attitudes could be remarkable for their time. He admitted his wife Frances as a member of one of his societies, at a time when women were normally kept firmly at home. As well as publishing works on medicine, Stukeley's major publications include:

- *Itinerarium Curiosum*, 1724, descriptions of monuments made while traveling in Britain since 1711, the 2nd volume was published after his death in 1776;

- *Stonehenge, a temple restor'd to the British Druids*, 1740;
- *Abury, a temple of the British Druids*, 1743;
- *Palaeographica Britannica*, 1743–1752 (three volumes), observation of various sites and monuments;
- *Memoirs of Sir Isaac Newton's Life*, 1752.

THE FOUNDERS

Archaeology achieved its maturity in the nineteenth century, with the development of more rigorous standards and a better idea of the passage of time since prehistory. Improvements in the scientific understanding of the world gave archaeologists new ways to interpret their evidence. Archaeology also began to develop as a profession in which people could earn a living and in which university training could create a continuous generation of new archaeologists working to the same standards. Archaeological remains came to be recognized as valuable in themselves and worth conserving or rescuing from the ravages of modern life.

Sir John Evans 1823–1908

Some people seem to be born with both energy and multiple talents. Sir John Evans was one. By profession he was a paper manufacturer, but he was also one of the leading archaeologists and geologists of his day. As well as being a fellow of the Royal Society, fellow and president of the Geological Society and the Society of Antiquaries, he was also a member of the Numismatic Society, and president at various times of the Royal Anthropological Institute, the Institute of Chemical Industry, the Egypt Exploration Fund and the British Association for the Advancement of Science. Not neglecting his business interests, he also helped to found the Paper Makers' Association.

His first key contribution to archaeology came in 1859. He went with the geologist Sir Joseph Prestwich to France to assess claims of early stone tools that provided a new chronology for mankind. The result was a paper presented at the Society of Antiquaries in that year establishing that humans had existed far back in prehistory, alongside extinct animals. This was a decisive nail in the coffin of a Biblical chronology for the past. As part of his work on this, he made use of experimental knapping of flint to make tools for himself, to better understand how man-made fractures differed from natural damage. He also drilled stone using soft drills of copper, bone, wood, and antler to show how some types of prehistoric stone tools could be made. Like many before, he also made use of ethnographic analogy to understand the stone tools being found from British prehistory. His knowledge of these tools was encyclopedic and he established the basic framework classifying them. He also turned his attention to bronze tools, with similar importance. His other important contribution was to the study of pre-Roman coins. In geology, he was the first scholar to identify the toothed beak and the bird-like characteristics of the fossil dinosaur Archaeopteryx, identifying it as key evidence for Darwin's and Wallace's recent ideas on evolution. His son, Arthur, would in his turn become a famous archaeologist, famous for his discoveries on Crete. Evans' major publications included:

- "On the occurrence of flint implements in undisturbed beds of gravel, sands, and clay" in *Archaeologia* 38: 280–307, 1860;
- *The Coins of the Ancient Britons*, 1864;
- "On portions of a cranium and of a jaw, in the slab containing the fossil remains of the archaeopteryx" in *Natural History Review* new series 5: 415–21, 1865;
- *The Ancient Stone Implements, Weapons and Ornaments of Great Britain*, 1872;
- *The Ancient Bronze Implements, Weapons and Ornaments of Great Britain and Ireland*, 1881.

Lord Avebury (Sir John Lubbock) 1834–1913

Like Evans, Avebury was a professional businessman, head of a banking firm. He was also a politician, elected as a Liberal MP in 1870, serving until his elevation to the House of Lords in 1900. Avebury served as president of the Institute of Bankers, of the British Association for the Advancement of Science, and of the Linnean Society of London. His concern for workers' welfare led him to found the Bank Clerks' Orphanage, a charity for bank employees and their dependents. His main political contribution was his drafting of the Bank Holidays Act in 1871, which created statutory holidays for the first time. He was a neighbor and friend of Charles Darwin, fully accepting his evolutionary ideas. It was only natural that he would be interested in natural history and geology, as well as archaeology. He published important works on zoology, being well known for his work on insects.

For Avebury, archaeology was part of the same field of endeavor, to understand the world through science, and the world of man was fully part of the natural world. His importance in archaeology is twofold. He was responsible for the Ancient Monuments Protection Act in 1882. This selected a list of sixty-eight ancient sites to be protected and properly recorded: the first attempt in Britain at giving legal protection to archaeological remains. In his survey of prehistory in 1865, he introduced two new terms to archaeology: the Paleolithic and the Neolithic, establishing the first definition of these two periods of the human past. As well as being a close friend of Darwin, he was also on good terms with General Pitt-Rivers (see following entry), marrying his daughter in 1884. Avebury believed firmly in popular education and was happy to publish books for a popular as well as a scholarly audience. His most important works were:

- *Prehistoric Times as Illustrated by Ancient Remains*, 1865, this remained the standard textbook for archaeology as late as 1913;
- *The Origin of Civilisation and the Primitive Condition of Man*, 1870, applying an evolutionary scheme of human cultural development;
- *Ants, Bees, and Wasps: a record of observations on the habits of the social Hymenoptera*, 1882;
- *The Senses, Instincts, and Intelligence of Animals*, 1888.

Augustus Pitt-Rivers 1827–1900

The man who is thought of as the first officially appointed, professional archaeologist in Britain, and who introduced modern methods of excavation and recording, spent most of his career in the army. Augustus Lane-Fox was an active army officer between 1845 and 1877, promoted to lieutenant general in 1882. He inherited the wealthy 43-square-mile estate of Cranborne Chase from a cousin in 1880 in return for taking the surname Pitt-Rivers. While being in charge of weapons testing in 1852, he began to collect firearms and other weapons, and studied how they had developed over time, and gave lectures on this in 1858. This interest in how to classify and order artifacts over time into a sequence of types was what he called typology, still one of the basic techniques of archaeology. His large anthropological and archaeological collections of artifacts were given to Oxford University and are now held in the Pitt-Rivers Museum. His army service took him to a posting in Ireland from 1862 to 1867. It was here that he first began to explore archaeological monuments. He saw that many monuments were being destroyed and became an early advocate for government action to preserve archaeological remains.

Back in England, from 1868, he surveyed and excavated hill forts in Sussex where he perfected the method of excavating by sections through stratigraphy at Cissbury. His work in Sussex identified and dated for the first time the flint mines of the Neolithic. Pitt-Rivers had worked with Sir John Lubbock to organize the International Congress of Prehistoric Archaeology in 1868, and as a noted advocate of state protection of monuments, was made the first Inspector of Ancient Monuments in 1883 under Lubbock's Ancient Monuments Protection Act. Until then, the only professional archaeologists in Britain were either a few museum curators or even fewer university professors.

His inheritance of Cranborne Chase not only gave him financial independence but also the right to excavate where he would on his own land. His excavations there provided a model for the future of field archaeology. Pitt-Rivers was determined to keep everything found in order to show the everyday life of people in the past, where earlier excavators would only keep the rare, beautiful, or valuable artifacts. His excavations were meticulously recorded, understanding that all excavation destroys the site it investigates and that a proper excavation report can be used by later archaeologists to reveal new information. The method of digging he advocated was open area excavation, understanding that small pits or narrow sections would not be enough to allow a proper interpretation of a site. He also advocated carrying out experiments to help interpret sites. At Cissbury in 1875, he had used antler picks to see how effective they had been in cutting the Neolithic galleries, and established that other tools would have had to be used with wooden handles to be effective. After excavation at Worbarrow in 1894, he came back three years later to excavate the ditches again to establish how they had eroded and refilled. This would help to interpret the ancient filling of ditches elsewhere and is a remarkable piece of early experimental field archaeology. Pitt-Rivers effectively founded modern excavation methods in Britain. He also believed strongly in the educational purpose of museums, opening up his own estate and its private museum to the public and deliberately setting out to make it attractive to poorer people to visit. Examples of his publications include:

- *The Instruction of Musketry*, 1854;
- *Primitive Warfare*, 1867–1869, three lectures published in the Journal of the Royal United Service Institution;
- *On the Evolution of Culture*, 1875, published in the Proceedings of the Royal Institution;
- *Excavations in Cranborne Chase, near Rushmore, on the Borders of Dorset and Wiltshire*, 1887–1898.

John Mortimer 1825–1911

While archaeology was slowly becoming a profession, using modern methods, the old amateur archaeologists were still active. One of the last, and best, of the traditional barrow diggers carrying on the tradition of excavating burial mounds that had been done since the eighteenth century was John Mortimer. By profession, Mortimer was a corn merchant in the chalk Wolds of Yorkshire, and his archaeological work was all within that area. Unlike most of the early archaeologists, he was not of professional or gentry status, and did not have any form of education beyond basic schooling. His concern with only local archaeology and his social standing made him an outsider, not part of the networks of scholarship, with little recognition from the national organizations of the day. For example, he was never made a fellow of the Society of Antiquaries. A class divide has always been a feature of archaeology, and continues in modified form to this day between those with a university education in archaeology and those without.

Mortimer first got interested in both archaeology and geology after visiting the Great Exhibition and the British Museum in 1851. He immediately set about collecting fossils and flint tools from the fields on the Wolds. Farming in the area was only recently switching to intensive crop growing and many earthworks still survived, although he noted that a large number (his estimate was around a quarter) were already being destroyed by ploughing. He began to survey the linear earthworks that marked prehistoric land boundaries on the Wolds, and from 1863 up to the end of his life excavated more than 360 barrows along with various flat cemeteries of the prehistoric to the Anglo-Saxon periods, and recovered more than 66,000 artifacts. Mortimer even built his own museum at Driffield in 1878 to house his finds and make them accessible to the public. He was insistent that the finds should remain in the East Riding as part of the heritage and identity of the area, a very modern concern with the role of archaeology and what we now call the sense of place. After his death, his collections were moved to the museum in Hull, the main city of the East Riding.

Although not as proficient as Pitt-Rivers, and not working up to a modern standard, nevertheless he collected everything he found and systematically recorded his excavations as well as the crop and soil marks he observed. He located all his sites on the map, noted the stratigraphy of the barrows, recorded sections and plans, and unusually for the time was able to recognize and record post and stakeholes under and within the barrows. Also in advance of his time, he made plaster casts of the stakeholes to determine the shape of the long-since rotted stakes and posts, and had samples of soil and human bone analyzed by specialists. Noting the stratigraphy of the barrows, he was able to spot possible burial structures that had rotted away and were now invisible. He could also be self-critical and went back to re-excavate sites he felt he had not adequately investigated early in his career.

His main weakness was not being able to interpret what he found. His assumptions about the wooden posts under the barrows being houses was wrong, and he could not place different barrows into a correct chronology within prehistory. Mortimer's achievements are all the more remarkable for being mostly self taught. His excavations were properly published in his one major work, along with accurate drawings of the finds by his teenage daughter Agnes, and still form an important record of barrows now destroyed by agriculture:

- *Forty Years' Researches in British and Saxon Burial Mounds of East Yorkshire*, 1905.

THE HEROIC AGE

Modern archaeology developed in the early twentieth century into a serious and well-established profession, with its own methodologies and theories. It would make great strides in understanding human development and culture. In a small discipline with relatively few professional practitioners, a few key people could leave a big mark and leave work of lasting importance.

Sir Mortimer Wheeler 1890–1976

One of the most publicly well-known archaeologists of the twentieth century, Sir Mortimer Wheeler began by studying classics at London University in 1907–1910. His working life was varied. His first job was with the Royal Commission on the Historical Monuments of England in 1913. This was interrupted by the First World War when he served with the Royal Artillery, seeing active service on the western front in 1917–1918. After the war, he worked for the National Museum of Wales from 1920, rising to be its director in 1924–1926. While there, he excavated at various Welsh sites, including Segontium and Caerleon. He moved to be Keeper of the London Museum in 1926, excavating at Lydney, Verulamium, and Maiden Castle. He was also one of the founders of the Institute of Archaeology in London in 1934 with the aim of training students in practical and scientific archaeological skills, and was its director from 1937, undertaking research on the Iron Age in Brittany. The Second World War saw him return to the Royal Artillery, rising to the rank of brigadier and serving in North Africa and Italy. Leaving the army in 1944, he went to be the director general of the Archaeological Survey of India from 1944 to 1948, excavating sites of the Indus culture at Harappa and Mohenjo-daro and modernizing Indian archaeology. He promoted the role of Indian archaeologists and universities, and in 1949–1950 helped to set up the

Pakistan archaeology department and national museum. His later excavations included Stanwick in northern England in 1951 and Charsadda in Pakistan in 1956. His final post was as secretary of the British Academy 1949–1968, revitalizing the body to provide funding for research worldwide.

He was married to Tessa Verney (born 1883) in 1914, an accomplished field archaeologist in her own right and one who deserves equal credit for his early excavations, but who died in 1936. Together, they updated and applied the rigorous approach of Pitt-Rivers. His innovation in field archaeology was the grid system of excavation with regular vertical baulks to help understand site stratigraphy. Publications followed promptly from all his excavations (unlike the habit of some of his contemporaries), and like Woolley he was happy to write for a popular audience. Wheeler was a keen publicist, some said of himself, but he would have said of archaeology which he understood needed public support if it was to thrive. This understanding may have come through having a father who was a journalist. He secured funding from the *Daily Mail* newspaper for his excavations at Caerleon in 1926 in return for exclusive access to reports of his finds. While excavating at Verulamium in 1930–1933, he made sure that his work was reported in the Pathe newsreels shown in cinemas at the time. At Maiden Castle, he opened the excavations to public tours and happily sold some of the many thousands of slingstones he had found on the site as souvenirs to help finance his work. His larger-than-life personality meant that he was a frequent performer on television, especially in the formative archaeology series of *Animal, Vegetable, Mineral* (1952–1960), *Buried Treasure* (1952–1958), *Chronicle* (from 1966) and other programs. His popularity was such that he was voted by the public as TV personality of the year in 1954. His use of the media was not new, but was thorough and highly successful. For many, Wheeler was the public face of archaeology in Britain, both authoritative and charismatic. Among his many publications were:

- *Prehistoric and Roman Wales*, 1925;
- *Verulamium: a Belgic and Two Roman Cities*, 1936;
- *The excavation of Maiden Castle, Dorset: second interim report*, 1936;
- *Maiden Castle, Dorset*, 1943;
- *The Indus Civilization*, 1953;
- *The Stanwick Fortifications, North Riding of Yorkshire*, 1954;
- *Archaeology from the Earth*, 1954, his thoughts about archaeology and its purpose, still valuable today;
- *Still Digging*, 1955, the first of his three autobiographies;

- *Alms for Oblivion*, 1966, another autobiography;
- *My Archaeological Mission to India and Pakistan*, 1976, his last autobiography.

Vere Gordon Childe 1892–1957

An Australian who spent his whole archaeological career in Britain, Gordon Childe was one of the most prominent archaeologists in the English-speaking world. He first came to Britain in 1914–1917 to study at Oxford University. He returned and remained in Britain from 1921. Childe was professor of archaeology at Edinburgh University from 1927 to 1946, and then director of the Institute of Archaeology from 1946 to 1956. He conducted excavations at Skara Brae, Maes Howe, Quoyness, and various Iron Age forts, always writing up and publishing his findings, but confessing to not enjoying excavation and only undertaking it with reluctance. He was also a famously poor lecturer but a superb researcher. His major work was to synthesize the research done up to his time and make sense of it in terms of a scheme of cultural evolution across the whole of Europe and the Middle East.

Childe thought deeply about how to explain cultural development. At first, he was happy to accept the migration of people as a cause, but then borrowed ideas from Marxism. He was politically an active and left-wing socialist. Childe had worked for the Australian Labor Party, and visited the Soviet Union in 1935 (but heavily criticized its invasion of Hungary in 1956), so it was only natural that he should apply Marxist ideas to archaeology. Marxism could help to explain why societies changed without invoking invasion and conquest. Following Marxist principles, he understood the importance of understanding the environment and how people got their food and materials from it as a necessary basis for other aspects of human culture. He also understood that societies would include diverse competing groups which could drive technological and social change. He defined two great changes in human culture since the end of the Ice Age: the development of farming and later the growth of cities, both happening in the Near East. Childe's "Neolithic Revolution" was the advent not only of farming but also of permanent settlement with long-lasting houses, pottery, and ownership of land. His "Urban Revolution" involved the rise of priests, kings, bureaucrats, artists, and specialist craftsmen in a hierarchical society using writing to keep records and develop literature, and monumental architecture. After Childe, archaeology could think big, across whole continents, and tackle great themes of human development. He thought deeply about the meaning of archaeological remains and what we could truly know about the past from our study of them.

Childe gained quick acceptance in Britain through the sheer force of his intellect, but his Marxism made him suspect in some quarters. Childe's political activities led to him being banned from entering the United States and his ideas were always better known in Europe, where he is acknowledged as one of the true greats of archaeology. Childe feared growing old and losing his intellectual capacity. He chose to leave life while still at the height of his fame and powers by committing suicide after returning to see family and friends in Australia. Childe published many works, especially for a popular audience, including:

- *The Dawn of European Civilization*, 1925, the first great overview of European prehistory in English;
- *The Danube in Prehistory*, 1929, making great use of the idea of cultures, not then a major part of British archaeological thinking;
- *Man Makes Himself*, 1936, his key work introducing the Neolithic and Urban Revolutions within a Marxist framework of analysis;
- *What Happened in History*, 1942;
- *Progress and Archaeology*, 1944;
- *Society and Knowledge*, 1956;
- *The Prehistory of European Society*, 1958.

Dorothy Garrod 1892–1968

Women were the second-class citizens of university scholarship. Cambridge University did not admit women to full membership of the university until 1948. In spite of this, in 1939, Dorothy Garrod became the first woman professor to be appointed at either Cambridge or Oxford Universities, becoming the Disney Professor of Archaeology at Cambridge: the oldest and most prestigious academic post in archaeology. Garrod was one of the most prominent archaeologists in Britain, and although her fieldwork lay outside Britain, she blazed a trail for women academics in higher education in the United Kingdom. She graduated in history from Cambridge University in 1916 and then studied archaeology, graduating in 1921. She worked on the Paleolithic in France under the legendary Abbé Breuil in 1922–1924. Garrod's own first excavation was of a Neanderthal site at Gibraltar in 1925 and she went on to excavate in Palestine at Shukba, where she discovered and defined the important Natufian culture in 1928. She also worked in Iraqi Kurdistan before working in various caves on Mount Carmel (such as Tabun) in Palestine in 1929–1934. This was her most famous project where she uncovered a sequence of 600,000 years spanning the time of the Neanderthals up to the Natufian and the origins of agriculture. She then worked in Anatolia and Bulgaria before becoming Disney Professor. After the war, she worked in France and produced a major correlation of chronology between the Middle East and northern Europe. Her last excavations were in Lebanon in 1958–1963. Her work formed the basis for prehistory in the Middle East. Garrod's perspective on the Paleolithic was worldwide, rather than only regional or local as most previous work had been. She was one of the first to suggest that modern humans originated outside Europe and brought Upper Paleolithic culture there from the east. Her leadership in Cambridge ensured that archaeology became a full undergraduate degree subject there for the first time. As a pioneering woman professor at Cambridge, she became a celebrated female academic, but never regarded herself as a feminist. However, and unusually, she did employ mostly local women as her laborers on the excavation at Mount Carmel, and her strongest partnerships were with other women archaeologists, especially in France. She published a great deal, including:

- *The Upper Palaeolithic Age in Britain*, 1926;
- *The Stone Age of Mount Carmel*, 1937.

Dame Kathleen Kenyon 1906–1978

Kathleen Kenyon was born into archaeology as her father, Sir Frederick Kenyon, was director of the British Museum. She graduated from Oxford in 1929 and worked with Gertrude Caton-Thompson (see list at the end of this chapter) at Zimbabwe and with Sir Mortimer Wheeler (see previous entry) at Verulamium in 1930–1935. Kenyon also worked on projects at Samaria in Palestine in 1931–1934, Jewry Wall in Leicester in 1936–1939, in Libya in 1948–1951, and in Jerusalem in 1961–1967, as well as other shorter excavations in Britain and elsewhere. However, her most famous excavations were at Jericho from 1951 to 1958. Jericho was revealed as the oldest continuously occupied settlement in the world (for at least 11,000 years), and a key site for understanding the origins of agriculture. Her work introduced a more rigorous approach to excavation and stratigraphy in the Middle East, and helped to prevent a too-literal equation of archaeological evidence and Biblical testimony. Her major importance in British archaeology was that she was a co-founder with Wheeler of the Institute of Archaeology in London, and was acting director of the institute from 1942 to 1946. The institute was the major center for academic archaeology outside Oxford and Cambridge, and a pioneer of scientific, applied archaeology. The excavation methods she learned from Wheeler were refined and perfected in her own excavations, and she became an expert in the refinement of pottery typology as an aid to dating sites and layers. Among her published books were:

- *Beginning in Archaeology*, 1952;
- *Digging Up Jericho*, 1957;
- *Archaeology in the Holy Land*, 1960.

Sir Grahame Clark 1907–1995

Early archaeologists understood that we cannot study past cultures in isolation from their environments. One of the most consistent advocates of this approach was Sir Grahame Clark. He was based in Cambridge University for his whole career, becoming Disney Professor of Archaeology from 1952 to 1974. His specialty was prehistory, and along with a group of friends, he took over a local archaeology society to make it into a national Prehistoric Society in 1935. His excavations in the Fens laid the foundations for our understanding of Neolithic settlements and stone tools in Britain. Clark firmly believed archaeology was not a study of past events or changes in culture. It was concerned with understanding how people lived in the past. Material culture allowed humans to survive in, and exploit, their environments. He saw human technology and subsistence as the basic necessities which allowed and determined the rest of human life. Clark advocated an interdisciplinary approach to the past, pioneered by his Cambridge University Fenland Research Committee in 1932 in which archaeologists, botanists, geographers, and geologists would work together. His work at the Mesolithic site of Star Carr in 1949–1951 was groundbreaking and revolutionized our view of the period in Britain. His vision, however, was never parochial. He believed in a world prehistory, in which archaeology should study not the development of one place or people but of the whole of humanity. In many ways, Clark anticipated later developments in archaeological theory in the 1960s with his interest in economic history and archaeology, but his role as a pioneer was somewhat eclipsed by the younger, more ambitious new generation. Some of his many publications were:

- *The Mesolithic Age in Britain*, 1932;
- *The Mesolithic Settlement of Northern Europe*, 1936;
- *Archaeology and Society*, 1939;
- *Prehistoric England*, 1940;
- *Prehistoric Europe: the Economic Basis*, 1952;
- *Excavations at Star Carr*, 1954;
- *World Prehistory: an Outline*, 1961;

- *The Identity of Man*, 1983;
- *Symbols of Excellence*, 1986;
- *Economic Prehistory*, 1989;
- *Space, Time, and Man: A Prehistorian's View*, 1992.

THE NEW GENERATION

The world of archaeology changed greatly in the late 1960s. New methods were becoming more widely available, such as radiocarbon dating which challenged the traditional chronologies and culture history built up over the previous hundred years. New ideas were being brought into archaeology from other disciplines, changing the way that archaeologists thought about and interpreted the past. The new generation was sometimes unfairly impatient and critical of the work of their forebears and they in turn would be criticized by younger colleagues with different attitudes.

David Clarke 1937–1976

The revolution in archaeological thinking in Britain began with David Clarke. Clarke graduated from Cambridge University in 1957, then did his doctoral research on Early Bronze Age Beaker pottery before being appointed to the staff of the university in 1966. His work on Beakers introduced a new rigorous approach to pottery studies, while his work on the Glastonbury settlement showed a new approach to understanding variability in spatial patterns on archaeological sites. The details of his work on both have had to be heavily modified since, but his major contribution was to archaeological thought. He soon published a book, *Analytical Archaeology*, which began a revolution in archaeological thinking in Britain. Clarke saw that human culture was the result of a complex web of interactions between people and specific aspects of their behavior such as technology, social structure, ideology or belief, etc. To try to make sense of this, Clarke used systems theory, borrowed from new thinking in geography. All parts of the system are ultimately interconnected with the others. Clarke wanted archaeologists to study the different parts of the system, such as social structures like family or hierarchy, religion, psychology or ideas, the economy, and technology, and identify how these affected each other to produce the cultures we see in the archaeological record. His ideas were soon being called the New Archaeology. This freed archaeologists to shed light on past cultures as living societies. It gave us concepts to help us think about the past, such as homeostasis (the long-term stability of a culture), feedback, adaptation, and variables as specific elements to be analyzed. Indeed, its critics often attacked the New Archaeologists' use of jargon and their use of theoretical models, flow-charts, statistics, and computer simulations.

Although Clarke had borrowed ideas from geography and elsewhere, he advocated that "archaeology is archaeology is archaeology." In other words, archaeologists must analyze the past using methods appropriate to the kinds of remains we find, and develop our own specific methodologies that would be unique to archaeology. The New Archaeology came as a revelation to many, and seemed to place archaeology on a more scientific path. Similar developments were happening in the United States, although of a slightly different nature. Clarke had a fertile mind, always developing his ideas. His early death robbed archaeology of a major figure, and he never had the chance to develop his ideas in response to critics who attacked them in the 1980s. These critics termed the approach of the late 1960s as processual archaeology and tended to equate it with its American version instead of reading closely what Clarke had written. Careful attention to Clarke shows his flexibility in applying his ideas, and that his ideas could easily accommodate the different perspectives of his critics. Clarke's publications included:

- *Analytical Archaeology*, 1968, one of the major works of archaeological theory;
- *Beaker Pottery of Great Britain and Ireland*, 1970;
- *Models in Archaeology*, 1972, an edited volume of work mostly by others who put Clarke's ideas into practice, but including his own *Glastonbury lake village. A provisional model of an Iron Age society and its settlement pattern*;
- *Archaeology: the Loss of Innocence*, 1973, published in the journal *Antiquity*;
- *Mesolithic Europe: The Economic Basis*, 1976;
- *Spatial Archaeology*, 1977.

Lord (Colin) Renfrew 1937–

Colin Renfrew graduated from Cambridge University in 1962, and became a lecturer at Sheffield University in 1965. He moved to Southampton University in 1972 and was then Disney Professor of Archaeology at the University of Cambridge from 1981 to 2004, and director of the McDonald Institute for Archaeological Research from 1990 to 2004. As a field archaeologist, his work has mostly been in Greece, specializing in the Bronze Age. Renfrew's major importance has been in archaeological theory, the reevaluation of our interpretations of the past and the fight against the illegal trade in antiquities. His first major reinterpretation was his use of the calibration of radiocarbon dates to show how changes in the cultures of western European often occurred earlier than, and independently of, the Middle East. Previously, many archaeologists had relied on making chains of links between sites and artifacts that showed how culture diffused from the eastern Mediterranean westward, and that the east was therefore the source of all civilization. Renfrew showed how these links were often not real and based on false similarities between sites and artifacts. This was a major advance in archaeology, freeing it to explain the past in ways that were no longer linked to notions of superiority and race. Another reinterpretation was his work on the origins of Indo-European languages, arguing that they originated in Anatolia, much earlier than previously accepted, and spread with the movement of farming into Europe from there. This theory has had less acceptance, as it contradicts the evidence of language specialists and historical linguistics. The majority view is still that the Indo-European languages spread during the Bronze Age from the lands to the north of the Black Sea (modern Ukraine and southern Russia).

Renfrew has always tackled some of the big questions about the human past and human identity, such as championing the use of catastrophe theory to explain dramatic cultural change. More recently, he has explored the approach of contemporary artists to making meaning out of material culture and argued that archaeologists could learn from this much about how people and the material world interact, define their identities, and make sense of their worlds. He has also made our analysis of religious ritual more rigorous through identifying the evidence it leaves behind in the archaeological record. Renfrew was made Lord Renfrew in 1991, enabling him to speak in Parliament on behalf of archaeology: the first archaeologist Parliamentarian since Lord Avebury. His major work politically has been in attempting to tackle the illegal trade in antiquities which encourages the destruction of archaeological sites and robs archaeologists of information about the past. His most important publications are:

- *The Emergence of Civilization: The Cyclades and the Aegean in The Third Millennium BC*, 1972;
- *Before Civilization: The Radiocarbon Revolution and Prehistoric Europe*, 1973;
- *Archaeology and Language: The Puzzle of the Indo-European Origins*, 1987;
- *Archaeology: Theories, Methods, and Practice*, 1991, written with Paul Bahn and the standard university textbook on archaeology;
- *Loot, Legitimacy and Ownership: The Ethical Crisis in Archaeology*, 2000;

- *Figuring It Out: What Are We? Where Do We Come From? The Parallel Visions of Artists and Archaeologists,* 2003;
- *Prehistory: The Making of the Human Mind,* 2008.

Ian Hodder 1948–

The second revolution in archaeological theory began in 1982 with a challenge to the dominant thinking by Ian Hodder. He pointed out that the attempt to create universal laws of human behavior was not supported by the evidence from anthropology. His own attempts to use the New Archaeology using statistics on African pottery were contradicted by the results he was finding. Hodder inspired a group of younger researchers eager to look for new questions and new sources of inspiration in archaeology, chiefly sociology and philosophy. They called the tradition they were reacting against "processual archaeology," and their views are known collectively as "post-processual archaeologies." Hodder had graduated from London in 1971, moving to Cambridge University for his doctoral research inspired by David Clarke, and then taught at Leeds University in 1974–1977, before returning to Cambridge from 1977–1999 where he developed his ideas. These ideas included placing archaeology into its contemporary world as a discipline practiced within particular social and political contexts. Archaeology therefore has a role to play in society today. He also saw that past cultures had their own historical origins and developments which made attempts to generalize about human behavior impossible. He has been a strong advocate of a collaborative approach to research rather than the traditional approach in the humanities of strongly personal research projects.

Hodder has been putting his ideas into practice at his long-term excavation at the major Neolithic site of Çatalhöyük in Turkey since 1993. This includes archaeology as a collaborative process involving dialogue between the collaborators, the past, and all those interested in the site, such as international women's groups who believe in the notion of the mother goddess. He also encourages his fieldworkers to be reflexive about their work, noting their own comments and feelings as part of the project archive. For Hodder, culture is meaningfully constituted. That is, objects have meanings for the people who make and use them, not simply practical uses. He is hostile to the traditional idea of archaeological cultures as too tied up with racial or national group identities. Importantly, he still insists on the primacy of the archaeological evidence, showing that the dialogue need not include accepting all and any views on the past, no matter how ludicrous. Since 1999, Hodder has been based at Stanford University in the United States of America, trying to introduce new ways of thinking to the tradition of anthropological archaeology of the United States, while the archaeologies he inspired have continued to evolve in different directions in Britain. Hodder's writings include:

- *Symbols in Action. Ethnoarchaeological Studies of Material Culture*, 1982, the key turning point away from Clarke's New Archaeology;
- *The Present Past: an Introduction to Anthropology for Archaeologists*, 1982;
- *Reading the Past: Current Approaches to Interpretation in Archaeology*, 1986;
- *The Domestication of Europe: Structure and Contingency in Neolithic Societies*, 1990;
- *Theory and Practice in Archaeology*, 1992, a set of his collected papers;
- *The Archaeological Process. An Introduction*, 1999;
- *Archaeology beyond Dialogue*, 2004, more collected papers;
- *The Leopard's Tale: Revealing the Mysteries of Çatalhöyük*, 2006;
- *At the Trowel's Edge: An Introduction to Reflexive Field Practice in Archaeology*, 2007, written with Asa Berggren;
- *Religion in the Emergence of Civilization. Çatalhöyük as a Case Study*, 2010;
- *Entangled: An Archaeology of the Relationships between Humans and Things*, 2012.

Other archaeologists

Some other important archaeologists whose careers or importance lay mostly outside Britain include:

- Sir Flinders Petrie 1853–1942: a key figure in creating many of the methods of modern archaeology, whose major work was done in Egypt and Palestine
- Margaret Murray 1863–1963: an ardent feminist archaeologist, who worked in Egypt and the Mediterranean, the first female British university lecturer in archaeology
- Sir Leonard Woolley 1880–1960: famous for his work in Mesopotamia, especially at Ur, and an early popularizer of archaeology and media celebrity of his day
- Gertrude Caton-Thompson 1888–1985: important for her work in the Middle East, and at the ruins of Great Zimbabwe where she demolished white racist interpretations of the site
- Peter Ucko 1938–2007: promoted aboriginal archaeologists in Australia, and created the World Archaeological Congress devoted to respect for indigenous Third World cultures

7

CONTROVERSIES AND SCANDALS

Archaeology is often controversial. The results of fieldwork are not always certain or obvious and archaeologists often disagree about the interpretation of their finds. Sometimes, the desire to make a name or prove a theory leads people astray into outright forgery and fake results. The remains of the past are also a form of heritage, used within the present for many purposes: financial, cultural, political, and so on. This can cause tensions between the needs of archaeology and the needs of others in society or with political authorities. Archaeology often comes into conflict with the desire of some to make financial gain out of the past, and the United Kingdom is a major worldwide hub for the international antiquities trade.

DISAGREEMENTS AMONGST ARCHAEOLOGISTS

The Antiquity of Early Man

In 1797, John Frere found stone tools in a quarry at Hoxne in Suffolk associated with the remains of extinct animals. He published his findings in the *Antiquaries Journal*, stating that they must have belonged to a time before the world we currently knew of. This hint of the antiquity of man before recorded history suggested that all was not well with the chronology that scholars were familiar with from the Christian Bible. Other similar finds were being made, and disputed by scholars anxious to defend the

Bible by questioning the reliability of the evidence. William Buckland, an Anglican priest and geologist, discovered the Paleolithic Paviland skeleton in 1823, believing it to be the burial of woman from the Roman period. Buckland was a firm creationist and suggested all the finds made so far were the intrusion of later stone tools or human bones into earlier deposits containing the extinct animals. John MacEnery, a Roman Catholic priest, found stone tools and extinct animals at Kents Cavern in Devon in 1825–1829, sealed under a geological deposit of cave breccia. He at first accepted the evidence but then allowed himself to be swayed by Buckland in assuming that these were also intrusive. Buckland had published an eloquent geological defense of creationism in 1836, yet was able to objectively look at the geological evidence and revise his views of the origin of recent deposits in Britain. By 1840, he accepted that deposits he thought had been left by the Biblical flood had in fact been deposited by glaciers in past ice ages. The major breakthrough happened in France with publication in 1847 of the finding of ancient stone tools by Boucher de Perthes near Abbeville in northern France. Similar finds were made in Britain by William Pengelly at Kents Cavern (excavating where MacEnery had left off) and Hugh Falconer at Brixham Cave. It was Falconer who invited the geologist Sir John Prestwich and archaeologist Sir John Evans to Abbeville to examine Boucher de Perthes' results. Their announcement of the validity of his work in 1859 marked the final academic acceptance of the antiquity of man, and the inability of the Bible to be seriously used as a guide to the chronology of humanity. Not long afterwards, in 1865, Sir John Lubbock published his book *Prehistoric Times as Illustrated by Ancient Remains* which gave mankind a deep prehistory for the first time. The final confirmation of man's place in nature and the possibility of a serious archaeological study of the development of the human species came with the publication by Charles Darwin of *The Descent of Man* in 1871.

Beginnings of the Neolithic: Adoption or Migration?

The beginning of farming has long been accepted as a major watershed in human development, perhaps the most important in the cultural evolution, not only of Britain but worldwide. This way of life replaced one based on hunting and gathering. This change from the Mesolithic to the Neolithic has traditionally been seen as a sharp and quick one, brought about by a migration of people into Britain bringing domestic animals and crops from the continent. This was questioned in the 1980s, in favor of a more gradual transition whereby farming was adopted by a largely indigenous population, and in which the people of the early Neolithic carried on a mobile lifestyle similar to the Mesolithic. In part, this was a result of having very little evidence for early Neolithic settlements in southern Britain, and a search for parallels in southern Scandinavia where the evidence is more complete. It is also very hard to find only one part of the continent with the same material culture as Britain and which would have been where people migrated from, although there are many similarities with a wide area from northern France through Belgium to the Netherlands. The post-processual emphasis on how people in the past felt and thought about their world led to a reluctance to accept migration and external explanations for cultural change. However, the evidence from the Mesolithic in Britain is very different from that from Scandinavia. There is no evidence for a gradual adoption of farming by Mesolithic groups, and the evidence is still for radically different lifestyles between the Mesolithic and Neolithic. Movement of people has to be taken seriously as part of the explanation for the beginning of the Neolithic in Britain. We know that the climate was beginning to cool down toward the end of the Mesolithic and this may have made the adoption of farming attractive in order to ensure a secure food supply. However, there is no evidence in Britain for contacts with farming groups by Mesolithic peoples. The latest research has involved the use of statistical methods to analyze the radiocarbon dates for the period. Being able to fine tune the dates is allowing a much better understanding of the evidence. This suggests that the Neolithic began around 4050 BC in the Thames estuary, spreading to south of the Wash and east of the Severn by 3900, then expanding rapidly to cover all Britain by 3700 BC. The best explanation for this is an initial migration by colonizers from the area between the Rivers Seine and Rhine (from Normandy to Flanders), followed by acculturation in the rest of Britain by the native inhabitants. The questions that still need resolving are whether there was one wave of colonization or successive waves, and whether they came from one geographical area or from several across a wider area. The debate can now move onto more interesting ground, not either migration or indigenous development, but the balance between the two and the relationships between incomers and natives.

Arthur: Fact or Fiction?

The figure of Arthur, known from Medieval literature and history, has long been controversial. The historical evidence is so slight that it cannot prove beyond doubt that Arthur (*Artorius* in Latin) was a historical figure. Two modern scholars made extensive reference to Arthur, assuming that he was a historic figure ruling in Britain in the early sixth century: the historian John Morris and archaeologist Leslie Alcock. By contrast, many historians are uncomfortable with fleshing out the meager documentary record, and some are overtly hostile, particularly David Dumville who was savage in his attack on John Morris's work. Alcock undoubtedly found an important high status site at South Cadbury belonging to the fifth and sixth centuries. The site had a historical association as being Arthur's capital of Camelot but the excavations could not prove this association, which is only based on the name of the nearby River Camel. Archaeological work has been done at various other sites that have a traditional historical or folklore association with Arthur. Castlesteads on Hadrian's Wall (Latin *Camboglanna*) was identified as Arthur's Camlann by the archaeologist Osbert Crawford in 1935 on the resemblance of its place-name. The Roman town of Colchester (Latin *Camulodunum*) has also been suggested as Camlann on the basis of its name. Arthur is an iconic figure in British culture, and provides a ready marketing brand to arouse interest among the press and media. The fragment of an inscription with the name *Artognou* was found in excavations at Tintagel in 1998. The excavators were careful not to say this was evidence of Arthur, as the name Artognou is an entirely different Welsh name. However, it was widely reported in the media as proof of Arthur at Tintagel. There is an undoubted appeal of Arthur stemming from his place in romantic literature, and as a symbol of Celtic nationhood. An overly zealous wish to establish Arthur as a real presence in archaeology and history is understandable. Equally, it is just as understandable that some will react strongly the other way to avoid what they see as contamination of "serious" history and archaeology by a figure from romantic fiction, associated with mysticism and nationalism. Both are equally strident and equally wrong. There has to be a possibility than a figure named Arthur existed and that we can speculate about what his role might have been, but we need always to admit that this is speculation, not hard fact, and that Arthur may after all be a Medieval mirage. We are forced to confront the uncertainties of archaeology and history, and the limits of what we can say about the past. This is uncomfortable but honest.

Anglo-Saxon Origins

The origins of England lie in the few hundred years after the end of the rule of the Roman Empire in Britain. The southeast of the island became the home of a northern Germanic culture and language that were brought over to Britain from across the North Sea. The traditional explanation for this was that Germanic migrants, later known as Anglo-Saxons, came over as a large-scale folk migration to Britain conquering, swamping, or driving out the native Britons. This explanation is one that is presented in the later historical documents which record the traditions of royal houses arriving and conquering in Britain.

Map of Britain during the Migration Period, courtesy of Donald Henson

It also felt comfortable in the late nineteenth century world of competing empires and new nations where invasion and conquest were a normal part of international relations. Since then, however, the size and nature of the migration of Germanic settlers to Britain in the fifth and sixth centuries have been the cause of much debate. Some archaeologists and historians still accept the picture painted in the later historical sources of a large-scale migration, although they no longer accept the idea of the expulsion of the native Britons. Others prefer to see only a small-scale immigration of elite kings and nobles, leading to an acculturation of the native Britons to a Germanic identity. Archaeologists have been especially attracted to this minimalist view. Many archaeologists have applied ideas from the study of prehistory, where the last thirty years have seen a move away from explaining cultural change through conquest and migration to the poorly documented migration period, for example, Chris Arnold whose study of the Anglo-Saxon kingdoms in 1988 argued for the elite conquest model. Francis Pryor in 2004 portrayed the Anglicization of southeastern Britain as merely a question of fashion with the Britons copying high status Anglo-Saxon taste in clothing and jewelry. On the other hand, place-name scholars and linguistic historians have been more accepting of mass migration, and a few British archaeologists and historians have looked at the evidence from Germany as well as Britain. A major study of Anglo-Saxon pottery in 1969 by John Myers showed the connections between not only cemeteries but individual pots in both Britain and northern Germany. A German archaeologist working in Britain, Heinrich Härke, has used the evidence of burial excavations to suggest that there is good evidence of Germanic incomers as a warrior elite in Britain, and argues for a large-scale movement of population, where the native Britons were simply swamped by incoming migrants. Historians and archaeologists are still deeply divided over this issue. Debate about the nature of migration, and the historically documented early Medieval migrations on the continent has been intense. One reviewer described Pryor's book of 2004 as "a great disappointment" and said of his analysis that "the results are ludicrous." It is clear that some migration did take place, and we need to study how it happened and how incoming migrants fitted into the existing order and eventually took it over. It is clear that different parts of Britain will have had different experiences. Large-scale migration will only apply to the southeast of modern England, while conquest and acculturation must be accepted for the north and west of the country. A resolution of the debate could come through the study of ancient and modern DNA. The results of such studies are capable of different interpretations, but it is clear that the Germanic immigrants did not

Anglo-Saxon royal jewelry, early seventh century shoulder clasp, Sutton Hoo. Photo, taken on 11 February 2011, is courtesy of Philip Pikart.

replace the native British but did form a large enough group to significantly alter the cultural balance in selected parts of southern and eastern Britain. Archaeologists need to develop a much more detailed understanding of migration as a process and be less simplistic in interpreting small samples of inadequate evidence.

The Archaeology of Now

Early in its development, archaeology tended to focus on prehistory and early periods with ruined remains we could tie to the historical record such as the Roman period. In fact, archaeology is not the study of the remote past, nor is it the study of ruins. Archaeology is the study of human material culture. It can therefore be used to study the very recent past, and even the present day. This is still controversial and the expansion of archaeology to cover ever later periods of the past has been resisted by many. An archaeology of contemporary times is even more contentious. Bristol University and Atkins Heritage came together in 2006 to excavate a 1991 Ford Transit van. This was not a buried van, but one still in use. It had been used by archaeologists and museum staff for more than fifteen years. The van was dealt with in the same way as a traditional archaeological site, using documentary research, oral histories, survey, planning, and excavation. The van

Excavating and recording the Transit van, photo courtesy of John Schofield

itself was a rare artifact by 2006, with only 110 vans still on the road, and was also significant in being one of the first in the UK to be built by robot. The project was widely reported in the newspapers and on television, and provoked mixed reactions among archaeologists with many opposed to it or highly skeptical of it. But this was partly the point, to provoke a reaction and make archaeologists think about what they do and why they do it. The project was also noticed by the public with equally divided opinion. One fear among archaeologists was that the project would seem so far removed from the stereotype of archaeology that it would appear frivolous and hold archaeologists up to ridicule. On the other hand, it did highlight very well the problems archaeology has with interpreting evidence, as was accepted by some of its critics. What the project also did was to raise the idea of an archaeology of contemporary life. This has been taken further in various ways. One project is looking at the archaeology of homelessness. This began in Bristol University and then moved to York University. An article about the project in the magazine *British Archaeology* featured homeless people on the cover of the magazine. This brought forth complaints from various members and readers about what was deemed appropriate for archaeology to investigate. The idea that archaeology only deals with the deep past is hard to shift from the minds of many. It took a seven-year-long project by the Council for British Archaeology (CBA) from 1995 to 2002, the Defence of Britain Project (in which 600 volunteers recorded nearly 20,000 military installations), to make the study of twentieth century military installations a respectable part of the discipline. The CBA has now launched a similar community project, Home Front Legacy (running from 2014 to 2018), aimed at recording the physical remains that relate to the First World War.

Theoretical Battles

Advances in scholarly theory often come about by a younger generation challenging the certainties of the establishment. The rise of post-processual ideas mirrored the rise of its predecessor, New Archaeology. Each began with new interpretations of archaeology challenging accepted ideas. In Britain, this was signaled with the publications of *Analytical Archaeology* by David Clarke in 1968 and of *Reading the Past* by Ian Hodder in 1986. The New Archaeologists were attacked by their predecessors in strong language. Jacquetta Hawkes described the New Archaeologists as "an introverted group of specialists enjoying their often rather squalid intellectual spells and ritual at the expense of an outside world to which they will contribute nothing that is enjoyable, generally interesting or of historical importance." Likewise, in a very similar way, the debates between the New Archaeologists and the post-processualists were often fierce, blunt, challenging, and personal. Christopher Chippindale wrote that post-processualism was "a game played by intellectuals for their own incomprehensible concepts of amusement, just as English persons of a certain type indulge in the incomprehensible performances and cruelties of croquet." A feature of scholarly debate is that each side tends to characterize the other in simplistic and very broad terms that emphasize the most extreme beliefs of the others. The use of different philosophical approaches means that each side simply shouts its beliefs at the other without any meaningful exploration of key issues. The objective scientific approach of New Archaeology has a place alongside the more subjective humanism of post-processualism. Together they both make archaeology stronger, if they can avoid their extreme excesses. These excesses are an assumption that we can be certain about what the archaeological record tells us and that all subjective opinions about the past are equally valid. Neither of these is true. Modern archaeology in Britain uses a mix of approaches, such as actor network theory or practice theory, in which New Archaeology systems approaches and post-processual individual agency both have a role. There are those who turn their back against theoretical debates and concentrate on excavating and conserving the remains of the past. Not all archaeology occurs within universities, and in Britain the work of archaeologists in heritage management is somewhat removed from much of the work of university researchers. The practice of field archaeology has developed in its own way, and new ideas have come from other sources. While some academics were calling for a politically engaged archaeology, the fieldworkers were practicing an archaeology that was increasingly engaging with local people and nonarchaeologists. This has tended to be done without reference to archaeological theory. The growth of public archaeology has transcended the theoretical debate, arising instead out of practice. Perhaps the next theoretical battle will no longer be within universities but between universities and the field archaeologists searching for alternative ways of thinking about their work.

Displays of Human Remains

Human remains can provoke strong reactions in people. We are shielded from much contact with, or views of, dead bodies in the modern world, either in reality or on our television screens. Yet archaeologists have a long history of finding, handling, and investigating human remains. The archaeology and museum professions have adopted post-modernist ideas over the last thirty years in which respect for the views and ideas of others is taken seriously. Many are therefore nervous about public reaction to the display of bodies in museums, or have highly empathetic reactions to the bodies themselves and wish to be sensitive to the once-living person the body represents. Some are quite overprotective. Museum of London guidelines suggest that human remains should be placed in displays in ways that give them some privacy. We might ask why an inert collection of bones with no living consciousness needs privacy. On the other hand, displays of ancient Egyptian mummies have long been accepted and have not caused such controversy. A major exhibition in Manchester tackled the issue of displaying past human remains head on. This was the minimalist, but intellectually complex, "Lindow Man: A Bog Body Mystery" exhibition held at Manchester Museum from 2008 to 2009. The body itself was displayed on its own, without its Iron Age background also being displayed. Instead the display highlighted the emotional responses of seven people, both professional and members of the public, to the body. A major conference was held, linked to the exhibition, to debate the issue of displaying human remains. The exhibition caused a great deal of controversy. This was not so much for its display of the body but for its lack of didactic content and its highlighting of seven different emotional responses to the body being given equal weight, including that of a modern, neo-pagan "druid." Those who believe we should display human remains believe that this can make the past more accessible and emotively powerful, placing people at the heart of the past instead of inert artifacts. The remains help to create empathy for the lives and times of others. Such displays may help to spark an interest in young people that will entice them into a future career dealing with the human body. A further gain from these displays is that they help visitors to confront and think about issues of mortality. Those who are opposed to the display of human remains feel that it is disrespectful to treat a human body as though it were an object, and that display of remains becomes a kind of "freak show." The way in which remains are displayed in museums can often be a way of reducing the remains to be simply another kind of object like pottery or swords, reducing the power of the body to move the visitor. Religious treatment of the dead body varies. Some religions feel that once the soul or living entity leaves the body then it has no further significance, while others believe that the dead body maintains a connection with the once-living person. Christian belief has tended to see the human remains as simply inert objects, although it has given saintly relics the power of healing and has had no problems displaying such relics for the last 2,000 years. The Human Tissue Act of 2004 in the United Kingdom lays down that consent must be sought for the display of bodies less than 100 years old, and the World Archaeological Congress adopted an accord on the display of human remains in 2005, which recognized the rights of communities to whom the remains belong to have the final say on whether they can be displayed or not. Some would extend these principles to all remains from the past, and that we should try to respect the beliefs of the people whose skeletons and artifacts we are uncovering. This is a problem when displaying prehistoric remains, whose religious beliefs we do not know and whose living descendants are hard to identify. Few studies have asked the public how they feel about human remains being on display. Those that have been done show high levels of public interest in these remains, and support for museums in displaying them. A study by the British Museum showed that three-quarters of its visitors expected to see skeletal remains and reacted positively to them. Visitors also thought that although the bodies should be respected they trusted the museum staff to get this right. The first exhibition of Lindow Man at Manchester Museum in 1987 holds the museum record for the greatest number of visitors ever to come to an exhibition.

DISPUTES BETWEEN ARCHAEOLOGY AND SOCIETY

The Elgin Marbles or the Parthenon Frieze?
One of the great treasures of the British Museum is a stone sculptured frieze that once ran around the top of the Parthenon in Athens. It was created by the workshop of Phidias, regarded as possibly the greatest of the

ancient Greek sculptors in the fifth century BC. The frieze, along with other remains, was removed by the Earl of Elgin in 1801–1812. Elgin was the British ambassador to the Ottoman Empire that ruled Greece at the time. He sold the sculptures to the British government in 1816, and they are now part of the collections of the British Museum. Of the whole frieze of 524 feet, around 247 feet are held by the British Museum while around 160 feet are held by the Greeks on display in the new Acropolis Museum. Some parts of the frieze are also held by a variety of other European museums. Elgin claimed he had the written authorization of the Ottoman Sultan in 1801 to remove the sculptures. He did not keep the original documents and the only copy that exists is possibly not accurate. Even this copy has wording which can be contested and used to show that Elgin had gone further than he was allowed in removing all the sculptures and shipping them to Britain. His actions were controversial at the time, being attacked by others such as the poet Lord Byron for defacing ancient monuments. Elgin defended his actions on the grounds that the sculptures were in danger of destruction had they remained where they were. It is ironic that the cleaning and conservation of the sculptures by the museum is now regarded as having damaged their original surfaces. The controversy over the sculptures began to escalate in 1983 when the Greek government asked for them to be returned to Athens and the ownership of the Greeks. The British Museum has consistently refused this. The museum maintains that the sculptures are part of the cultural heritage of mankind, and that it shows the artistic heritage of Greece to a world audience. The Greeks on the other hand feel that a symbolic part of their identity is missing. Athens has a key symbolic role as the cradle of Greek civilization (although in fact many other areas of the Greek world were similar "cradles"), and the Parthenon is a crucial surviving part of a city that many look to as the originator of democracy (albeit in ancient Greece in which women and slaves were excluded from voting). This symbol of ancient Athenian democracy is a vital symbol of Greek democracy in the modern era. National identity in Greece is particularly strong, only achieving recognition internationally as a nation in 1830 after an eight-year revolt against the Ottoman Empire. The British Museum fears that to return the marbles would open the floodgates to other demands for the return of artifacts and lead to the impoverishment of museums which would be unable to communicate a variety of culture to transnational audiences. Many arguments have been used by both sides to support their position, including mutual attacks on the other's ability to adequately care for the sculptures (such as the damaging cleaning by the British Museum in the 1930s or the levels of pollution eroding the marble in modern Athens). The key issue, though, is ownership of the remains of the past. This ownership confers a feeling of deep connection with a symbolic past, as well as bringing the right to the economic benefits of heritage tourism. There are many in Britain who agree with returning the sculptures, and there would be a good case archaeologically for reuniting all parts of the Parthenon as a single monument. Nevertheless, the British Museum, and others, are great collections of world culture and seeing the world as one rather than as separate nations is a worthwhile purpose. The dispute pits the role of the past in national and ethnic identities against the role of its remains in helping us to understand the achievements of mankind through scholarship and science. It also helps to cast light on the practices of antiquarians of the seventeenth to the nineteenth centuries who acquired many thousands of artifacts from other cultures for the museums and great houses of Europe and America, in ways which would now be deemed unacceptable by the archaeological and museum professions.

Archaeology and Developer Funding

Post-war redevelopment in London saw office blocks being built on top of many archaeological remains. By 1988, a new phase of development was engulfing Bankside. At that time in England, known or suspected archaeological sites might be excavated if they were thought to be important, with funding granted from a limited budget by English Heritage. When a modern office block on the site of the Rose Theatre was being taken down for new building, an excavation was mounted to see if any remains of the Rose had survived. They had, and were revealed to a blaze of media publicity in 1989. This attracted thousands of visitors to the site, including many actors and actresses. These included people such as Sir Ian McKellen, Dame Peggy Ashcroft, and Dustin Hoffman. This in itself generated more publicity for the excavation. A campaign to save the remains was soon mounted, which highlighted the limited role of archaeology in rescuing sites about to be destroyed. Eventually, the developers agreed to an extension of time for the excavations, and a redesign of their office building to protect the parts of the site not yet excavated. The Rose Theatre was not the only site in Britain under threat, and many sites were completely lost, but the near loss of the remains of the Rose and the protest by high profile public figures led to a review of the system of protection for the historic environment. The result was Planning Policy Guidance 16 (PPG16). Equivalents were later issued in the rest of the United Kingdom: a separate PPG16 for Wales in 1990 and National Planning Policy Guideline 5 in Scotland in 1994. The ethos behind PPG16 and equivalents is that Britain is an old, long-settled nation where the remains of the past are abundant yet finite. They are constantly being eroded and destroyed by natural and human processes.

The most visible of these is new building in towns, and of roads, pipelines, railways in the countryside. Every act of destruction is irreversible and is a loss of knowledge of the past. The assumption in the PPG16 was that remains had to be undisturbed and that building plans would be altered to protect the remains (called mitigation). If they could not be protected, then they would be excavated or surveyed, an act of preservation by record. The costs of mitigation, excavation, or survey were paid by the developer. The system has since been modified in England with a new planning framework in force, but the principle has been kept, that developers pay for archaeology in advance of their work. The amount of money spent on this area of archaeology rose rapidly and many more archaeologists found employment in fieldwork. Archaeology has become a necessary part of the planning process, and become much more professional as a result. On the other hand, the new system has had some negative effects. Archaeological companies now compete for fieldwork and often drive down their costs, and workers' salaries. They may work in areas of the country they know little about and have few local contacts. Their reports are often hard to find, produced for developers and not published in conventional archaeological sources (and are known as "grey literature"). The amount of fieldwork done since 1990 has been enormous with a resulting avalanche of data that is very hard for archaeologists to take in and use on a national basis. The sheer number of finds produced by these excavations has led to a crisis in storage, where many museums no longer have the space to store what the field units produce. However, the gains far outweigh the problems. Archaeology is now accepted as a profession and archaeological evidence is revealing ever more about Britain's past. The latest National Planning Policy Framework for England now states the aim of archaeology no longer as simply trying to preserve the remains of the past but to advance society's knowledge and understanding of its past. We have a lot to thank a few famous actors for.

Access to Stonehenge

The stones at Stonehenge are a powerful site that stirs the imagination. They are unique, set amid the open downland, monumental in scale, and mysterious in that we don't know exactly how they were used or what meaning they carried for those who built them. Stonehenge was almost certainly a place of religious celebration, and we have been very ready in modern times to associate them with various aspects of belief. They symbolize a premodern purity, free of the ills that we see around us and somehow untainted by the material world which some would like to reject. Various modern groups therefore feel they have a connection with the site or take special meaning from being at the site. The site was associated with the ancient druids by antiquarians in the seventeenth century, but we know that it was abandoned more than a thousand years before the druids are recorded in history. That does not stop the modern Ancient Order of Druids (founded in 1781) from seeing Stonehenge as its own special temple. What we do know is that the midsummer and midwinter solstices were important to the builders and users of the site in prehistory. Alternative, and counter culture, groups have often sought to gather at Stonehenge at the solstices to celebrate their own identities and ways of life. The main focus for these groups became the Stonehenge Free Festival, held each year from 1972 until 1984. At its height, this attracted more than 60,000 people. Such large numbers were damaging the site and open access to the stones was restricted from 1977. Concerns about conserving the site from erosion led to a complete ban on access to the stones in 1985. Some groups wanting to attend the free festival and celebrate the summer solstice, however, still tried to gain access to the site. Around 450 people were intercepted by police and security staff in fields about eight miles away from the site. The result became known as the Battle of the Beanfield. A heavy-handed police and security response resulted in the police later being adjudged in court to have been guilty of assault, criminal damage, and wrongful arrest. The battle highlighted the role of archaeologists as guardians of the remains of the past. Their concern to safeguard the physical condition of remains can lead them to assume the arrogant position of expert elites, restricting the rights of others to engage with heritage on their own terms. Conservation of the past can conflict with the desire of people to make the monuments of the past an active part of their lives. If the remains of the past belong to the nation, then surely the people have a right to visit them. On the other hand, the remains may be fragile or in danger of being damaged, in which case the archaeologists surely have a responsibility to protect them. This is not an easy conundrum to solve.

The Battle over Seahenge

People's desire to respect and make use of a monument came into direct conflict with the authority of archaeologists in a quiet corner of the east of England in 1999. An unusual wooden circle was revealed by erosion on the coast at Holme-next-the-Sea in 1998–1999, soon popularly called Seahenge. Analysis revealed it was built in spring or early summer 2049 BC in a salt marsh. Fifty-five close-set posts, 10 feet high, were arranged in a circle 21 feet across. The circle had one small sealed entrance facing the midwinter sunset and facing back to midsummer sunrise at the opposite side of the circle. In the middle of the circle was an upside down tree stump set into the ground, invisible from the outside. The site was not a henge, but is so far unique. One theory is that it was a site where bodies would be placed to rot down before burial, but this is unlikely given the absence of human bone. Another is that the alignment enables a journey of the sun under the earth from sunset to sunrise as an emblem of rebirth. The site was completely excavated and removed, controversially so. Once it had been uncovered by the sea, the wooden structure would rot away quite quickly. English Heritage decided to fund the full excavation of the structure. This provoked protests at the site from various groups after the story made the national and international news. The description of the site by a journalist as the "Stonehenge of the sea" led to thousands of people coming to see it. Local residents were anxious about the loss of a potential tourist site, as well as feeling that outsiders funded by a national agency were depriving them of their local heritage. Other protests were by modern neo-pagans who objected to the removal on religious grounds. The site was in a National Nature Reserve, and the visitors and protesters at the site were disturbing colonies of wading birds, leading wildlife organizations to support the removal of the site by excavation. English Heritage did try to negotiate with the protesters but with no success. Both sides resorted to the courts, English Heritage to bar the protesters from the site and the protesters to gain access to it. Eventually the site was fully excavated at a high standard under difficult environmental conditions and completely removed. This allowed for a very detailed study of the timbers, yielding a great deal of information about how it was built, when, and by whom (a community that could send at least fifty-one separate people to work the timbers with their own bronze axes). The remains have now been conserved and are housed at the local museum in King's Lynn. Nearby, along the beach, was another structure of two concentric timber circles surrounding a hurdle-lined pit containing two oak logs, dating to 2400–2030 BC. This may be the eroded remains of a burial mound. Although this was also threatened with destruction by the sea, the timbers were left in place and exposed to the sea to be worn away. The whole dispute shows how a legitimate desire to record and conserve archaeological remains can come into conflict with others who see the sites not as objects of scientific study but as either part of their own local heritage and identity or as spiritual places. To most archaeologists, neo-pagan beliefs are not descended from Early Bronze Age religion and their claims of a connection with these sites is not "authentic." Archaeologists then feel that their authority is threatened and their specialist role diminished.

FAKES AND FORGERY

The Piltdown Forgery

The discovery of teeth, skull, and jawbone fragments with stone tools at Piltdown in East Sussex caused a sensation in 1912. Britain had at last yielded evidence of an early hominin, named *Eoanthropus dawsoni*, in honor of the original finder, Charles Dawson. The skull fragments look quite modern, while the jaw was more ape-like. Here was the classic missing link between humans and apes. As more hominin remains were found worldwide, none resembled Piltdown Man as he was popularly known. Piltdown remained both unique and odd, and diverted academic research away from a true consideration of human origins. Scientific tests in the 1940s suggested that the bones were relatively young. A proper study was then done on the remains, published in 1953, exposing them to be an elaborate fraud. The skull fragments were human, but the jaw had come from an orangutan, and the teeth modified to make them look more human. All had been stained to make them seem as though they had come from ancient gravel deposits. What made people accept the discovery was that they were investigated and announced by Arthur Smith Woodward, the respected Keeper of Geology at the Natural History Museum. Ever since the announcement by Darwin and Wallace of a mechanism for evolution and the acceptance of the antiquity of man, people had been searching for "the missing link" between humans and apes. The fact that this link was found in Britain was pleasing to national pride and also made people less inclined to look too closely at the finds. Woodward was almost certainly taken in by Dawson, and believed in the truth of the finds. However, he was not a specialist in primate fossils and so more easily deceived than others may have been. Dawson was an amateur archaeologist and geologist. No further finds were made at Piltdown after his death in 1916, and he is known to have found many other fossils and artifacts now proven to be fakes. The skull fragments may be from a Medieval burial disturbed by gravel digging and given to Dawson in 1908. The teeth in the jaw had been filed down to resemble those of a genuine 500,000-year-old early hominin found in 1907 at Heidelberg. Among the finds at Piltdown was a shaped piece of fossil bone from an elephant, evidence of early tool-making. In fact, the fossil bone had been shaped by a steel knife and was part of the hoax. The stone tools found at the site had also been artificially stained and were planted at the site. A few people had reservations about the finds from the beginning, even identifying correctly the human skull with ape jaw combination as false. A

German anthropologist even pointed to the jaw as being from an orangutan with the teeth filed down. Of course, as a foreigner, he was ignored and it took a further thirty years for British scientists to announce the forgery. The whole story shows just how prepared scholars are to believe the evidence they desperately want in order to support their scientific theories and view of the world. However, it was also science that ultimately was able to prove the forgery beyond any doubt.

ARCHAEOLOGY VERSUS COMMERCE

Maritime Treasure Hunting

Underwater archaeology presents unique technical challenges. Possibly the greatest of these is faced when excavating shipwrecks. There are also legal obstacles in that wrecks may be in international waters. International conventions on dealing with wrecks are not always enforced. A UNESCO Convention on the Protection of the Underwater Cultural Heritage was adopted in 2001, but this has yet to be ratified by the United Kingdom. However, in United Kingdom territorial waters, it is an offense to dive on, survey, excavate, or interfere with a designated underwater wreck. These wrecks are designated for their archaeological, historical, or artistic worth. Other wrecks may be designated as war graves under the protection of the Ministry of Defence. But, there is a long-standing practice of commercial salvage of wrecks, and people can claim to be working within the law of salvage while looting sites for their artifacts to sell on the antiquities market. Modern deep-sea diving technology allows any wreck to be visited, but is highly expensive. Those salvaging such sites need to sell finds on the open market to recover their costs, or to make a profit. The controversy about this has intensified in recent years because the British government has signed deals with commercial companies to salvage historic wrecks in international waters. The first agreement of this kind was made in 2002, between the UK government and an American company, Odyssey Marine Exploration, over the wreck of HMS *Sussex*. The *Sussex* was a Royal Navy warship launched in 1693. She had only a short life, foundering in a storm off the coast of Spain in 1694 with the loss of almost 500 men. Among her cargo was a shipment of gold coins, meant to be a subsidy to a British ally in the war then going on against the French. Odyssey works to a high professional standard, carrying out a great deal of research in both documentary sources and in surveying the sea floor. However, they are a profit-making organization. The deal with the government laid down that Odyssey would get 80 percent of the proceeds up to $45 million, 50 percent from $45 million to $500 million, and 40 percent above $500 million, with the British government getting the rest. Work began in 2005 but was halted in 2006 to allow negotiations with the government of Spain and the region of Andalucia to ensure the wreck would be investigated according to Spanish requirements. Spain eventually withheld its agreement and work on the wreck has not gone ahead. The agreement with Odyssey was criticized by many archaeologists and MPs on the grounds that the artifacts recovered would be sold on the open market, and that the depth of the wreck would make proper archaeological survey or excavation impossible (the *Sussex* lies at a depth of 2,600 feet). Also, salvage operations usually only target salable materials and may ignore artifacts that would be of interest to archaeologists. A further concern to some is that wrecks are often the graves of the sailors and passengers on board, and marine treasure hunting is seen as a form of grave robbing, although it is not clear how that differs from archaeological excavation of cemeteries on land. On the other hand, some archaeologists were willing to work with the project to try to ensure it was done to an acceptable standard of fieldwork. Odyssey's work would ensure that at least some information was recovered from a site that would otherwise not be investigated. Various major archaeological organizations in Britain have cooperated with Odyssey in the past. The key issue in the controversy is whether it is right that the remains of the past should be recovered for financial gain. The issues are still live. The British government signed another deal with Odyssey in 2011 to recover 200 tons of silver from the SS *Gairsoppa*, sunk during the Second World War 300 miles southwest of Ireland and lying at 15,000 feet on the bed of the Atlantic. The government would get 20 percent of the silver with 80 percent going to Odyssey. Around 110 tons of silver ingots have been recovered from the wreck at an estimated value of £250 million ($400 million).

Metal Detecting and Archaeology

Metal detecting grew greatly as a hobby in Britain in the 1960s. Archaeologists quickly became concerned about the extraction of artifacts from the ground without proper recording and excavation. Information about the finds was therefore lost and knowledge of them was not preserved for future study. Their extraction could also disturb or destroy archaeological structures or layers. There are many agents of the destruction of sites through removal of artifacts, such as plowing by farmers, coastal erosion, or the casual taking of items by walkers or tourists. However, it was metal detecting for the sale of artifacts or for private collections that was the most obvious target for attack by archaeologists.

The law on ownership of finds is different in different parts of the United Kingdom. In Scotland, all lost or abandoned property with no clear owner is legally the property of the Crown. Any objects found by archaeologists, metal detectorists, or others have to be declared. The Crown then decides whether to exercise its right to ownership or return the objects to the finder. The Crown's rights are exercised by the Scottish government through the Scottish Archaeological Finds Allocation Panel. In England and Wales, finds are the legal property of the landowner, apart from those legally defined as "treasure" (all gold and silver until 1996, and a wider range of finds after that date). Archaeologists or metal detectorists must have the landowner's permission to work on their land and can ask for the landowner's agreement that they may keep and own any finds. The exception is detecting on a Scheduled Ancient Monument, where consent must be given by English Heritage. By the 1970s the number of metal detectorists had grown significantly and the Council for British Archaeology led a high-profile campaign in 1979, the STOP campaign, aimed at banning metal detecting. A few archaeologists recognized that aggressive confrontation was not the right response. Tony Gregory, the county archaeologist for Norfolk, worked with local detectorists to record their finds (24,000 metal detecting finds in 1977). Gregory pointed out that most archaeologists were from the university-educated middle class, while most detectorists tended to be working class and lacked university education. Gregory felt that archaeology was being highly exclusive, elitist, and protective of its professional identity, seeing the detectorists as unworthy outsiders only interested in money rather than knowledge. He also pointed out that the academic training of archaeologists made it hard for them to communicate effectively with nonacademics.

A report by the Council for British Archaeology in 1995 found that there could be up to 30,000 detectorists, organized either independently or in one of 250 clubs. These were making an estimated 400,000 finds of artifacts dating from before 1600 each year, and that less than 10 percent of these were being recorded. Nearly 200 acts of detecting illegally on Scheduled Ancient Monuments had been recorded between 1988 and 1994, and 74 percent of field units had experienced illegal raids by detectorists on archaeological sites. On the other hand, where finds were reported there was a clear benefit for archaeology. In 1970 there were only 1,150 known coins of the pre-Roman tribe of the Iceni, centered in Norfolk. By 1994, this had grown to 13,000 known coins, largely found through metal detecting.

People digging sites to find treasure is not a new problem. Examples can be found in Medieval times of the Crown safeguarding its right to gold and silver finds by prosecuting local people who had been found looting ancient sites, such as at Wroxeter in 1292. One key modern episode that helped to change attitudes was the pillaging of the site of Wanborough Roman temple in Surrey. Coins had been found on the site in 1983 by responsible detectorists who reported their finds to the local museum. Unfortunately, the location of the site was made public and hoards of detectorists then came to loot the site. Around forty looters took away a possible total of £2 million of Roman coins, causing great damage to the archaeological structure and layers of the site. Only five were eventually arrested, in 1986, and three convicted, given fines of only £250, £400, and £1,000 each. The grounds for prosecution were theft from the Crown, that is a breach of the then-law of Treasure Trove. The coins would be trove only if they were deposited with the intention to recover them. On archaeological grounds, this was unlikely as they were probably votive offerings at a temple. A reasonable archaeological opinion on the site would therefore acquit the looters of wrongdoing! Looting of Wanborough has continued ever since, although this is now condemned by the local metal detecting clubs. Another example of serious looting is at the Roman site of Icklingham in Suffolk. In the 1980s, a hoard of Romano-British bronze artifacts was illegally taken from the site, which has continued to be raided since. Up to fifty people have been prosecuted over the last thirty years, with fines varying from £38 to £500. In one raid in 2007 a single looter dug more than 200 holes in the site.

Eventually, lobbying by archaeologists, with partial agreement from detectorists, persuaded Parliament to pass the Treasure Act in 1996. This made it a criminal offense not to report the finding of treasure, which was redefined to include any object of at least 10 percent silver or gold and over 300 years old, with any associated nonprecious objects and all coin hoards of whatever metal also over 300 years old. The Act has since been extended to cover all prehistoric metal objects. To cope with the expected flood of reporting, the government funded the Portable Antiquities Scheme in 1997. This was extended nationwide to cover the whole of England and Wales in 2003, and was based largely on the example set by Tony Gregory in the 1970s in Norfolk. The Scheme was accepted by most metal detectorists, especially the influential National Council for Metal Detecting (NCMD), who had their own code of conduct to make sure detectorists acted responsibly. A voluntary Code of Practice of Responsible Metal Detecting was agreed in 2006 between archaeologists and detectorists. However, relations between the two sides are still marred by suspicion and by the loud voices of a few highly antagonistic members of both sides. A report into illegal detecting, called nighthawking, in 2009 alienated many detectorists who felt that once again archaeologists were seeking to attack and ban their activities. This was not the intention. The report focused on illegal activity at 240 archaeological sites (6 percent of archaeological excavations) between 1995 and 2008.

Archaeologists have to accept that metal detecting has many benefits. It provides information from areas not being researched by archaeologists, recovers information from the plow-zone which would otherwise be destroyed, yields information about new types of finds, and vastly increases our knowledge about certain types of artifact and periods of the past. Moreover, it empowers people to engage with the past directly for themselves, which is one reason why some archaeologists oppose it. Detecting weakens professional control of archaeology. Its problems are that it is random in only producing information where there are active detectorists, and is very much focused on finding artifacts rather than sites or structures. The real problem is no longer how to control metal detecting but how to stop the illegal looting of sites, an activity condemned by both archaeologists and metal detectorists.

The Antiquities Trade

Of course, many early archaeologists and antiquarians can also be accused of looting. Certainly the Greeks see the Earl of Elgin as having looted the Parthenon frieze and the work of others in the eighteenth and nineteenth centuries is equally suspect. Dealing in archaeological remains and cultural heritage is still big business, with easy communications and travel across the globe leading to an intense worldwide market for antiquities. Looting today is more likely to be done by local people in parts of the world where government control is weak or where war creates conditions in which theft and destruction can flourish. Ancient sites are often in rural areas of the Third World where local people live in poverty. Selling antiquities taken from the ground will earn much-needed income for them and their families, far more than they could earn through farming or other activity. However, most of the income from the trade goes to the middle men (including professional thieves) and auction houses. It is the insatiable greed of the wealthy art collectors which makes the trade possible, not the action of the local looters. London is a major center for the international trade in cultural artifacts with its concentration of auction houses and art dealers, such as Christie's and Bonhams (Sotheby's began as a British auction house until its transfer to the United States in 1983). Antiquities sold through auction houses are often (and may be mostly) illegally acquired. Archaeological awareness of the illegal trade in antiquities was greatly raised by the Illicit Antiquities Research Centre from 1996 to 2007. This was part of the McDonald Institute for Archaeological Research at Cambridge University, set up under Lord Renfrew to monitor and report upon the damage caused to cultural heritage by the international trade in antiquities. Its work has been continued by the Trafficking Culture research program at Glasgow University in the Scottish Centre for Crime and Justice Research.

The United Kingdom government has a mixed record on dealing with the antiquities trade. It has not signed the 1954 UNESCO Convention for the Protection of Cultural Property in the Event of Armed Conflict (also known as the Hague convention). Nor has it signed up to the Convention on Stolen or Illegally Exported Cultural Objects of 1995 issued by the International Institute for the Unification of Private Law (UNIDROIT), aimed at restoring stolen antiquities to their original owners and preventing people from buying illegally obtained antiquities. On the other hand, the efforts of archaeologists finally paid off in 2002 when the United Kingdom government at last signed the 1970 UNESCO Convention on the Means of Prohibiting and Preventing the Illicit Import, Export and Transfer of Ownership of Cultural Property, designed to prevent excavation and export of objects of cultural heritage without the permission of the governments in which they are found. Also, in 2003, Parliament passed the Dealing in Cultural Objects Act, which made it a criminal offense to deal in any cultural object that has been illegally excavated or removed.

The Middle East as the cradle of civilizations is an obvious target for looters and the political and military instability in the region in recent years has given them plenty of scope for their activities. Stealing antiquities in other countries is a problem for Britain since the United Kingdom has widespread international links and is actively involved in military action in various parts of the world. On the other hand, when University College London bought a large collection of rare Mesopotamian pottery from a Norwegian antiquities collector, who himself had bought them on the open market believing them to be legitimate finds, it did act under United Nations sanctions that made it illegal to deal in stolen artifacts from Iraq. An inquiry showed that the bowls had most likely been looted from Iraq and the University was forced to return them, but not to an Iraqi museum but to the original collector who was the legal owner of them. Widespread looting also took place after the United Nations sanctioned invasion of Afghanistan. In a two-year period, the government recovered more than three tons of looted antiquities smuggled into the United Kingdom.

One famous example of the nature of the trade is the Sevso treasure. A hoard of six late Roman silver items was bought by Sotheby's in London in 1981 from a dealer in Vienna. Five more items from the hoard were then also bought with financial investment from the Marquis of Northampton. The total amount spent was £2,788,000. In 1984, a further four items were bought for an additional £5,300,000. The items had paperwork that showed them to be legal exports from Lebanon, yet these were proved to be forged export licenses. New licenses were obtained by lawyers (but also forged) and the items were put on sale at Sotheby's in New York. Court action was then taken by Lebanon, Yugoslavia, and Hungary who each claimed the items had been illegally dug up in their own countries. A court ruled in 1993 that none of these claims were valid and the items could not be sold as they had no legal provenance but that they legally belonged to the Marquis of Northampton. The Marquis was innocent of any wrongdoing, having given money for their acquisition in good faith, believing them to be legally obtained artifacts. Scientific evidence showed that the items had most likely originated in Hungary.

Another case to make the headlines was the finding in 2010, at Crosby Garrett in Cumbria, by a metal detectorist of an exceptional Roman brass ceremonial cavalry helmet and visor. This would have been used in military equestrian pageants and sporting events. Although broken into pieces, it was remarkably complete. It was found on its own with no other finds, was not gold or silver, and was not prehistoric. This meant that it fell outside the scope of the Treasure Act. The landowner and finder promptly put the helmet up for sale through the Christie's auction house in London. Various archaeologists pleaded or negotiated with the landowner and finder to agree a private sale to a museum, but with no success. The National Council of Metal Detectorists also agreed that this exceptional artifact should be held for public benefit in a museum. The Tullie House Museum and Art Gallery in Carlisle raised £1.7 million to try to buy the helmet at the public auction. Unfortunately, it was outbid by an anonymous, private collector who paid £2.3 million for it. The helmet was restored by Christie's. They would not allow it to be analyzed and conserved archaeologically, although Christie's did allow the helmet and the conservation records to be seen by archaeologists. The owner has loaned the helmet for exhibition at the Royal Academy of Arts and to Tullie House, but it mostly resides as an object of private contemplation hidden away from public view.

It is not only excavated artifacts and ancient works of art that are being stolen. Many houses have historic fittings or architectural features such as fire surrounds or staircase banisters that are now the object of outright theft. These objects can be sold in the architectural salvage markets or be sold as antiques ending up anywhere in the world. These may not seem to be the concern of archaeology, but archaeologists are increasingly studying historic buildings and these items are artifacts of human manufacture every bit as capable of telling us about the past as Roman or prehistoric objects. One report in the *Daily Telegraph* newspaper (8 January 2005) estimated the scale of the thefts in the United Kingdom at £300 million a year.

8

CURRENT AND
RECENT RESEARCH

Part of the excitement of archaeology is that new discoveries are always being made, even in a heavily investigated country with a long tradition of field work like Britain. In this chapter, we see how the earliest settlement of Britain is being pushed back into earlier times, and how its very shape and existence as an island have been subject to global forces of climate change. New research is also throwing new light on sites we already think we know a lot about. New work at Stonehenge is revolutionizing our views of a very familiar monument, while new finds farther north in Orkney are revealing equally important and contemporary ritual sites of a very different kind. The importance of waterlogged sites is reflected in work in the east of England (Must Farm) and intensive excavation is revealing ever more about life in Roman Britain (Silchester and *Vindolanda*). The excavation of some sites, such as Bamburgh, is revealing as much about previous excavations as it is about the site's own history. Recent spectacular finds have included both incredibly wealthy burials (Prittlewell) and the poor burials of the formerly very powerful (King Richard III).

As well as recovering the island story of Britain's past, archaeological practice has evolved in recent years in important ways that have made it ever more socially accessible and important. Archaeology has been a constant presence of British television and this has helped to feed a growing interest in working with local communities, also supported by the growing presence of archaeology online. An important new role for the subject is as a form of therapy, with one important new initiative giving archaeological fieldwork a vital role to play in rehabilitating wounded soldiers. Archaeology therefore has a wider purpose than simply helping us to find out about the past. Britain's current population may also have much it could learn from the past of its previous inhabitants as revealed by archaeologists and this chapter will end with a look at what some of those lessons might be.

PREHISTORIC BRITAIN

Early Hominins Reach the Far Northwest of Europe

For much of its past, Britain has been the far northwest of the European mainland, connected to the rest of Europe across the North Sea and English Channel. Early hominins moved into Britain from the south after their migrations out of Africa. Discoveries at various sites in the last few years have gradually pushed the date of earliest hominin presence in Britain farther and farther back in time. The current earliest presence is the subject of a major joint research project by the British Museum, the Natural History Museum, and Queen Mary University of London looking at the coast of Norfolk in the east of Britain. The focus of the research is at the site of Happisburgh (pronounced "Hazeborough"), first exposed by coastal erosion. Some seventy-eight flint artifacts (cores and simple flakes) were excavated from site 3 in 2001–2005. These are the oldest archaeological finds from Britain. They are also evidence of the most northerly presence in the world of hominins of such an early date. The sediments they were found in were left by a marshy river estuary, flowing through a pine and spruce woodland with some open grassland. The climate was beginning to cool and was a little colder than Britain is today. Animals roaming the land included mammoth, horse, elk, red deer, and hyena. Which species of hominin made the core and flakes is unknown, but it may have been *Homo antecessor*. The flints were left behind during one of two interglacial epochs, either 866,000 to 814,000 or 970,000 to 936,000 years ago.

The flint artifacts would in themselves be a cause for celebration. However, the story took an even more dramatic turn in 2013. Continuing erosion along the beach uncovered depressions in the sediments underneath the beach sand. These turned out to be the oldest hominin footprints to have been found outside Africa. There were around 150 prints left behind by a small family group of at least five individuals, including children and adults. They left their prints in the mudflats of a tidal estuary, now under a sandy beach. Sadly, the same erosion that uncovered the footprints has now washed them away, but not before they were recorded in detail by the archaeologists. Twelve of the prints were sharp enough to reveal the height of one of the adults at 5 feet 8 inches, and weighing approximately 8 stones (112 lbs.). Analysis of the mud suggests the prints are of a similar age to the flint artifacts found nearby.

Climate Change Is Not New

That Britain had once been connected across the North Sea to Germany and Denmark by a low-lying dry plain was first suggested in 1913 by the geologist Clement Reid. The shallowest point of the North Sea had for generations been known as the Dogger Bank and this long-vanished plain was given the name of Doggerland by Bryony Coles in 1998, who made the first modern study of the lost land. That Doggerland had been dry land and a place of prehistoric settlement was made evident by the find of a

Map of Doggerland during the Early Mesolithic, courtesy of Donald Henson

Mesolithic antler harpoon in 1931 dredged up during fishing off the coast of Britain. Coles' research showed that sea levels had risen by 400 feet since the end of greatest extent of the last Ice Age. The rocks under the North Sea are a major source of oil and gas. Seismic data are used to map the oil and gas reservoirs, and the idea of using them to map the drowned landscape of Doggerland was floated in 2001. Research since then has been led by the archaeologists at the University of Birmingham, especially through the North Sea Palaeolandscapes Project from 2005 to 2008. They have had access to 9,000 square miles of seismic records covering the western part of Doggerland and have been able to use advanced three-dimensional computer graphics to interpret the data. What has been revealed is a landscape of rivers, lakes, and coastlines available to the post-glacial settlers of northern Europe. In this land were ten major river estuaries and at least one salt marsh drained into a large lake (later an arm of the sea). There were twenty-four other lakes and a total of 1,000 miles of rivers and streams along with various low hills and valleys. There is still much to do and a wider area of the North Sea needs to be explored in the same detail. Finding evidence for human settlement from what is now the bed of the North Sea will be difficult, but we now have a good idea of the land connecting Britain with the rest of Europe until that connection was lost around 8,500 to 8,000 years ago. Further investigation of Doggerland will also help us to understand processes involved in inundation of the land by the sea, so important in a world of global warming. Birmingham University researchers have continued their work in other offshore areas of Britain such as the Bristol Channel and the Irish Sea.

Landscapes of the Living and the Dead

Stonehenge is probably the most iconic site in British archaeology. It is both unique and has been the focus of study since the seventeenth century. The site itself is of great interest, but it belongs within a fascinating landscape of monuments of the Late Neolithic and Early Bronze Age and it can only be understood in relation to these other sites. This relationship was studied by a major collaboration between the universities of Sheffield, Manchester, Bournemouth, Bristol, and University College London from 2003 to 2009, the Stonehenge Riverside Project; and is still the focus of ongoing research.

The Stonehenge we see now is merely the end product of a long history of building and remodeling. Current research has modified the traditional history of the site through careful excavation and reinterpretation of earlier excavation records. It is still best to think of Stonehenge as having gone through five phases of building and rebuilding. Stonehenge I was begun in 3000–2920 BC, and consisted of fifty-six pits in a circle, originally holding bluestone pillars from the Preseli Hills in southwest Wales, inside an embanked ditch enclosing a circle 330 feet across. Cremation burials were placed in the pits and elsewhere inside the circle in this and later phases. Sixty-three cremations are now known at Stonehenge, making it the largest cremation cemetery of its period. Stonehenge II was a modification of the site in 2620–2480 BC, when massive trilithons (two upright stones, up to 24 feet tall, joined by a lintel across the top) were arranged in a horseshoe inside a circle 100 feet across of sandstone columns joined together with lintels. The bluestones were moved to form two arcs between the outer circle and the horseshoe. The trilithon horseshoe was aligned with its open side facing midsummer sunrise and its closed side facing midwinter sunset. An embanked avenue was built as part of Stonehenge III in 2480–2280 BC, leading from the site to the River Avon, and bluestones were rearranged again to form a circle inside the trilithon horseshoe. In 2280–2020 BC (Stonehenge IV), the bluestones outside the horseshoe were arranged in a circle and the innermost bluestone circle was changed into an oval. The last phase, Stonehenge V, saw the digging of two outer circles of pits (the Y and Z holes) between 1680 and 1520 BC. These do not seem to have been finished and the site was then abandoned.

Various other important sites lie within the 10 square miles of the World Heritage Site and wider landscape of Stonehenge. The most important of these is Durrington Walls, some two miles away. This was originally thought to be a major henge monument. It is surrounded by a circular bank (98 feet wide) and internal ditch (18 feet deep by 59 feet wide), with two surviving entrances at the northwest and southeast. Inside it, two wooden circles were found during excavations in the 1960s. The southern circle was built around 2600 BC and has four concentric rings of wooden posts oriented towards midwinter sunrise (the mirror image of Stonehenge's orientation towards midwinter sunset). However, the Stonehenge Riverside project has revealed its true nature as a settlement, abandoned around 2450 BC although the site itself continued in use until 2300 BC. Seven houses (16 feet square) were excavated in an area with around 80,000 cow, sheep, and especially pig bones. These are the waste from feasting, most likely during summer and at midwinter. Isotope analysis of the cattle bones shows that while most were coming from the local area, a few were possibly from as far away as northern Britain. Intriguingly, one of the houses was of the same size, shape, and internal layout as the contemporary houses at Skara Brae in Orkney. A short avenue heads from the southern circle towards midsummer sunset and leads to the River Avon. Farther along the Avon the river can be left by the avenue which leads towards Stonehenge. Durrington Walls and Stonehenge seem to be two halves of a complex in the Late Neolithic which somehow symbolizes, enacts, or commemorates a religious journey from life to death, and in which Durrington Walls was the site of major midwinter feasting linked with ceremonies at Stonehenge.

The links between Stonehenge–Durrington Walls and the rest of Britain, such as southwest Wales or the far north of Britain, must surely indicate some kind of political or social relationships that reflect the power of the communities living in Wessex at this time. Some archaeologists believe that prehistoric people used Stonehenge as a site of healing where the religious power of the stones or their provision of access to the gods or spirit world would enable healing of the sick, much as Christian saints and relics have the same allure to many today. Others disagree as the evidence for this is very slim.

Religious activity in the area of Stonehenge goes back even further than Stonehenge itself. A cursus nearly 2 miles long and over 300 feet wide was built between 3630 and 3375 BC. This has a long barrow at the eastern end and is aligned so that the sunrise at the spring and autumn equinoxes appears to rise from the barrow. Contemporary with Stonehenge III and later are around 260 Early Bronze Age round barrows within a two mile radius, often grouped in "cemeteries," such as:

- King Barrow Ridge, fourteen round barrows on a ridge to the east of Stonehenge;
- Normanton Down, two small long barrows and an enclosure, with more than fifty round barrows overlooking Stonehenge from the south, including the Bush Barrow burial;
- Winterbourne Stoke, a 275-foot-long barrow and thirty-two Early Bronze Age round barrows.

Some of the burials in these barrows were spectacularly rich. The most famous is the Bush Barrow burial half a mile south of Stonehenge and excavated in 1808. An adult male was buried there with a decorated lozenge-shaped sheet of gold a little over seven inches long on his chest, presumably attached to his clothing. Other finds were a smaller golden lozenge, over an inch long, a golden belt hook, a polished stone mace-head with bone rings and mounts from some kind of haft, and three bronze daggers. The wooden hilt of the smallest dagger had been inlaid with thousands of tiny gold studs. By his shoulders was a bronze axe-head wrapped in cloth. More recent finds have been even more spectacular.

The Amesbury Archer burial was excavated in 2002, just three miles from Stonehenge, and proved to be exceptional even by Early Bronze Age standards. The burial was of an adult man aged around forty. He was not that healthy, having a mouth abscess and knee injury, but he was buried with over 100 individual grave goods, the largest number of such goods from the period in Britain. These goods included five beakers, three copper knives (imports from France or Spain), sixteen flint arrowheads, flint and metal working tools, stone wristguards, boar tusks, a shale belt ring, and golden hair ornaments. The burial was dated to between 2400 and 2200 BC. The biggest surprise about the man was his origin. Chemical analysis of his teeth showed that he had grown up in central Europe north of the Alps. A nearby body of a younger man in his twenties shared the same abnormal fusing of bones in the foot and is assumed to be a near relative.

A year later, in 2003, the Boscombe Bowmen burial (Wiltshire), also about three miles from Stonehenge, was excavated. Inside the grave was the body of a man with three young children. The disturbed bones of a teenager and two other adults were arranged above and below the bodies. Grave goods were eight beakers of an early continental style, a boar tusk, five flint arrowheads, other flint tools, and a bone toggle. The bones in the skulls of the adults and the teenager all share similar features and they were probably all closely related to each other. Analysis of the teeth of the adult men shows that they grew up somewhere in the west of Britain, most likely either in Wales or the Lake District. The burials are probably of a similar date to the Amesbury Archer, around 2300 BC. Given that some of the stones at Stonehenge came from southwest Wales, could this burial show further contact between people living in these two areas?

Other sites in the area include:

- Woodhenge, six concentric rings of wooden posts, surrounded by a bank and ditch, aligned on midsummer sunrise and midwinter sunset;
- a newly found bluestone henge at the end of the Stonehenge avenue where it meets the River Avon;
- Robin Hood's Ball, a causewayed enclosure two-and-a-half miles from Stonehenge;
- Vespasian's Camp, an Iron Age hill fort, two miles to the southeast of Stonehenge, enclosing 37 acres, with a large Mesolithic settlement underneath the hill fort;
- a Mesolithic post setting that may show religious use of the area going back many thousands of years before Stonehenge.

Religion and Power in the Far North

Ness of Brodgar is a six-acre site between the Stones of Stenness and the Ring of Brodgar in Orkney. Excavations since 2003 by the Orkney Research Centre for Archaeology in the University of the Highlands and Islands have revealed a type of site that was unique in the Neolithic of Britain. A complex of stone buildings on a large scale was built on a narrow strip of land cut off by a 300-yard-long wall up to 20 feet wide. An early phase of many buildings, each perhaps belonging to a different community in the island, was begun around 3200 BC. This was replaced around 2600 BC by one massive building 82 feet long by 65 feet wide, with 15-foot-thick walls. Inside this building was a chamber less than 20 feet wide, very similar to the burial chamber at nearby Maes Howe. Moreover, the building was aligned to face Maes Howe. The Ness was deliberately closed down and partly demolished around 2300 BC with a massive feast using 500 cattle. A wide range of different kinds of Grooved Ware pottery was found, suggesting that people came to the site from a range of different communities. The walls of the buildings were decorated with incised or painted lozenge and chevron patterns. The finding of red, orange, and yellow paints is very rare at sites of this period. Other rare finds include a baked clay object that may be a figurine and stone roofing tiles. The excavation of the site is still ongoing, and more is still to be discovered. Orkney has long been special for its Late Neolithic archaeological remains, and now has a religious or political meeting place of a kind that has been found nowhere else. People entering the Ness would have to pass through either the Ring of Brodgar or the Stones of Stenness, and these previously separate sites (along with Maes Howe) can now be seen as part of an impressive landscape created as part of the centralization of power and identity in Late Neolithic Orkney.

Bronze Age Life Revealed

Research by Cambridge University since 1999 on the eastern side of the Flag Fen basin in the southeast of Britain at Bradley Fen and Must Farm has uncovered precious evidence of a Bronze Age landscape (some two miles away from the previously excavated site at Flag Fen). This landscape lies under twenty feet of later fenland sediments, only revealed because of the modern quarrying of clay for brick making. Large open-area excavation has uncovered remains from the Neolithic onward, preserving features that elsewhere have eroded away. Burial mounds, houses, fences, and other evidences of settlement such as fish weirs and eel traps were situated on dry land near a low-lying river. The Late Neolithic and Early Bronze Age landscape even preserved the hoof-prints of animals grazing by the river. By 1300 BC the fens were beginning to drown in an increasingly wet climate. It was now that large numbers of bronze artifacts began to be deposited in the fenland waters. The most recent research has concentrated at Must Farm where a wooden bridge/trackway was built over a small stream around 1240 BC, left to collapse, and replaced by an oval enclosure and wooden building that burnt down around 850 BC. The fire preserved a remarkably intact assemblage of the kind that does not normally survive, including carbonized textiles (such as clothing), green or blue glass beads, stone querns and flint tools, spindle whorls, metal sickles, gouges, spears, razors, rings, punches, awls and pots still containing food, fish, and grain. This is not all. Among the Late Bronze Age finds are nine logboats dating from 1300 to 700 BC, some of which were deliberately scuttled in the river. Bronze Age life is revealed here as nowhere else in Britain.

HISTORIC BRITAIN

Life and Death of a Roman Town

A long-term research project by Reading University has been uncovering the development of the Roman town of Silchester (Latin *Calleva Atrebatum*) since 1974. This has built upon a twenty-year excavation by the Society of Antiquaries from 1890 to 1909 and has helped to make Silchester one of the best understood Roman sites in Britain. The town is a typical Roman *civitas* (tribal) capital (of the Atrebates). It was mapped out in the first century, with a central forum, baths, temples, and amphitheater. The Roman town replaced a late Iron Age town of 72 acres that had been established in the first century BC. The early levels of the Roman town have evidence of native-style round houses alongside rectangular Roman-style buildings and must have been built with native Britons as owners. The late Iron Age inhabitants seemingly traded with the Roman Empire and excavations have yielded evidence of Roman-style food and artifacts well before the Roman conquest of Britain. After the conquest, the population included silversmiths, money lenders, tanners, dyers, and farmers. There was also a *mansio*, a hotel for Imperial officials, and an Imperial brickworks was nearby. Even a small tribal capital was connected with the rest of an Empire which stretched all the way to Egypt and the Egyptian god Serapis was worshiped in the town. The later levels have a building with an outside font which may be one of the earliest churches to be found in Britain. The town was fortified with a stone wall in the third century and seems to have continued into the fifth or sixth century when dykes were erected to defend the area against Anglo-Saxon attack. What makes Silchester special and of great value to archaeologists is that it was eventually abandoned and never built on thereafter. The ruins therefore survive to be excavated without having been damaged or erased by later construction.

Lives and Letters on the Edge of Empire

Vindolanda lies to the south of Hadrian's Wall and began in 85 when a series of wooden forts was built. The last of these was rebuilt in stone at the same time as the building of the Wall. This seems to have been later decommissioned and native round houses were built on the site until a new stone fort was built in 212. There is a civilian settlement or vicus outside the fort, with evidence of temples and industrial activity. Excavations began there in the 1930s, led by Eric Birley, and have been carried on ever since by his son Robin and grandson Andrew. As well as the usual finds from Roman sites, such as 500 tons of pottery, the presence of waterlogged ground has revealed rare organic evidence of life in Roman times, such as clothing, hair, and the famous Vindolanda tablets. These are the oldest surviving written documents from Britain, in the form of thin slivers of wood (birch, alder, or oak) folded in half and used for writing letters in black ink with pens by the army garrison. The first tablets were found in 1973 and there are now well over 750 fragile examples, and more are still being found and translated. They provide what archaeology seldom yields, which are the voices of people from the past. Their state of preservation means that infrared photography has been used to reveal the contents, which are in a handwritten style that is quite hard to decipher. Most of the tablets date from between 92 and 102. The garrison of the fort was the 9th Batavian cohort and many of the tablets were from the archive of its commander Flavius Cerialis or his wife Sulpicia Lepidina. They give precious information about military supplies, clothing, social life, and language. Among the most famous of the letters is one from Claudia Severa to Sulpicia inviting her to visit her for her birthday celebrations, the earliest known Latin writing by a woman. Another letter was a plea from a foreign civilian possibly to the provincial governor for redress for having been wrongly flogged by one of the soldiers. The cold weather on the frontier is surely reflected in the letter recording the sending of sandals with socks and underpants to one of the soldiers. One letter refers to obtaining supplies of leather from Catterick, and we know from archaeological excavation that Catterick did have a tannery at this period. Vindolanda is a special site, and the letters make it exceptional.

Searching for the Origins of England

At Bamburgh there is a high rock outcrop on the coast, currently occupied by a nine-acre castle. This was originally a native British stronghold taken over in the sixth century by incoming Anglian kings and becoming a residence of the Kings of Northumbria. The Medieval castle was built after 1086, and was in royal hands from 1095 to 1610. It was badly damaged during the Wars of the Roses, in 1464, and has been heavily restored since the eighteenth century and is still a private residence. A long-term program of excavation by the Bamburgh Research Project has been investigating the early Medieval remains since 1996. This has followed earlier excavations (never published) by Brian Hope-Taylor in 1959–1962 and 1970–1974. Hope-Taylor's site office had remained shut and untouched since he was last at the site in 1974. It was reopened in 2001 and its contents have helped to interpret Hope-Taylor's findings. His own trenches have also been reexcavated to help interpret his records: an example of the archaeology of archaeology! The excavations have found Romano-British and earlier occupation as far back as the Neolithic, a native British and Anglo-Saxon cemetery, a seventh-century wooden hall (possibly a gatehouse and later rebuilt in stone), and areas of early ninth century metalworking and mixing of mortar. The cemetery began as a burial place for British Christians, then for the pagan Anglians, and finally for their newly Christianized descendants. Analysis of the bones suggests that they were high status aristocrats from various locations within the kingdom. One burial may even have been of an Irish Scot, who will have attached himself to King Oswald during Oswald's exile among the Scots in the seventh century. The high status of the site is confirmed by the finding of gold objects and very high quality pattern welded swords.

All that Glitters Is Often Gold

The migration period between the end of Roman Britain and the richly documented Medieval period is still producing archaeological surprises. Two recent finds have caught the public imagination through the quality of craftsmanship they reveal and the dim light they shed on Britain's early history.

The Staffordshire hoard was discovered by a metal detectorist, Terry Herbert, in 2009 near Lichfield in Staffordshire. He promptly reported the find to the Portable Antiquities Scheme and archaeologists were able to recover the largest hoard of Anglo-Saxon gold and silver ever found. This amounted to more than fourteen pounds of gold and silver, nearly 4,000 items. Most were weapon and armor fittings and many were decorated and inlaid with garnets to a very high standard of craftsmanship. A further eighty-one items were found in 2012. Among the items are various Christian crosses and one Christian inscription. The decorative fittings had been stripped from their original weapons, helmets, and shields. It is not yet known why they were buried, nor their exact date. Nothing else has been found near the hoard and it does not seem to have been buried in or near any kind of building or structure. The hoard is a mix of objects from the 100 years before its deposition, most likely very early in the eighth century. It looks like booty gathered in war, and its location is in the heart of the Anglian Kingdom of Mercia, a powerful and aggressive state at this period. As treasure the hoard was valued at £3,280,000, and £900,000 of this was found by donations from the public to ensure the hoard could be bought by the Birmingham and Stoke-on-Trent museums. The items are still being studied and it will be years before the full story of the hoard can be told. All credit should go to Terry Herbert for reporting his find. In previous decades, this hoard may have simply been sold and lost to archaeology.

Road widening at Prittlewell in Southend in Essex in 2003 was due to affect a known Anglo-Saxon cemetery, discovered in the early twentieth century. Archaeologists working in advance of the road building uncovered one of the most spectacular burials found in Britain. It turned out to be an untouched burial chamber (16 feet square and 5 feet deep), wood lined with artifacts still hanging from nails in the wall or arranged on its floor. The roof of the chamber had long since fallen in and allowed soil to fill the space. Meticulous and delicate excavation recovered items that in previous decades would have been lost, such as finely woven gold thread. For the excavators from Museum of London Archaeology, it would be the find of their lives. The burial turned out to be of an extremely wealthy and powerful person from the early seventh century. The sandy soils have eroded away the bones of the burial, but it is assumed from the weapons in the grave that this is the burial of a man. Some of the artifacts buried with him are unique, such as an iron-framed folding stool, gold foil crosses, and a Byzantine flagon. Others are of kinds that rarely survive, for example, wooden buckets held together with iron bands, wooden cups with decorated gold leaf ornamentation, a well-preserved lyre, gaming pieces and dice, exquisite glass jars, and an iron standard. The golden crosses and the hollow golden belt buckle which may have held a Christian relic reveal the man's religion. Some of the artifacts are clearly imports from Italy or the eastern Mediterranean, possibly gifts brought to Britain by the early Christian mission from Rome. Years of post-excavation analysis of the more than 100 artifacts will reveal more about this important burial. The wealth of the burial suggests he may have been a King of the East Saxons. He would then have to be either King Saeberht who died in 616 or King Sigeberht who died in 653 as the other Kings of East Saxons in this period remained pagans.

Rethinking Richard

King Richard III is one of the most well-known kings of England, partly because of his immortalization by Shakespeare. He was the last king of the royal House of York, who deposed his nephew to take the throne. He in turn was defeated and killed at the Battle of Bosworth in Leicestershire, on 22 August 1485, by Henry Tudor, Earl of Richmond (henceforth King Henry VII). The Wars of the Roses (raging on and off since 1455) had at last been settled, and the Tudor dynasty of King Henry VII began to reign. A new, post-Medieval period of English was about to begin. This key battle has been commemorated both in Shakespeare and since 1974 at a visitor center on the battlefield. At least everyone thought it was the battlefield, until a new theory was put forward by Peter Foss in 1985 that the battle had actually been fought somewhere else. Foss' work was a landmark in the application of landscape archaeology to battlefields. An archaeological and historical survey by the Battlefields Trust from 2005 to 2010 found evidence for where the battlefield actually was, close to where Foss had suggested, nearly two miles away from the visitor center. The evidence included musket and cannon shot, the largest amount ever found on a Medieval battlefield.

A suggestion by a member of the Richard III Society, Philippa Langley, led to an excavation in 2012 in the car park in the middle of the town of Leicester. Philippa suggested that this could be a site of the burial of Richard III. It was known that, after the Battle of Bosworth, he was taken to Leicester and buried in the choir of the church of a friary in the city. The excavation by the University of Leicester soon found the remains of the friary and a grave in what had been the choir. The grave was shallow, and poorly dug. The body had been placed in it without a coffin or shroud and seemingly had its hands tied together. The grave was also too short and the head of the body was propped up against the end. The bones were of a man of slender build, 5 feet 8 inches high, with evidence of weapon injuries to the skull and body. Chemical analysis of the bones showed he had a diet rich in meat and fish, and was therefore of the upper strata of society. Radiocarbon dates placed his death between 1455 and 1540. Moreover, he had a curved spine. An analysis of his DNA showed that it matched that of two living female relatives of Richard III. There could be no doubt that this was the body of the King. Public interest in the burial was immense. The archaeologists had decided that should he be found then he would be reburied in Leicester cathedral, the nearest major burial place to where he was found. However, others disagree with this and would like Richard to be buried in York where he was based as his king's lieutenant before he became king, and close to where he grew up at Middleham in Yorkshire. The debate between the two sides has even been taken to the High Court. The passions of the Wars of the Roses seem to be still alive and well in the twenty-first century!

Current archaeological work in Britain is not only concerned with field investigation of the past. There is an increasing acceptance that archaeology has a public service role. Archaeologists depend on public support for their funding, and they have not only interesting stories but also important and relevant information from the past that can help us live our lives in the present. There are many projects aiming to engage more people with archaeology through fieldwork. Only a few are highlighted below.

PRACTICING ARCHAEOLOGY

Televising Archaeology

Archaeology has long been a staple of television schedules in Britain. The earliest television archaeology was the quiz show *Animal, Vegetable, Mineral?* which ran from 1952 to 1960, starring the leading archaeologist Glyn Daniel and often featuring Sir Mortimer Wheeler (see chapter 6). The success of this series led to a documentary strand, *Buried Treasure*, since when archaeology has hardly ever been off Britain's TV screens. The long-running documentary series *Chronicle* (1966 to 1991) was followed by the even longer-running live excavation series *Time Team* (1994–2015). *Time Team* has especially appealed to a young audience of children and teenagers. An unpublished survey by the author of the terrestrial television channels broadcasting in Britain in 2003 showed that there were 62 archaeology series with 377 broadcast episodes and one-off programs broadcast over 121 hours during the year. The popularity of archaeology does rise and fall but public interest in archaeology programs is still steady. Topics like ancient Egypt and Rome are always popular, and recent programs have covered a wide variety of subjects such as the underwater archaeology of shipwrecks, prehistoric religion, Biblical archaeology, heritage walks through Britain's landscapes, precious or intriguing artifacts found by the public, a prehistoric tsunami, Medieval battlefield archaeology, and archaeological approaches to historic architecture. Continual exposure on television has made a few archaeologists into well-recognized figures. It has also made archaeological methods and approaches more well known, and fosters a continuing interest in Britain's past among all ages and backgrounds.

Community Archaeology

Public interest in archaeology is nothing new. The earliest local archaeology societies were being formed in the 1840s, with a big expansion in the number of societies after the Second World War. Through these societies, people can take part in their own research projects, carrying out survey and excavation for themselves. Many local societies have a proud record of fieldwork and publication, and work to a high standard of expertise. In more recent times, professional archaeologists have begun working with local communities. Sometimes, this will be with an already-established society, but can also lead to the creation of new local groups. There is both a top-down and a bottom-up approach to this kind of community archaeology. The top-down projects are those where the public is invited to take part in a professionally funded and run field project, either alongside professional work or as a community project specifically for local people. Bottom-up projects are ones where local groups have their own research and invite or pay for professional help with specific aspects of the archaeology.

A series of community archaeology projects has taken place in the city of Manchester and its surrounding urban areas. These began with the "I Dig Moston" project of 2003–2004, excavating the remains of Moston Hall and involving the Moston and District Archaeology and Social History Society, who became a key partner of the later Dig Manchester project. Dig Manchester involved work at four excavations from 2005 to 2008 in different parts of the city of Manchester, run by the Greater Manchester Archaeological Unit (based at the University of Manchester) with the support of the city council and the Heritage Lottery Fund. The university wanted to use the project to persuade children from deprived neighborhoods to think about applying to higher education. However, the project also involved people of all ages from 3 to over 80, local people, schools, and various other socially or economically disadvantaged groups, such as an arts group for adults with mental health problems, children with autism, disabled groups, and people struggling to find employment. The most recent project is Dig Greater Manchester, running from 2012 to 2016, now organized by the Centre for Applied Archaeology at the University of Salford and funded by the ten local authorities in Greater Manchester and one in Lancashire. This aims to include nearly 10,000 young people and adults over four years at a range of sites from the Medieval to the modern industrial period.

That Britain is an island is sometimes forgotten in that most archaeological research has focused on inland sites. However, there is a long coastline around Britain that varies from high stone cliffs to sandy beaches to low-lying estuaries and mud flats. Much of this coastline is actively eroding or is subject to damaging storms and floods. Sites of all periods of the past are being revealed and then destroyed by this coastal erosion. Work by Archaeology Scotland from 1997 led to a major project between the Scottish Coastal Archaeology and the Problem of Erosion (SCAPE) Trust and the University of St. Andrews in 2001. This project is Shorewatch. Support and training are given to local people and groups to monitor their own coastline, record and survey sites before they are lost, and in some cases excavate them. There are possibly up to 12,000 sites at risk of erosion along the Scottish coast, ranging from Mesolithic shell middens to Second World War defenses. A similar scheme, known as Arfordir (Welsh for coastline), has been set up in Wales, run by three of its Archaeological Trusts: Dyfed, Glamorgan-Gwent, and Gwynedd.

Accessing Archaeology Online

The fast-changing nature of modern technology is allowing more people than ever before to engage with Britain's past. One example of how archaeologists are now using this technology is the Archwilio smartphone app (*archwilio* is Welsh for "to explore"). All four Welsh Archaeological Trusts have come together to produce the app. They each have custody of the Historic Environment Records (HERs) for their area, which contain all the information about approximately 100,000 archaeological sites in Wales. The information has been available online for some time, but the smartphone app was launched in 2013 to allow more people to use the records, and to be able to use them when actually in the landscape to find information about where they are standing. Modern technology allows users to interact and upload their own information. One project that makes the most of this is Know Your Place, by Bristol City Council and the University of Bristol. The Know Your Place website was launched in 2011 and allows users to see information from the HER as well as historic maps of the locality. But, it goes further than this and invites local people to upload their own information, images, and memories of places within Bristol. This enhances the HER with local knowledge, and it allows local people to create added value for the places they cherish. It can help to empower people to identify with their heritage. The historic environment then becomes a living place of memories and lives instead of only an archaeological place of structures, walls, and streets.

Helping People through Archaeology

Archaeologists today are more aware than ever before that their activities are not some kind of private hobby, but have real popularity with others, and can serve a real purpose in people's lives. One remarkable project is using archaeology in a very direct way as therapy to help people back into life and employment after serious trauma. This began as a pilot project in 2011 devised by Sergeant Diarmaid Walshe of the 1st Battalion The Rifles and Richard Osgood of the Defence Infrastructure Organisation. It was aimed at helping wounded servicemen and women who had returned from active service in Afghanistan. The pilot was so successful it led to the creation of Operation Nightingale and the founding of the Defence Archaeology Group in 2012. Working closely with the professional field unit of Wessex Archaeology, Operation Nightingale aims to provide viable rehabilitation for wounded soldiers. Archaeology provides both physical dexterity and technical skills that can be highly valued outside the discipline, and a social environment of teamwork which is valuable for improving mental health and restoring the ability to live in civilian society. Archaeology and soldiering have much in common, and many key early archaeologists had a military background such as Lieutenant General Augustus Pitt-Rivers (see chapter 6) and Brigadier Sir Mortimer Wheeler (see chapter 6). Field archaeology is helping to restore fitness, confidence, and self-esteem to soldiers with the physical and psychological scars of war. The project began by working on Salisbury Plain, much of which is owned by the Ministry of Defence and is a major army training area as well as one of the richest areas of Britain during later prehistory. The project has now widened to include work elsewhere in Britain. Sites excavated include an Iron Age midden at East Chisenbury, a Roman building at Caerwent, an Anglo-Saxon cemetery at Barrow Clump, and the wreck of a Second World War USAAF Liberator bomber.

LEARNING LESSONS?

Modern archaeological research is keen to show how it can be of value to modern society. Can modern Britons look back on their long past as revealed by archaeology and learn any lessons for today? We can see that climate change is a constant feature in the past. Being in a turbulent maritime climatic zone provides modern Britons with a constant topic of conversation. Instead of bemoaning their weather, perhaps people should revel in its unpredictable, ever-changing nature, and treat seriously its potential to change where and what is built in Britain's landscape. Flooded houses in low-lying areas or beneath steep hillsides are a common feature on Britain's television news screens. People build for today, unmindful that their climate is not constant and that they need to build with one eye on the past to have homes for the future.

It is easy to see Britain as an island, somehow detached from the continent, and therefore not really part of Europe. A simple look at the past shows how much Britons owe to their fellow Europeans and how much they have relied on them throughout the past, as a market for their goods, as a source of enrichment for their culture and of new people for their genetic stock. Taking a European perspective also helps Britain to be a little less self-centered as a nation. It is on the edge of Europe, not at its center. Britain has often accepted aspects of continental culture and given them a particularly British twist. Britain's contributions back to the rest of Europe have often been crucial. It was Anglo-Saxon and Celtic missionaries who helped secure Christianity in much of northern and western Europe in the seventh and eighth centuries, and brought with them a renewed vigor in art and craftsmanship. Britain could ask itself what it could contribute to Europe today.

Within Britain, there is a long history of regional imbalance with some regions being centers of power and more obviously wealthy than others. For sensible geographical reasons, the southeast has often fulfilled this role. However, this current dominance of the area around London has not always been the case. Other regions have been able to challenge its advantage of nearness to the continent and transport along the Thames. Wessex, the Orkneys, the industrial coalfields have at times been the centers of Britain. Archaeological understanding of why other areas can sustain trade, economic surplus, and political power is in its infancy. One clear factor, though, seems to be transport links with other wealthy areas outside or within Britain. Do modern transport links help or hinder the current dominance of the southeast? How can other parts of Britain generate the wealth needed to catch up with living standards in London? Perhaps Britain's policy makers should ask an archaeologist.

Throughout the archaeological past we can see a Britain that is culturally diverse. Styles of monument, of house, of religious practices, types of economy, and types of artifacts have always varied between different parts of the island. The differences are both from north to south and from east to west. Being an island means having four ends and four faces to the world. We tend to think islands should look inwards to the center and forget that movement along the coasts has been easier than movement across the land for most of its past. The Medieval creation of England, Scotland, and Wales fixed identities that until then had been fluid and capable of being reshaped along different geographical lines. Would links between Orkney and Wessex in the Late Neolithic have created a sense of a common island identity, or would they have reminded people of the differences between the far north and the far south? Perhaps people should beware of others who peddle simple identities and remind themselves of the multiple cultures that make Britain and its past such an exciting kaleidoscope of sites, artifacts, landscapes, and ways of life.

The archaeological remains of Britain are extensive, deep in time, and highly varied. This book has only showcased a small and not always representative snapshot of what can be seen. Britain's archaeological heritage is rich, fascinating, and unique. It helps to explain who Britons are and their journey into the modern world. Of course, it is also a wonderful reason for enticing people to its shores to explore what to them will be an exotic other. That many come to Britain for its heritage is shown by recent research that heritage tourism contributes £26.4 billion to the UK economy each year, a bigger amount than car manufacturing or film making. Britain may not offer its visitors sun-drenched sandy beaches, but it can offer a rich heritage well worth exploring.

EPILOGUE

Finding Out More

VISITING SITES AND MONUMENTS

Major Organizations

Various organizations look after archaeological sites and monuments and open them to the public to visit. Some of these work across Britain while others work in one or more of the individual nations within Britain. Some sites may be free to visit, while others will have an entrance fee. Likewise, some may be an archaeological structure with facilities, a visitor center or museum, while others will be unattended ruins or remains.

Cadw

The Welsh word *cadw* means to protect, and the Cadw service is an arm of the Welsh government which cares for Wales' historic environment. One of its functions is to care for sites and monuments that are in the care of the state, and it opens these for the public to visit.

http://cadw.wales.gov.uk/?lang=en

English Heritage

English Heritage is in the process of being reorganized, and the section that deals with managing and opening to the public the sites and monuments in state care will become a separate charitable trust. Currently, information about these sites can still be found at the website http://www.english-heritage.org.uk/.

Historic Houses Association

Many historic houses, castles and gardens in Britain are privately owned. About one-third of these (around 500) are open to the public. They range from small historic properties to large and iconic stately homes.

http://www.hha.org.uk/

Historic Scotland

Care of sites under the protection of the state in Scotland is the responsibility of Historic Scotland, which has more than 300 sites that the public can visit.

http://www.historic-scotland.gov.uk/

Museums Association

Most museums in Britain are members of the Museums Association, and information about them is available through subscription to their yearbook. Information about this can be found at http://www.museumsassociation.org/home.

National Trust

The National Trust was founded in 1895 and is an independent charity, but with statutory protection for its activities. Its mission is to preserve and protect historic places and spaces for ever, for everyone. The ideals of its founders were that people of all backgrounds would benefit from access to uplifting and inspiring spaces and places. It now owns large areas of open countryside and coastline as well as historic houses and gardens.

https://www.nationaltrust.org.uk/

National Trust for Scotland

The National Trust for Scotland is a separate organization from the National Trust, set up in 1931 to fulfill a similar purpose, to preserve and conserve Scotland's natural and human heritage.

http://www.nts.org.uk/Home/

RECONSTRUCTED ARCHAEOLOGICAL SITES

There are many museums, sites, and open-air heritage centers in Britain. It is not possible to list them all. However, there are a few sites that contain reconstructions of archaeological buildings based on excavated evidence. A selection of the most well known is listed below.

Arbeia Roman Fort (Tyne and Wear)

An excavated Roman fort with some partially reconstructed buildings.

http://www.twmuseums.org.uk/arbeia.html

Butser Ancient Farm (Hampshire)
An Iron Age experimental archaeology center.
http://www.butserancientfarm.co.uk/
Castell Henllys (Pembrokeshire)
A reconstructed Iron Age hill fort.
http://www.pembrokeshirecoast.org.uk/default.asp?PID=261
Scottish Crannog Centre (Perthshire)
A reconstructed Iron Age lake dwelling.
http://www.crannog.co.uk/
West Stow Anglo-Saxon Village (Suffolk)
Reconstructions of Anglo-Saxon buildings on the site of an excavated settlement.
http://www.weststow.org/

MAJOR EVENTS

Festival of Archaeology
This festival is organized by the Council for British Archaeology every July and is made up of more than a thousand local events all over the country put on by museums, excavation units, local societies, universities, and others. The emphasis is on family friendly activities and sometimes there is access to sites or artifacts not normally open to the public. Information about the festival can be found at http://www.archaeologyfestival.org.uk/.

Heritage Open Days
Coordinated by English Heritage every September, Heritage Open Days aim to bring local history to life through tours, events, and activities, and enable free access to historic, architectural, and cultural properties that are usually closed to the public or that charge for admission.
http://www.heritageopendays.org.uk/

History Live!
This was formerly known as the Festival of History and is organized every year by English Heritage over one weekend in July at Kelmarsh Hall in Northamptonshire. The event focuses on reenactment of all periods in British history over the last 2,000 years. Information is posted on the English Heritage website, for 2014 at http://www.english-heritage.org.uk/daysout/events/history-live2014/.

Jorvik Viking Festival
There are also local and regional heritage or archaeology festivals at different times across Britain. It is always worth checking whether a town or

place you wish to visit has such a festival during the year. One of the biggest is the Jorvik Viking Festival, held over a week every February and organized by York Archaeological Trust. Information about this is posted on their website at http://jorvik-viking-centre.co.uk/festivals/.

Scotland's Festival of History

The major Scottish reenactment festival is held in August at Chatelherault, near Hamilton in Lanarkshire, and covers all periods of Scottish history. More information can be found at http://www.lanarkmedieval festival.co.uk/.

Scottish Archaeology Month

Scotland has its own archaeology festival run by Archaeology Scotland. This is run every September and includes a range of activities, including free talks, tours, exhibitions, workshops, and hands-on events. Information about the Month is posted on the Archaeology Scotland website at http:// www.archaeologyscotland.co.uk/.

GETTING INVOLVED

Excavation Opportunities

Current Archaeology

The *Current Archaeology* magazine's website has a wide range of information about archaeology and opportunities to take part in it or study it.
http://www.archaeology.co.uk

CBA

The Council for British Archaeology website is the first port of call for anyone interested in archaeology in Britain. A comprehensive listing of excavation opportunities is available in its Briefing section at http://www .britisharchaeology.org/fieldwork.

Past Horizons

Details of fieldwork in both Britain and worldwide are available at the online magazine *Past Horizons*, http://www.pasthorizons.com/world projects.

TORC

The Training Online Resource Centre is another source of opportunities for taking part in fieldwork, as well as for finding courses and events.
http://www.torc.org.uk/

LEARNING MORE ABOUT BRITAIN'S ARCHAEOLOGY

Finding the Latest News

BAJR (The British Archaeological Jobs Resource)

BAJR is a useful website, privately produced by David Connolly, with various web resources, adverts for jobs, a discussion forum, information about publications, archaeological tools, and courses.

http://www.bajr.org/

British Archaeology

The Council for British Archaeology is the UK-wide association for all archaeological organizations and individuals interested in archaeology. It acts as the national voice for archaeology to government and the media. Their magazine *British Archaeology* is published every two months, and has articles about the latest finds and debates within British archaeo-logy. It is free to CBA members, otherwise subscription details can be found on their website, http://new.archaeologyuk.org/british-archaeology-magazine/.

Current Archaeology

The magazine *Current Archaeology* is the longest running independent popular magazine about archaeology in Britain, founded in 1967 by Andrew Selkirk. It often focuses on the latest discoveries, and has a sister magazine *Current World Archaeology*.

http://www.archaeology.co.uk/ and http://www.world-archaeology.com/

Explorator

A simple online, weekly email chronicle of latest discoveries and news in worldwide archaeology, including Britain, is provided direct to your email in-box. Subscription is free and by email.

http://groups.yahoo.com/group/Explorator/

Learning More about Sites

Official records of archaeological remains are known as historic environ-ment records. These are held both nationally and locally in Britain. Many have been made available to the public online.

Beresford's Lost Villages

This is a new website delivering information about the shrunken and deserted Medieval villages of England.

http://www.dmv.hull.ac.uk/

Canmore

The database of the Royal Commission on the Ancient and Historical Monuments of Scotland (RCAHMS) has more than 300,000 sites listed and is made available through the Canmore website.

http://www.rcahms.gov.uk/canmore.html

Coflein

The online database for the National Monuments Record of Wales is available through the Coflein website (coflein meaning memory-line in Welsh) by the Royal Commission on the Ancient and Historical Monuments of Wales.

http://www.coflein.gov.uk

Heritage Gateway

Those local historic environment records that are held by local authorities in England and are available online can be searched through the Heritage Gateway website.

http://www.heritagegateway.org.uk

PastScape

PastScape is a website of English Heritage which gives access to the 400,000 records in the National Monuments Record for England.

http://www.pastscape.org.uk

PastMap

The RCAHMS makes available its historic environment information from its own and local authority databases through an interactive map of Scotland at the PastMap website.

http://www.pastmap.org.uk

BIBLIOGRAPHY

The following bibliography is highly selective. There is a very large amount written about British archaeology and this listing only scratches the surface. It includes all the works used in the writing of the text of this book, along with some other selected key works. References are listed under the chapter and section they refer to.

GENERAL ARCHAEOLOGY OF BRITAIN

A great many accessible and popular books on various aspects of archaeology are published by Shire Publications. These are written by acknowledged authorities in their field and offer concise summaries of academic knowledge for a lay audience. Only a few of their books are listed below. For more details see their website, http://www.shirebooks.co.uk/Archaeology/. Many Shire books are now out of print but are still highly sought after and contain a wealth of information about Britain's archaeology and heritage. A full list of their past publications is available at http://www.shirebooks.co.uk/pdf/45years.pdf.

Alcock, N. W., Barley, M. W., Dixon, P. W., & Meeson, R. A. (1996). *Recording timber-framed buildings: An illustrated glossary.* York: Council for British Archaeology.

Ashmore, P. (1995). *Ancient Scotland 4000–750 BC.* London: Batsford and Historic Scotland.

Bewley, R. (1994). *Prehistoric settlements*. London: Batsford and English Heritage.

Cunliffe, Sir B. (2013). *Britain begins*. Oxford: Oxford University Press.

Currie, C. (2005). *Garden archaeology: A handbook*. York: Council for British Archaeology.

Darvill, T. (2010). (2nd ed.) *Prehistoric Britain*. London: Routledge.

Dellino-Musgrave, V. (2012). *Marine archaeology: A handbook*. York: Council for British Archaeology.

Dyer, J. (1993). *Discovering prehistoric England*. Princes Risborough: Shire Publications.

Hunter, J., & Ralston, I. (2009). (2nd ed.) *The archaeology of Britain: An introduction from earliest times to the twenty-first century*. London: Routledge.

Langmaid, N. G. (1978). *Prehistoric pottery*. Princes Risborough: Shire Publications.

Parsons, D. (1998). *Churches and chapels: investigating places of worship*. York: Council for British Archaeology.

Pollard, J. (ed.) (2008). *Prehistoric Britain*. London: Wiley-Blackwell.

Reid, M. L. (1993). *Prehistoric houses in Britain*. Princes Risborough: Shire Publications.

Reynolds, P. (1987). *Ancient farming*. Princes Risborough: Shire Publications.

Schofield, J., Carman, J., & Belford, P. (2011). *Archaeological practice in Great Britain: A heritage handbook*. New York: Springer.

Wright, P. (2009). *On living in an old country: The national past in contemporary Britain*. Oxford: Oxford University Press.

TIME

Aston, M. (1985). *Interpreting the landscape: Landscape archaeology and local history*. London: Routledge.

Aston, M. A., & Gerrard, C. M. (2013). *Interpreting the English village: Landscape and community at Shapwick, Somerset*. Oxford: Windgather Press.

Gerrard, C., & Aston, M. (2007). *The Shapwick Project, Somerset: A rural landscape explored*. Society for Medieval Archaeology Monograph 25, London: Maney Publishing.

Hoskins, W. G. (1955). *The making of the English landscape*. London: Hodder & Stoughton.

Johnson, M. (2006). *Ideas of landscape*. London: Wiley-Blackwell.

Muir, R. (2000). *Reading the landscape: Fieldwork in landscape history*. Exeter: Exeter University Press.

Pryor, F. (2011). *The making of the British landscape: How we have transformed the land, from prehistory to today*. London: Penguin Books.

Rackham, O. (1986). *The history of the countryside: The full fascinating story of Britain's landscape*. London: J. M. Dent & Sons.

Yorke, T. (2008). *British architectural styles: An easy reference guide*. Newbury: Countryside Books.

PLACE

Aston, M., & Bond, J. (2000). *The landscape of towns*. Stroud: Sutton Publishing.

Blair, J. (2007). *Waterways and canal-building in Medieval England*. Oxford: Oxford University Press.

Crowe, N. (1994). *Canals*. London: Batsford and English Heritage.

Fox, C. (1932). *The personality of Britain*. Cardiff: National Museum of Wales.

Morriss, R. K. (1999). *The archaeology of railways*. Stroud: Tempus.

Ottaway, P. (1992). *Archaeology in British towns: From the Emperor Claudius to the Black Death*. London: Routledge.

Ransom, P. J. G. (1979). *The archaeology of canals*. Tadworth: World's Work.

Rippon, S. (2012). *Historic landscape analysis: Deciphering the countryside*. York: Council for British Archaeology.

Taylor, C. (1979). *Roads and tracks of Britain*. London: J. M. Dent & Sons.

Wagstaff, J. M. (1987). *Landscape & culture: Geographical & archaeological perspectives*. Oxford: Blackwell.

PEOPLE

Cherryson, A., Crossland, Z., & Tarlow, S. (2012). *A fine and private place: The archaeology of death and burial in post-Medieval Britain and Ireland*. Leicester: Leicester University Press.

Hills, C. M. (1986). *The blood of the British*. London: George Philip.

Hutton, R. (2013). *Pagan Britain*. Yale: Yale University Press.

Miles, D. (2006). *The tribes of Britain: Who are we? And where do we come from?* London: Phoenix House.

Mytum, H. (2000). *Recording and analysing graveyards*. York: Council for British Archaeology.

Oppenheimer, S. (2006). *The origins of the British: A genetic detective story*. London: Constable and Robinson.

Price, G. (ed.) (2000). *Languages in Britain and Ireland*. Oxford: Blackwell.

Rodwell, W. J. (1989). *Church archaeology*. London: Batsford and English Heritage.

Stringer, C. (2007). *Homo Britannicus: The incredible story of human life in Britain*. London: Penguin Books.

Sykes, B. (2006). *The blood of the isles*. London: Bantam Press.

Woodward, A. (1992). *Shrines and sacrifices*. London: Batsford and English Heritage.

CHAPTER 2. LONG-SETTLED ISLANDS

Ice Age Colonizers (13,800 BC)

Barton, N. (2000). *Stone Age Britain*. London: Batsford and English Heritage.

Lawson, A. J. (1991). *Cave art*. Princes Risborough: Shire Publications.

Pettitt, P., & White, M. (2012). *The British Palaeolithic*. London: Routledge.

Stuart, A. J. (1988). *Life in the Ice Age*. Princes Risborough: Shire Publications.

Timms, P. (1974). *Flint implements of the Old Stone Age*. Princes Risborough: Shire Publications.

Hunter-Gatherer Utopia (9650 BC)

Conneller, C., & Warren, G. (2006). *Mesolithic Britain and Ireland: New approaches*. Stroud: The History Press.

Milner, N., & Woodman, P. (eds.) (2005). *Mesolithic studies at the beginning of the 21st century*. Oxford: Oxbow Books.

Reynier, M. (2005). *Early Mesolithic Britain*. British Archaeological Reports British Series 393, Oxford: Archaeopress.

Wickham-Jones, C. (1996). *Scotland's first settlers*. London: Batsford and Historic Scotland.

Wymer, J. (1991). *Mesolithic Britain*. Princes Risborough: Shire Publications.

First Farmers (4050 BC), Ritual and Hierarchy (3250 BC), and Farms, Forts, and Kings (1450 BC)

Many popular and even academic works on the later prehistory of Britain are based on the old period divisions of the Neolithic, Bronze Age, and Iron Age, even though they are not an accurate reflection of the changes in society and economy of this time, and do not fit into the chapter structure adopted in this book. References below are therefore grouped according to the traditional chronology.

Neolithic

Burl, A. (1979). *Prehistoric stone circles*. Princes Risborough: Shire Publications.

Burl, A. (1983). *Prehistoric astronomy and ritual*. Princes Risborough: Shire Publications.

Burl, A. (1991). *Prehistoric henges*. Princes Risborough: Shire Publications.

Gibson, A. (1986). *Neolithic and Early Bronze Age pottery*. Princes Risborough: Shire Publications.

Grinsell, L. V. (1983). *Barrows in England and Wales*. Princes Risborough: Shire Publications.

Holgate, R. (1991). *Prehistoric flint mines*. Princes Risborough: Shire Publications.

Malone, C. (2001). *Neolithic Britain and Ireland*. Stroud: Tempus.

Mercer, R. J. (1990). *Causewayed enclosures*. Princes Risborough: Shire Publications.

Saville, A. (ed.) (2011). *Flint and stone in the Neolithic Period*. Oxford: Oxbow Books.

Whittle, A. (2003). *The archaeology of people: Dimensions of Neolithic life*. London: Routledge.

Whittle, A. W. R., Healy, F. M. A., & Bayliss, A. (2011). *Gathering time: Dating the Early Neolithic enclosures of Southern Britain and Ireland*. Oxford: Oxbow Books.

Bronze Age

Barber, M. (2003). *Bronze and the Bronze Age: Metalwork and society in Britain c. 2500–800 BC*. Stroud: Tempus.

Brück, J. (2001). *Bronze Age landscapes: Tradition and transformation*. Oxford: Oxbow Books.

Parker Pearson, M. (2005). *Bronze Age Britain*. London: Batsford and English Heritage.

Pearce, S. (1984). *Bronze Age metalwork in Southern Britain*. Princes Risborough: Shire Publications.

Pryor, F. (1982). *Fengate*. Princes Risborough: Shire Publications.

Iron Age

Collis, J. (2003). *The Celts: Origins, myths and inventions*. Stroud: Tempus.

Cunliffe, B. (1995). *Iron Age Britain*. London: Batsford and English Heritage.

Cunliffe, B. (2004). *Iron Age communities in Britain*. London: Routledge. (4th ed.)

Cunliffe, B., & Koch, J. T. (2010). *Celtic from the West: Alternative perspectives from archaeology, genetics, language, and literature*. Oxford: Oxbow Books

Cunliffe, B., & Koch, J. T. (2013). *Celtic from the West 2: Rethinking the Bronze Age and the arrival of Indo-European in Atlantic Europe*. Oxford: Oxbow Books.

Dixon, N. 2004 *The crannogs of Scotland: An underwater archaeology*. Stroud: Tempus.

Dyer, J. (1981). *Hillforts in England and Wales*. Princes Risborough: Shire Publications.

Elsdon, S. M. (1989). *Later prehistoric pottery in England and Wales*. Princes Risborough: Shire Publications.

Harding, D. W. (2004). *The Iron Age in northern Britain: Celts and Romans, natives and invaders*. Abingdon: Routledge.

Harding, D. W. (2009). *The Iron Age round-house: Later prehistoric building in Britain and Ireland*. Oxford: Oxford University Press.

Haselgrove, C., & Moore, T. (2007). *The later Iron Age in Britain and beyond*. Oxford: Oxbow Books.

Megaw, R., & Megaw, J. V. S. (1986). *Early Celtic art in Britain and Ireland*. Princes Risborough: Shire Publications.

Ritchie, J. N. G. (1988). *Brochs of Scotland*. Princes Risborough: Shire Publications.

Ritchie, W. F., & Ritchie, J. N. G. (1985). *Celtic warriors*. Princes Risborough: Shire Publications.

CHAPTER 3. TWO THOUSAND YEARS OF HISTORY

Roman Interlude (43 AD)

Anderson, A. S. (1984). *Roman military tombstones*. Princes Risborough: Shire Publications.

Bagshawe, R. (1979). *Roman roads*. Princes Risborough: Shire Publications.

Bédoyère, G. de la (1988). *Samian Ware*. Princes Risborough: Shire Publications.

Bédoyère, G. de la (1992). *Roman towns in Britain*. London: Batsford and English Heritage.

Bédoyère, G. de la (1993). *Roman villas and the countryside*. London: Batsford and English Heritage.

Bédoyère, G. de la (2010). *Roman Britain: A new history*. London: Thames and Hudson.

Bennett, J. (1988). *Towns in Roman Britain*. Princes Risborough: Shire Publications.

Bishop, M. C., & Coulston, J. C. (1989). *Roman military equipment*. Princes Risborough: Shire Publications.

Breeze, D. (1983). *Roman forts in Britain*. Princes Risborough: Shire Publications.

Casey, P. J. (1980). *Roman coinage in Britain*. Princes Risborough: Shire Publications.

Dyson, S. (2003). *The Roman countryside*. London: Gerald Duckworth.

Green, M. J. (1983). *The gods of Roman Britain*. Princes Risborough: Shire Publications.

Hanley, R. (2000). *Villages in Roman Britain*. Princes Risborough: Shire Publications.

Hobbs, R., & Jackson, R. (2010). *Roman Britain*. London: British Museum.

Ireland, S. (2008). *Roman Britain: A sourcebook*. London: Routledge.

Johnson, P. (1995). *Romano-British mosaics*. Princes Risborough: Shire Publications.

Johnston, D. E. (1983). *Discovering Roman Britain*. Princes Risborough: Shire Publications.

Johnston, D. E. (1983). *Roman villas*. Princes Risborough: Shire Publications.

Jones, B., & Mattingly, D. (2002). *An atlas of Roman Britain*. Oxford: Oxbow Books.

Ling, R. (1985). *Romano-British wall painting*. Princes Risborough: Shire Publications.

Mattingly, D. (2007). *An imperial possession: Britain in the Roman Empire 54 BC–AD 409*. Harmondsworth: Penguin Books.

McWhirr, A. (1982). *Roman crafts and industries*. Princes Risborough: Shire Publications.

Millett, M. (1995). *Roman Britain*. London: Batsford and English Heritage.

Milne, G. (1995). *Roman London*. London: Batsford and English Heritage.

Perring, D. (2002). *The Roman house in Britain*. London: Routledge.

Potter, T. W. (2002). *Roman Britain*. London: British Museum.

Rook, T. (1992). *Roman Baths in Britain*. Princes Risborough: Shire Publications.

Salway, P. (2000). *Roman Britain: A very short introduction*. Oxford: Oxford University Press.

Swann, V. G. (1988). *Pottery in Roman Britain*. Princes Risborough: Shire Publications.

Todd, M. (ed.) (2008). *A companion to Roman Britain*. London: Wiley-Blackwell.

Migrations and Kingdoms (410 AD)

Arnold, C. J., & Davies, J. L. (2000). *Roman and early Medieval Wales*. Stroud: History Press.

Carver, M. (ed.) (2003). *The cross goes north*. York: York Medieval Press.

Collins, R. (2004). *Debating late antiquity in Britain AD 300–700*. British Archaeological Reports British Series 365, Oxford: Archaeopress.

Dark, K. R. (2001). *Britain and the end of the Roman Empire*. Stroud: Tempus.

Driscoll, S., Geddes, J., & Hall, M, A, (2010). *Pictish progress*. Leiden and Boston: Brill.

Foster, S. (2004). *Picts, Gaels and Scots: Early historic Scotland*. London: Batsford.

Fraser, I. (2008). *The Pictish symbol stones of Scotland*. Edinburgh: RCAHMS.

Gerrard, J. (2013). *The ruin of Roman Britain: An archaeological perspective*. Cambridge: Cambridge University Press.

Harden, J. (2010). *The Picts*. Edinburgh: Historic Scotland.

Henderson, G., & Henderson, I. (2004). *The art of the Picts: Sculpture and metalwork in early Medieval Scotland*. London: Thames & Hudson.

Henson, D. (2006.) *The origins of the Anglo-Saxons*. Hockwold-cum-Wilton: Anglo-Saxon Books.

Higham, N. J. (2007). *Britons in Anglo-Saxon England*. London: Boydell & Brewer.

Hunter, F. (2007). *Beyond the edge of empire: Caledonians, Picts and Romans*. Rosemarkie: Groam House Museum.

James, E. (2001). *Britain in the first millennium*. London: Arnold Publishing.

Jessup, R. (1974). *Anglo-Saxon jewellery*. Princes Risborough: Shire Publications.

Kennett, D. H. (1978). *Anglo-Saxon pottery*. Princes Risborough: Shire Publications.

Lang, J. (1978). *Anglo-Saxon sculpture*. Princes Risborough: Shire Publications.

Laing, L. (2006). *The archaeology of Celtic Britain and Ireland: Circa AD 400–1200*. Cambridge: Cambridge University Press.

Seaborne, M. (1994). *Celtic crosses of Britain and Ireland*. Princes Risborough: Shire Publications.

Welch, M. (1992). *Anglo-Saxon England*. London: Batsford and English Heritage.

Williams, H. (2006). *Death and memory in early Medieval Britain*. Cambridge: Cambridge University Press.

Yeoman, P. (1995). *Medieval Scotland*. London: Batsford and Historic Scotland.

Medieval Monarchies (865 AD)

Aston, M. (2013). *Interpreting the landscape: Landscape archaeology and local history*. London: Routledge.

Barrett, J. H. (2003). *Contact, continuity, and collapse: The Norse colonization of the North Atlantic*. Turnhout: Brepols.

Brown, R. A. (1989). *Castles*. Princes Risborough: Shire Publications.

Coppack, G. (1990). *Abbeys and priories*. London: Batsford and English Heritage.

Coppack, G. (2006). *Abbeys and priories*. Stroud: Tempus.

Crabtree, P. J. (2001). *Medieval archaeology: An encyclopedia*. London: Routledge.

Creighton, O. H., & Higham, R. (2003). *Medieval castles*. Princes Risborough: Shire Publications.

Creighton, O. H., & Higham, R. (2005). *Medieval town walls: An archaeology and social history of urban defence*. Stroud: Tempus.

Fawcett, R. (1995). *Scottish abbeys and priories.* London: Batsford and Historic Scotland.

Foster, S. (2004). *Picts, Gaels and Scots: Early historic Scotland.* London: B. T. Batsford.

Gaimster, D. R. M., & Stamper, P. (1997). *The Age of transition: The archaeology of English culture 1400–1600.* Oxford: Oxbow Books Limited.

Gerrard, C. M. (2003). *Medieval archaeology: Understanding traditions and contemporary approaches.* London: Routledge.

Giles, K., & Dyer, C. (2005). *Town and country in the Middle Ages: Contrasts, contacts and interconnections, 1100–1500.* London: Maney Publishing.

Hadley, D. M. (2001). *Death in Medieval England: An archaeology.* Stroud: Tempus.

Hall, D. (1982). *Medieval fields.* Princes Risborough: Shire Publications.

Hall, R. (1990). *Viking Age archaeology.* Princes Risborough: Shire Publications.

Haslam, J. (1985). *Early Medieval towns in Britain.* Princes Risborough: Shire Publications.

Haslam, J. (1989). *Medieval pottery.* Princes Risborough: Shire Publications.

Hindle, B. P. (1982). *Medieval roads.* Princes Risborough: Shire Publications.

Hindle, B. P. (1990). *Medieval town plans.* Princes Risborough: Shire Publications.

Hinton, D. A. (1982). *Medieval jewellery.* Princes Risborough: Shire Publications.

Hinton, D. A. (2005). *Gold and gilt, pots and pins: Possessions and people in Medieval Britain.* Oxford: Oxford University Press.

Kenyon, J. (2005). *Medieval fortifications.* Leicester: Leicester University Press.

Kerr, M., & Kerr, N. (1983). *Anglo-Saxon architecture.* Princes Risborough: Shire Publications.

Kinross, J. (1984). *Discovering castles in England and Wales.* Princes Risborough: Shire Publications.

Laing, J. (1988). *Anglo-Saxon sculpture.* Princes Risborough: Shire Publications.

Lucas, A. (2006). *Wind, water, work: Ancient and Medieval milling technology.* Leiden and Boston: Brill.

McNeill, T. (1992). *Castles.* London: Batsford and English Heritage.

Morris, M. (2003). *Castle: A history of the buildings that shaped Medieval Britain.* London: Windmill Books.

Quiney, A. (2003). *Town houses of Medieval Britain.* Yale: Yale University Press.

Pepin, D. (1994). *Discovering cathedrals.* Princes Risborough: Shire Publications.

Richards, J. D. (1991). *Viking Age England.* London: Batsford and English Heritage.

Rigby, S. H. (2008). *A companion to Britain in the later Middle Ages.* London: Wiley-Blackwell.

Rippon, S. (2008). *Beyond the Medieval village.* Oxford: Oxford University Press.

Ritchie, A. (1995). *Viking Scotland.* London: Batsford and Historic Scotland.

Roberts, B. J. (1982). *Village plans.* Princes Risborough: Shire Publications.

Roberts, K. (2006). *Lost Farmsteads: Deserted rural settlements in Wales.* York: Council for British Archaeology.

Rowley, T. (1997). *Norman England.* London: Batsford and English Heritage.

Rowley, T., & Wood, S. (1995). *Deserted villages.* Princes Risborough: Shire Publications.

Schofield, J., & Vince, A. G. (2003). (2nd ed.) *Medieval towns: The archaeology of British towns in their European setting*. Leicester: Leicester University Press.

Steane, J. (2003). *The archaeology of the Medieval English monarchy*. London: Routledge.

Szarmach, P. E., Tavormina, T. M., & Rosenthal, J. T. (2013). *Medieval England: A social history and archaeology from the Conquest to 1600 AD*. London: Routledge.

Wheatley, A. (2004). *The idea of the castle in Medieval England*. York: York Medieval Press.

Williamson, T. (2004). *Shaping Medieval landscapes: Settlement, society, environment*. Oxford: Windgather Press.

Wilson, D. (1985). *Moated sites*. Princes Risborough: Shire Publications.

Wright, G. N. (1994). *Discovering abbeys and priories*. Princes Risborough: Shire Publications.

Reformation and Revolution (1521 AD)

Alcock, L. W., & Hall, L. (1994). *Fixture and fittings in dated houses 1567–1763*. York: Council for British Archaeology.

Draper, J. (1984). *Post-Medieval pottery*. Princes Risborough: Shire Publications.

Foard, G. (2012). *Battlefield archaeology of the English Civil War*. British Archaeological Reports British Series 570, Oxford: Archaeopress.

Gaimster, D. R. M., & Gilchrist, R. (eds.) (2003). *The Archaeology of reformation, 1480–1580*. London: Maney.

Gaimster, D. R. M., & Stamper, P. (1997). *The Age of transition: The archaeology of English culture 1400–1600*. Oxford: Oxbow Books.

Harrington, P. (1992). *Archaeology of the English Civil War*. Princes Risborough: Shire Publications.

Harrington, P. (2004). *English Civil War archaeology*. London. Batsford.

Tabraham, C., & Grove, D. (1995). *Fortress Scotland and the Jacobites*. London: Batsford and Historic Scotland.

Industrial Advance and the Modern World (1760 AD)

Atkinson, R. L. (1987). *Copper and copper mining*. Princes Risborough: Shire Publications.

Atkinson, R. L. (1989). *Tin and tin mining*. Princes Risborough: Shire Publications.

Barker, D., & Cranstone, D. (eds.) (2004). *The archaeology of industrialization*. Society of Post-Medieval Archaeology Monographs 2, London: Maney.

Barton, D. A. (1995). *Discovering chapels and meeting houses*. Princes Risborough: Shire Publications.

Gale, W. K. V. (1994). *Ironworking*. Princes Risborough: Shire Publications.

Lawrence, S. (2003). *Archaeology of the British: Explorations of identity in the United Kingdom and its colonies 1600–1945*. London: Routledge.

Lowry, B. (1996). *20th century defences in Britain: An introductory guide*. York: Council for British Archaeology.

Newman, R., Cranstone, D., & Howard-Davis, C. (2001). *The historical archaeology of Britain: Circa 1540–1900*. Stroud: Sutton Publishing.

Palmer, M., Nevell, M., & Sissons, M. (2012). *Industrial archaeology: A handbook*. York: Council for British Archaeology.

Saunders, A. (1997). *Channel defences*. London: Batsford and English Heritage.

Sekers, D. (1994). *The Potteries*. Princes Risborough: Shire Publications.

Smith, P. L. (1993). *Discovering canals in Britain*. Princes Risborough: Shire Publications.

Stratton, M., & Trinder, B. (1997). *Industrial England*. London: Batsford and English Heritage.

Stratton, M., & Trinder, B. (2000). *Twentieth century industrial archaeology*. Abingdon: Taylor and Francis.

Vince, J. (1993). *Discovering watermills*. Princes Risborough: Shire Publications.

Williams, M. (1991). *The slate industry*. Princes Risborough: Shire Publications.

Williams, R. (1989). *Limekilns and limeburning*. Princes Risborough: Shire Publications.

Willies, L. (1994). *Lead and leadmilling*. Princes Risborough: Shire Publications.

CHAPTER 4. PREHISTORIC SITES AND FINDS

Information about the World Heritage Sites and those on the Tentative List can be found on the UNESCO website at http://whc.unesco.org/en/statesparties/GB/. Information on sites is also available through the historic environment records available for England at PastScape, http://www.pastscape.org.uk/, for Scotland at Canmore, http://www.rcahms.gov.uk/canmore.html, and for Wales at Coflein, http://www.coflein.gov.uk.

Dyer, J. (2001). *Discovering prehistoric England: A gazeteer of prehistoric sites*. Princes Risborough: Shire Publications.

Hovell, G. (2009). *Visiting the past: A guide to finding and understanding Britain's archaeology*, Stroud: The History Press.

Quinn, T. (2011). *Britain's best historic sites*. London: New Holland Publishers.

Taylor, T. (2005). *The Time Team guide to the archaeological sites of Britain & Ireland*. London: Channel 4.

ICE AGE COLONISERS

Boxgrove
Roberts, M. B., & Parfitt, S. A. (1999). *Boxgrove: A Middle Pleistocene hominid site at Eartham Quarry, Boxgrove, West Sussex*. London: English Heritage.
Cheddar Gorge
Bello, S., Parfitt, S., & Stringer, C. (2011). "Gough's Cave, Somerset." *British Archaeology* 118: 12–19.

Creswell Crags

Bahn, P., & Pettit, P. (2009). *Britain's oldest art: The Ice Age cave art of Creswell Crags*. London: English Heritage.

Jenkinson, R. D. S. (1984). *Creswell Crags: Late Pleistocene sites in the East Midlands*. British Archaeological Reports British Series 122, Oxford: Archaeopress.

Nash, G. H., Calsteren, P. van, Thomas, L., & Simms, M. J. (2012). "A discovery of possible Upper Palaeolithic parietal art in Cathole cave, Gower peninsula, South Wales." *Proceedings of the University of Bristol Spelaeological Society* 25 (3): 327–336.

Paviland Cave

Aldhouse-Green, S. (2000). *Paviland Cave and the Red Lady: A definitive report*. Liverpool: Western Academic & Specialist Press.

Aldhouse-Green, S. (2001). "Great sites: Paviland Cave." *British Archaeology* 61 [available at http://www.archaeologyuk.org/ba/ba61/feat3.shtml, accessed 19 March 2014].

Sommer, M. (2008). *Bones and ochre: The curious afterlife of the Red Lady of Paviland*. Cambridge: Harvard University Press.

HUNTER-GATHERER UTOPIA

Aveline's Hole

Conneller, C. (2006). "Death." In C. Conneller and G. Warren, *Mesolithic Britain and Ireland: New approaches* (pp. 148–157). Stroud: Tempus Publishing.

Schulting, R., & Wysocki, M. (2002). "The Mesolithic human skeletal collection from Aveline's Hole: A preliminary note." *Proceedings of the University of Bristol Spelaeological Society* 22 (3): 255–68.

Broom Hill

O'Malley, M., & Jacobi, R. M. (1978). "The excavation of a Mesolithic occupation site at Broomhill, Braishfield, Hampshire 1971–1973." *Rescue Archaeology in Hampshire* 4: 16–38.

Cheddar Man

Barham, L., Priestley, P., & Targett, A. (1999). *In search of Cheddar Man*. Stroud: Tempus.

Sykes, B. (2006). *Blood of the isles* (pp. 27–29). London: Bantam Press.

Culverwell

Palmer, S. (1999). *Culverwell Mesolithic habitation site, Isle of Portland, Dorset: Excavation report and research studies*. British Archaeological Reports, British Series 287, Oxford: Archaeopress.

Goldcliff

Bell, M., & Neumann, H. (1997). "Prehistoric intertidal archaeology and environments in the Severn Estuary, Wales." *World Archaeology* 29 (1): 95–113.

Scales, R. (2007). "Footprint tracks of people and animals." In M. Bell, *Prehistoric coastal communities: The Mesolithic in western Britain* (pp. 139–157). York: Council for British Archaeology.

Howick

Richards, J. (2011). "Britain's oldest house?" *BBC history* [available at http://www.bbc.co.uk/history/ancient/archaeology/oldest_house_01.shtml, accessed 10 March 2014].

Waddington, C. (2007). "Rethinking Mesolithic settlement and a case study from Howick." In C. Waddington & K. Pedersen, *Mesolithic studies in the North Sea basin and beyond: Proceedings of a conference held at Newcastle in 2003* (pp. 101–113). Oxford: Oxbow Books.

Waddington, C. (ed.) (2007). *Mesolithic settlement in the North Sea basin: A case study from Howick, northeast England*. Oxford: Oxbow and English Heritage.

Morton

Candow, R. (1989). "Prehistoric Morton: The story of the Mesolithic discoveries on Morton Farm on Tentsmuir in North East Fife." In E. M. Wilson, *Aspects of antiquity: A miscellany by members of the Archaeological Section of the Abertay Historical Society (pp. 43–48)*. Dundee: Abertay Historical Society.

Coles, J. M. (1971). "The early settlement of Scotland: Excavations at Morton, Fife." *Proceedings of the Prehistoric Society* 37 (2): 1971.

Star Carr

Cark, J. G. D. (1954). *Excavations at Star Carr: An early Mesolithic site at Seamer near Scarborough, Yorkshire*. Cambridge: University Press.

Milner, N., Conneller, C., Taylor, B., & Schadla-Hall, R. T. (2012). *The story of Star Carr*. York: Council for British Archaeology.

Milner, N.; Taylor, B.; Conneller, C., & Schadla-Hall, T. (2013). *Star Carr: Life in Britain after the Ice Age*. York: Council for British Archaeology.

Star Carr archaeology project, http://starcarr.com/ [accessed 19 March 2014].

Warren Field, Crathes

Gaffney, V., et al. (2013). "Time and a place: A luni-solar 'time-reckoner' from 8th millennium BC Scotland." *Internet Archaeology* 34.

Murray, H. K., Murray, J. C., & Fraser, S. M. (2009). *A tale of the unknown unknowns: A Mesolithic pit alignment and a Neolithic timber hall at Warren Field, Crathes, Aberdeenshire*. Oxford: Oxbow Books.

FIRST FARMERS

Balbridie

Ralston, I. (1982). "A timber hall at Balbridie farm: The Neolithic settlement of north east Scotland." *Aberdeen University Review* 49: 238–49.

Rowley-Conwy, P. (2002). "Great sites: Balbridie." *British Archaeology* 64: 22–24 [available at http://www.archaeologyuk.org/ba/ba64/feat3.shtml, accessed 19 March 2014].

Belas Knap Chambered Tomb

Grinsell, L. V. (1978). *Belas Knap long barrow*. London: Her Majesty's Stationery Office.

Parsons, J. (2002). "Great sites: Belas Knap." *British Archaeology* 63 [available at http://www.archaeologyuk.org/ba/ba63/feat3.shtml, accessed 6 July 2014].

Cissbury Flint Mines

Holgate, R. (1991). *Prehistoric flint mines*. Princes Risborough: Shire Books.

Russell, M. (2000). *Flint mines in Neolithic Britain*. Stroud: Tempus Publishing.

Duggleby Howe

Clarke, D. V., Cowie, T. G., & Foxon, A. (1985). *Symbols of power at the time of Stonehenge* (pp. 64–66, 247–248). Edinburgh: National Museum of Antiquities of Scotland.

Gibson, A., Bayliss, A., Heard, H., Mainland, I., & Ogden, A. R. (2009). "Recent research at Duggleby Howe, North Yorkshire." *Archaeological Journal* 166: 39–78.

Kinnes, I., Schadla-Hall, T., Chadwick, P., & Dean, P. (1983). "Duggleby Howe reconsidered." *Archaeological Journal* 140: 83–108.

Loveday, R. (2002). "Duggleby Howe revisited." *Oxford Journal of Archaeology* 21 (2): 135–146.

Folkton Chalk Drums

Clarke, D .V., Cowie, T. G., & Foxon, A. (1985). *Symbols of power at the time of Stonehenge* (pp. 248–249). Edinburgh: National Museum of Antiquities of Scotland.

Longworth, I. H. (1999). "The Folkton Drums unpicked." In R. Cleal & A. MacSween, *Grooved Ware in Britain and Ireland* (pp. 83–88). Neolithic Studies Group Seminar Papers 3, Oxford: Oxbow Books.

Middleton, A., Young, J. R., & Ambers, J. (2004). "The Folkton Drums: Chalk or cheese?" *Antiquity* 78 (299) [available at http://antiquity.ac.uk/projgall/middleton/index.html, accessed 19 March 2014]

Great Langdale Stone Quarry

Bradley, R., & Edmonds, M. (1993). *Interpreting the axe trade: Production and exchange in Neolithic Britain*. Cambridge: Cambridge University Press.

Claris, P., Quatermaine, J., & Woolley, A. R. (1989). "The Neolithic Quarries and Axe Factory Sites of Great Langdale and Scafell Pike: A New Field Survey." *Proceedings of the Prehistoric Society* 55: 1–25.

Maesmor macehead

Clarke, D. V., Cowie, T. G., & Foxon, A. (1985). *Symbols of power at the time of Stonehenge* (pp. 171, 255). Edinburgh: National Museum of Antiquities of Scotland.

Rotten Bottom Bow

Sheridan, A. (1992). "A longbow from Rotten Bottom, Dumfriesshire, Scotland." *Newswarp* 12: 13–15.

Rudston Ritual Complex

Chapman, H. P. (2003). Engaging with a Neolithic monument in its landscape setting using GIS. *Oxford Journal of Archaeology* 22 (4): 345–356.

Clark, P. A. (2004). *The Neolithic ritual landscape of Rudston* [available at http://www.archaeology.look-here.co.uk/GypseyRace/RudstonNeo/files/RudstonPaper.pdf, accessed 28 October 2013].

Dymond, D. P. (1966). "Ritual monuments at Rudston, east Yorkshire, England." *Proceedings of the Prehistoric Society* 32: 86–95.

Manby, T. (1988). "The Neolithic period in eastern Yorkshire." In T. Manby (ed.), *Archaeology in Eastern Yorkshire* (pp. 35–88). Sheffield: University of Sheffield.

Riley, D. N. (1988). "Air survey of Neolithic sites on the Yorkshire Wolds." In T. Manby (ed.), *Archaeology in Eastern Yorkshire* (pp. 89–93). Sheffield: University of Sheffield.

Street House Long Cairn

Vyner, B. E. (1984). "The excavation of a Neolithic cairn at Street House, Loftus, Cleveland." *Proceedings of the Prehistoric Society* 50: 151–195.

Vyner, B. E., Ambers, J., Healey, E., Innes, J., Jelley, D., Nye, S., Parker, S., & Turner, J. (1988). "The Street House Wossit: The excavation of a Late Neolithic and Early Bronze Age palisaded ritual monument at Street House, Loftus, Cleveland." *Proceedings of the Prehistoric Society* 54: 173–202.

Trethevy Quoit Portal Dolmen

Barnatt, J. (1982). *Prehistoric Cornwall: The ceremonial monuments*. Wellingborough: Turnstone Press.

Weatherhill, C. (1997). *Cornovia: Ancient sites of Cornwall and Scilly*. Tiverton: Cornwall Books.

West Kennet Long Barrow

Bayliss, A., Whittle, A., & Wysocki, M. (2007). "Talking about my generation: The date of the West Kennet long barrow." *Cambridge Archaeological Journal* 17 (Supplement S1): 85–101.

Thomas, J., & Whittle, A. (1986). "Anatomy of a tomb—West Kennet revisited." *Oxford Journal of Archaeology* 5 (2): 129–154.

Windmill Hill Causewayed Enclosure

Cleal, R. (2002). "Great sites: Windmill Hill." *British Archaeology* 67 [available at http://www.archaeologyuk.org/ba/ba67/feat3.shtml, accessed 19 March 2014].

Smith, I. F. (1959). "Excavations at Windmill Hill, Avebury, Wilts, 1957–8." *Wiltshire Archaeological and Natural History Magazine* 57: 149–162.

Smith, I. F. (1965). *Windmill Hill and Avebury: Excavations by Alexander Keiller, 1925–1939*. Oxford: Clarendon Press.

Whittle, A., Pollard, J., & Grigson, C. (1999). *The harmony of symbols: The Windmill Hill causewayed enclosure, Wiltshire*. Oxford: Oxbow Books.

York Hoard

Clarke, D. V., Cowie, T. G., & Foxon, A. (1985). *Symbols of power at the time of Stonehenge* (pp. 172, 252). Edinburgh: National Museum of Antiquities of Scotland.

RITUAL AND HIERARCHY

Arbor Low

Barnatt, J. (1996). *Arbor Low: A guide to the monuments*. Matlock: Peak District National Park.

Barnatt, J., & Smith, K. (2004). *The Peak District: Landscapes through time*. Macclesfield: Windgather Press.

Edmonds, M., & Seaborne, T. (2001). *Prehistory in the Peak*. Stroud: Tempus Publishing.

Avebury

Brown, G., Field, D., & McOmish, D. (eds.) (2005). *The Avebury landscape: Aspects of the field archaeology of the Marlborough Downs*. Oxford: Oxbow Books.

Burl, H. A. W. (1976). *Prehistoric Avebury*. Yale University Press.

Edelman, I. (1995). *Discovering Avebury*. Princes Risborough: Shire Publications.

Gillings, M., & Pollard, J. (2004). *Avebury*. London: Duckworth.

Gillings, M., Pollard, J., Wheatley, D., & Peterson, R. (2008). *Landscape of the megaliths: Excavation and fieldwork on the Avebury monuments*. Oxford: Oxbow Books.

Malone, C. (1989). *Avebury*. London: Batsford and English Heritage.

Pollard, J., & Reynolds, A. (2002). *Avebury: The biography of a landscape*. Stroud: Tempus.

Smith, I. F. (1965). *Windmill Hill and Avebury: Excavations by Alexander Keiller, 1925–1939*. Oxford: Clarendon Press.

Whittle, A. (1993). "The neolithic of the Avebury area: Sequence, environment, settlement and the monuments." *Oxford Journal of Archaeology* 12 (1):29–53.

Balnuaran of Clava Burial Cairns

Barclay, G. J. (1991). "The clearing and partial excavation of the cairns at Balnuaran of Clava, Inverness shire, by Miss Kathleen Kennedy, 1930–31." *Proceedings of the Societies of Antiquaries of Scotland 120*: 17–32.

Bradley, R. (2000). *The good stones: A new investigation of the Clava Cairns*. Edinburgh: Society of Antiquaries of Scotland.

Big Moor

Barnatt, J. (1986). "Bronze Age remains on the East Moors of the Peak District." *Derbyshire Archaeological Journal* 106: 18–100.

Machin, M. L. (1975). "Further excavations of the enclosure of Swine Sty, Big Moor, Baslow." *Transactions of the Hunter Archaeological Society* 10 (3): 204–211.

Richardson, C. G. S., & Plant, M. (1969). "Excavations at Swine Sty, Big Moor, 1967–8." *Transactions of the Hunter Archaeological Society* 9 (4): 261–263.

Calanais Stone Circle (Callanish, Western Isles)

Ashmore, P. (2002). *Calanais: The standing stones*. Edinburgh: Historic Scotland.

Ponting, G. (2002). *Callanish and other megalithic sites in the Outer Hebrides*. Glastonbury: Wooden Books.

Castlerigg Stone Circle

Waterhouse, J. (1985). *The stone circles of Cumbria*. Chichester: Phillimore.

Dover Boat

Clark, P. (2004). *The Dover Bronze Age boat*. Swindon: English Heritage.

Great Orme Copper Mines

Dutton, A., & Fasham, P. J. (1994). "Prehistoric copper mining on the Great Orme, Llandudno, Gwynedd." *Proceedings of the Prehistoric Society* 60: 245–286.

Jenkins, D. A., & Lewis, C. A. (1991). "Prehistoric mining for copper in the Great Orme, Llandudno." In P. Budd, B. Chapman, C. Jackson, R. Janaway, & B. Ottaway (eds.), *Archaeological Sciences 1989* (pp. 151–161). Oxford: Oxbow Monograph 9.

O'Brien, W. (1996). *Bronze Age copper mining in Britain and Ireland*. Princes Risborough: Shire Publications.

Grimes Graves

Barber, M., Field, D., & Topping, P. (1999). *The Neolithic flint mines of England*. Swindon: English Heritage.

Green, B. (1993). *Grime's Graves*. London: English Heritage.

Russell, M. (2000). *Flint mines in Neolithic Britain*. Stroud: Tempus.

Topping, P. (2003). "Great sites: Grimes Graves." *British Archaeology* 72 [available at http://www.archaeologyuk.org/ba/ba72/feat2.shtml, accessed 19 March 2014].

Kilmartin Glen

Abernethy, D. (1998). *Kilmartin Glen project*. Glasgow: University of Glasgow.

Abernethy, D. (2000). *Prehistoric monumentality in the Kilmartin Glen, Mid Argyll*. Glasgow: University of Glasgow.

Cook, M., et al. (2010). "Excavations at Upper Largie Quarry, Argyll & Bute, Scotland: New light on the prehistoric ritual landscape of the Kilmartin Glen." *Proceedings of the Prehistoric Society* 7: 165–212.

Mold Gold Cape

Clarke, D. V., Cowie, T. G., & Foxon, A. (1985). *Symbols of power at the time of Stonehenge* (pp. 114, 277–278). Edinburgh: National Museum of Antiquities of Scotland.

Mount Stuart Jet Necklace

Clarke, D. V., Cowie, T. G., & Foxon, A. (1985). *Symbols of power at the time of Stonehenge* (pp. 156, 289). Edinburgh: National Museum of Antiquities of Scotland.

Orkney

Ritchie, A. (1995). *Prehistoric Orkney*. London: Batsford and Historic Scotland.

Wickham-Jones, C. (2007). *Orkney: A historical guide*. Edinburgh: Birlinn.

Orkney: Barnhouse

Richards, C. (2005). *Dwelling among the monuments: The Neolithic village of Barnhouse, Maeshowe passage grave and surrounding monuments at Stenness, Orkney. Cambridge:* Cambridge University Press.

Orkney: Maes Howe

Ashmore, P. J. (1990). *Maes Howe*. Edinburgh: Historic Scotland.

Childe, V. G. (1955). "Maes Howe." *Proceedings of the Societies of Antiquaries of Scotland* 88: 155–72.

MacKie, E. W. (1997). "Maeshowe and the winter solstice: Ceremonial aspects of the Orkney Grooved Ware culture." *Antiquity* 71 (272): 338–359.

Richards, C. (2005). *Dwelling among the monuments: The Neolithic village of Barnhouse, Maeshowe passage grave and surrounding monuments at Stenness, Orkney*. Cambridge: McDonald Institute Monographs.

Orkney: Ring of Brodgar

Downes, J., & Richards, C. (2008). "Ring of Brodgar, Orkney (Stenness parish), excavation." *Discovery and Excavation in Scotland, New series* 9: 136–7.

Ritchie, J. N. G. (1988). "The Ring of Brodgar, Orkney." In C. L. N. Ruggles, *Records in stone: Papers in memory of Alexander Thom (pp. 337–50)*. Cambridge: Cambridge University Press.

Orkney: Skara Brae

Childe, V. G., & Clarke, D. V. (1983). *Skara Brae*. Edinburgh: Her Majesty's Stationery Office.

Clarke, D., & Maguire, P. (2000). *Skara Brae: Northern Europe's best preserved Neolithic village*. Edinburgh: Historic Scotland.

Richards, C. (1991). "Skara Brae: Revisiting a Neolithic village in Orkney." In W. Hanson & E. Slater (eds.), *Scottish archaeology: New perceptions* (pp. 24–43). Aberdeen: Aberdeen University Press.

Shepherd, A. (2000). "Great sites: Skara Brae." *British Archaeology* 55 [available at http://www.archaeologyuk.org/ba/ba55/ba55feat.html, accessed 19 March 2014].

Orkney: Stones of Stenness

Richards, C. (2005). *Dwelling among the monuments: The Neolithic village of Barnhouse, Maeshowe passage grave and surrounding monuments at Stenness, Orkney*. Cambridge: McDonald Institute for Archaeological Research.

Ritchie, J. N. G., & Marwick, E. W. (1975). "The Stones of Stenness, Orkney." *Proceedings of the Society of Antiquaries of Scotland* 107: 1–60.

Silbury Hill

Field, D. (2003). "Great sites: Silbury Hill." *British Archaeology* 70 [available at http://www.archaeologyuk.org/ba/ba70/feat2.shtml, accessed 19 March 2014].

Leary, J., & Field, D. (2010). *The story of Silbury Hill*. London: English Heritage.

Whittle, A. W. R. (1997). *Sacred mound, holy rings: Silbury Hill and the West Kennet palisade enclosures*. Oxford: Oxbow.

Towie Stone Ball

Clarke, D. V., Cowie, T. G., & Foxon, A. (1985). *Symbols of power at the time of Stonehenge* (pp. 54, 254). Edinburgh: National Museum of Antiquities of Scotland.

FARMS, FORTS, AND KINGS

Birdlip Mirror
Green, C. (1949). "The Birdlip early Iron Age burials: A review." *Proceedings of the Prehistoric Society* 15: 188–190.

Staelens, Y. J. E. (1982). "The Birdlip Cemetery." *Transactions of the Bristol and Gloucestershire Archaeological Society* 100: 19–31.

Camulodunum Oppidum
Hawkes, C. F. C., & Crummy, P. (1995). *Colchester Archaeological Report 11: Camulodunum 2*. Colchester: Colchester Archaeological Trust.

Capel Garmon Firedog
Fox, Sir C. (1939). "The Capel Garmon firedog." *Antiquaries Journal* 19 (4): 446–448.

National Museum Wales. (n.d.). *Discovering the Celtic Iron Age in Wales: The Capel Garmon firedog* [available at http://www.museumwales.ac.uk/en/2348/].

Castell Henllys
Mytum, H. C. (1988). *Castell Henllys: A visitor's guide*. York: Department of Archaeology, University of York.

Mytum, H. C. (1999). "Castell Henllys." *Current Archaeology* 161: 164–171.

Danebury hill fort
Cunliffe, B. (1993). *Danebury*. London: Batsford and English Heritage.

Cunliffe, B. (2011). (3rd ed.) *Danebury hillfort*. Stroud: The History Press.

Dartmoor Settlements and Field Systems
Fleming, A. (2007). *The Dartmoor reaves: Investigating prehistoric land divisions*. Oxford: Windgather Press.

Gerrard, S. (1997). *Dartmoor*. London: Batsford and English Heritage.

Eildon Hill Hill Fort
Armit, I. (1998). *Scotland's hidden history*. Stroud: Tempus.

Owen, O. A. (1992). "Eildon Hill North." In J. S. Rideout, O. A. Owen, & E. Halpin, *Hillforts of southern Scotland* (pp. 21–72). Edinburgh: AOC Scotland.

Fiskerton Causeway
Naomi, F., & Parker Pearson, M. (2003). *Fiskerton: An Iron Age timber causeway with Iron Age and Roman votive offerings*. Oxford: Oxbow Books.

Flag Fen Settlement and Field System
Pryor, F. (1991). *Flag Fen: Prehistoric Fenland centre*. London: Batsford and English Heritage.

Pryor, F. (2001). *The Flag Fen basin: Archaeology and environment of a Fenland landscape*. London: English Heritage.

Pryor, F. (2005). *Flag Fen: Life and death of a prehistoric landscape*. Stroud: Tempus.

Pryor, F., & Bamforth, M. (2007). *Flag Fen, Peterborough:Excavations and research, 1995–2007*. Oxford: Oxbow Books.

Gurness Broch
Armit, I. (2003). *Towers in the North: The Brochs of Scotland*. Stroud: Tempus.

Fojut, N. (1993). *The brochs of Gurness and Midhowe*. Edinburgh: Historic Scotland.

Hedges, J. W. (1987). *Bu, Gurness and the brochs of Orkney, part 2: Gurness*. British Archaeological Reports, British series 164, Oxford: Archaeopress.

Hasholme Boat

Hull Museums. (2008). "Hasholme boat" [available at http://www.hullcc.gov.uk/museumcollections/behind-the-scenes/behindthescenesdetail.php?irn=477].

Millet, M., & McGrail, S. (1987). "The archaeology of the Hasholme logboat." *Archaeological Journal* 144: 69–155.

Hengistbury Head

Cunliffe, B. W. (1978). *Hengistbury Head*. London: Elek Books.

Culniffe, B. W. (1987). *Hengistbury Head, Dorset, Volume 1: The prehistoric and Roman settlement, 3500 BC–AD 500*. Oxford: Oxford University Press.

Hoodless, W. A. (2005). *Hengistbury Head*. Poole: Poole Historical Trust.

Jarlshof

Ashmore, P. J. (2002). *Jarlshof: A walk through the past*. Edinburgh: Historic Scotland.

Ritchie, A. (2003). "Great sites: Jarlshof." *British Archaeology* 69: 20–23 [available at http://www.archaeologyuk.org/ba/ba69/feat3.shtml, accessed 19 March 2014].

Lindow Man

Faulkner, N. (2009). "Who killed Lindow Man?" *Current Archaeology* 233: 22–28.

Joy, J. (2009). *Lindow Man*. London: British Museum Press.

Kenyon, D., & Neave, R. (1987). *Lindow Man: His life and times*. Manchester: Manchester Museum.

Stead, I. M., Bourke, J., & Brothwell, D. (1986). *Lindow Man: The body in the bog*. London: British Museum Press.

Little Woodbury

Bersu, G. (1940). "Excavations at Little Woodbury, Wiltshire: part 1, the settlement as revealed by excavation." *Proceedings of the Prehistoric Society* 6: 30–111.

Brailsford, J. W. (1949). "Excavations at Little Woodbury: Part IV, supplementary excavation, 1947." *Proceedings of the Prehistoric Society* 15: 156–168.

Brailsford, J. W., & Jackson, J. W. (1948). "Excavations at Little Woodbury: Part II, the pottery; Part III, the animal remains." *Proceedings of the Prehistoric Society* 14: 1–23.

Hill, J. D. (2000). "Great sites: Little Woodbury." *British Archaeology* 54 [available at http://www.archaeologyuk.org/ba/ba54/ba54feat.html, accessed 19 March 2914].

Llyn Cerrig Bach

Fox, Sir C. (1946). *A find of the early Iron Age from Llyn Cerrig Bach, Anglesey*. Cardiff: National Museum of Wales.

National Museum Wales. (n.d.). *Discovering the Celtic Iron Age in Wales: Artefacts from Llyn Cerrig Bach* [available at http://www.museumwales.ac.uk/en/2363/].

Parker Pearson, M. (2000). "Great sites: Llyn Cerrig Bach." *British Archaeology* 53 [available at http://www.archaeologyuk.org/ba/ba53/ba53feat.html, accessed 19 March 2014].

Maiden Castle Hill Fort

Sharples, N. M. (1991). *Maiden Castle: Excavations and field survey 1985–6*. London: English Heritage.

Wheeler, R. E. M. (1943). *Maiden Castle, Dorset*. London: Society of Antiquaries of London.

Mam Tor Hill Fort

Coombs, D. G., & Thompson, F. H. (1979). "Excavation of the hillfort of Mam Tor, Derbyshire." *Derbyshire Archaeological Journal* 99: 7–51.

Mousa Broch

Armit, I. (2003). *Towers in the north: The brochs of Scotland*. Stroud: Tempus.

Fojut, N. (1982). "Is Mousa a broch?" *Proceedings of the Society of Antiquaries of Scotland* 111: 220–8.

Hamilton, J. (1983). *The brochs of Mousa and Clickhimin*. Edinburgh: Her Majesty's Stationery Office.

Oakbank Crannog

Dixon, T. N. (1984). "Oakbank crannog." *Current Archaeology* 90: 217–220.

Dixon, T. N. (2000). *Crannogs of Loch Tay*. Edinburgh: Scottish Trust for Underwater Archaeology.

Peelhill Hoard

Coles, J. M., & Scott, J. G. (1965). "The Late Bronze Age hoard from Peelhill, Strathaven, Lanarkshire." *Proceedings of the Society of Antiquaries of Scotland* 96: 136–44.

Roos Carr Figurines

Hull City Council 2008 *Hull Museums Collections: Roos Carr Figures: Faces from the past* [available at http://www.hullcc.gov.uk/museumcollections/collections/storydetail.php?irn=484, accessed 20 February 2014].

Snettisham Hoards

Green, B. (1991). "Snettisham treasure." *Current Archaeology* 126: 260–262.

Stead, I. M. (1993). "Snettisham." *Current Archaeology* 135: 97–102.

Stead, I. M. (1991). "The Snettisham Treasure: Excavations in 1990." *Antiquity* 65 (248): 447–465.

Uffington White Horse

Miles, D., Palmer, S., Lock, G., Gosden, C., & Cromarty, A. M. (2003). *Uffington White Horse and its landscape: Investigations at White Horse Hill, Uffington, 1989–95 and Tower Hill, Ashbury, 1993–4*. Thames Valley Landscape Series 18, Oxford: Oxford University School of Archaeology.

Witham Shield

James, S., & Rigby, V. (1997). *Britain and the Celtic Iron Age*. London: British Museum Press.

Jope, E. M. (1971). "The Witham shield." *British Museum Quarterly* 35 (1): 61–69.

CHAPTER 5. HISTORIC SITES AND FINDS
ROMAN INTERLUDE

Antonine Wall Frontier

Breeze, D. J. (2006). *The Antonine Wall*. Edinburgh: John Donald.

Hanson, W. S., & Maxwell, G. S. (1983). *Rome's north west frontier: The Antonine Wall*. Edinburgh: Edinburgh University.

Robertson, A. S. (2001). *The Antonine Wall: A handbook to the surviving remains*. Glasgow: Glasgow Archaeological Society.

The Antonine Wall: Frontiers of the Roman Empire, http://www.antoninewall.org/history.php [accessed 19 March 2014].

Bath Temple and Baths

Cunliffe, B. (1971). *Roman Bath discovered*. London: Routledge.

Cunliffe, B. (1996). *Roman Bath*. London: Batsford and English Heritage.

Cunliffe, B. (2000). *Roman Bath discovered*. Stroud: Tempus Publishing.

Gerrard, J. (2008). "The end of Roman Bath." *Current Archaeology* 217: 24–31.

Bignor Villa

Aldsworth, F. G., & Rudling, D. R. (1995). "Excavations at Bignor Roman villa, 1985–1990." *Sussex Archaeological Collections* 133: 103–188.

Frere, S. (1982). "The Bignor villa." *Britannia* 13: 135–195.

Henig, M. (2000). "Great sites: Bignor Roman villa." *British Archaeology* 51 [available at http://www.archaeologyuk.org/ba/ba51/ba51feat.html, accessed 19 March 2014].

Caerleon Fort and Amphitheatre

Boon, G. C. (1972). *Isca, the Roman legionary fortress at Caerleon, Monmouthshire*. Cardiff: National Museum of Wales.

Boon, G. C. (1987). *The legionary fortress of Caerleon-Isca*. Caerleon: Roman Legionary Museum.

Knight, J. K. (1994). *Caerleon Roman Fortress*. Cardiff: Cadw.

Deskford Carnyx

Carnyx & Co. http://www.carnyxscotland.co.uk/about/about_carnyx_co [accessed 19 March 2014].

National Museums Scotland. (n.d.). *Deskford carnyx* [available at http://www.nms.ac.uk/highlights/objects_in_focus/deskford_carnyx.aspx, accessed 19 March 2014].

Hadrian's Wall Frontier

Bédoyère, G. de la (1998). *Hadrian's Wall: A history and guide*. Stroud: Tempus.

Birley, A. (2002). *Garrison life at Vindolanda: A band of brothers*. Stroud: The History Press.

Birley, R. (2012). *Vindolanda guide: The home of Britain's finest treasures*. Greenhead: Roman Army Museum Publications.

Bishop, M. C., & Dore, J. N. (1988). *Corbridge excavations of the Roman fort and town 1947–80*. London: English Heritage.

Breeze, D. J. (2006). *Handbook to the Roman Wall*. Newcastle: Society of Antiquaries of Newcastle upon Tyne.

Breeze, D. J., & Dobson, B. (2000). *Hadrian's Wall*. (4th ed.) London: Penguin Books.

Burton, A. (2004). *Hadrian's Wall path*. London: Aurum Press.

Crow, J. (2012). *Housesteads Roman fort*. London: Batsford and English Heritage.

Dore, J. N. (1989). *Corbridge Roman site*. London: English Heritage.

Hodgson, N. (2011). *Chesters Roman fort*. London: English Heritage.

Johnson, S. (1989). *Hadrian's Wall*. London: Batsford and English Heritage.

Wilmott, T. (2005), *Birdoswald Roman fort*. London: English Heritage.

Hinton St. Mary Mosaic

BBC. (2010). *A history of the world: Hinton St. Mary mosaic* [available at http://www.bbc.co.uk/ahistoryoftheworld/objects/VfupdXVjTM6crACGDU-6uA, accessed 1March 2014].

Painter, K. S. (1967). "The Roman site at Hinton St. Mary, Dorset." *British Museum Quarterly* 3 (31): 15–31.

Pearce, S. (2008). "The Hinton St. Mary mosaic: Christ or emperor?" *Britannia* 39: 193–218.

Hoxne Hoard

Bland, R., & Johns, C. (1993). *The Hoxne treasure: An illustrated introduction*. London: British Museum Press.

Johns, C. (2010). *The Hoxne late Roman treasure: Gold jewellery and silver plate*. London: British Museum Press.

Spitalfields Woman

Thomas, C. (1999). "Laid to rest on a pillow of bay leaves." *British Archaeology* 50 [available at http://www.archaeologyuk.org/ba/ba50/ba50feat.html].

Tre'r Ceiri Hill Fort

Hogg, A. H. A. (1962). "Garn Boduan and Tre'r Ceiri, excavations at two Caernarvonshire hill-forts." *Archaeological Journal* 117: 1–39.

MIGRATIONS AND KINGDOM

Snyder, C. A. (1997). "A gazetteer of sub-Roman Britain (AD 400–600): The British sites." *Internet Archaeology* 3 [available at http://intarch.ac.uk//journal/issue3/snyder/toc.html, accessed 19 March 2104].

Aberlemno Pictish Stone

Cummins, W. A. (1999). *The Picts and their symbols*. Stroud: Sutton Publishing.

Fraser, J. E. (2006). *The Pictish conquest: The Battle of Dunnichen 685 and the birth of Scotland*. Stroud: Tempus.

Laing, L. (2000). "The chronology and context of Pictish relief sculpture." *Medieval Archaeology* 34: 81–114.

Cadbury Castle Fort

Alcock, L. (1995). *Cadbury Castle, Somerset: The early Medieval archaeology.* Cardiff: University of Wales Press.

Barrett, J. (2000). *Cadbury Castle, Somerset: The late prehistoric and early historic archaeology.* London: English Heritage.

Tabor, R. (2008). *Cadbury Castle: The hillfort and landscapes.* Stroud: The History Press.

Cannington Cemetery

Rahtz, P., Hirst, S. M., & Wright, S. M. (2000). *Cannington cemetery: Excavations 1962–3 of prehistoric, Roman, post-Roman and later features at Cannington Park Quarry, near Bridgwater, Somerset.* Britannia Monograph 17, London: Society for the Promotion of Roman Studies.

Canterbury St. Martin's Church

Fisher, E. A. (1962). *The greater Anglo-Saxon churches: An architectural-historical study* (pp. 355–362). London: Faber and Faber.

Jenkins, F. (1965). "St. Martin's church at Canterbury: A survey of the earliest structural features." *Medieval Archaeology* 9: 11–15.

Taylor, H. M., & Taylor, J. (1965). *Anglo-Saxon architecture, Volume 1* (pp. 143–145). Cambridge: Cambridge University Press.

Dunadd Fort

Lane, A., & Campbell, E. (2000). *Excavations at Dunadd: An early Dalriadic capital.* Oxford: Oxbow Monographs.

Lane, A., & Campbell, E. (n.d.). *Dunadd: An early Dalriadic capital,* http://www.gla.ac.uk/schools/humanities/research/archaeologyresearch/projects/dunadddigitalarchive/ [accessed 19 March 2014].

Franks Casket

Webster, L. (2012). *The Franks Casket: Objects in focus.* London: British Museum Press.

Lindisfarne Gospels

Backhouse, J. (1981). *The Lindisfarne Gospels.* Oxford: Phaidon.

Brown, M. P. (2010). *The Lindisfarne Gospels and the early Medieval world.* London: The British Library.

Mucking Settlement and Cemetery

Clark, A. (1993). *Excavations at Mucking, volume 1: The site atlas.* English Heritage Archaeological Report 20, London: English Heritage.

Hamerow, H. (1993). *Excavations at Mucking, volume 2: The Anglo-Saxon settlement.* English Heritage Archaeological Report 21, London: English Heritage.

Hirst, S., & Clark, D. (2009). *Excavations at Mucking, volume 3: The Anglo-Saxon cemeteries.* London: Museum of London Archaeology.

Jones, W., & M. U. (1974). "The early Saxon landscape at Mucking, Essex." In T. Rowley (ed.) *Anglo-Saxon settlement and landscape.* British Archaeological Reports British Series 6, Oxford: Archaeopress: 20–35.

Offa's Dyke
Hill, D., & Worthington, M. (2003). *Offa's Dyke: History and guide.* Stroud: Tempus.
Noble , F. (ed. M. Gelling) (1983). *Offa's Dyke reviewed.* British Archaeological Reports, British Series 114, Oxford: Archaeopress.

Ruthwell Cross
Cassidy, B. (1993). *The Ruthwell Cross: Papers from the colloquium sponsored by the Index of Christian Art.* Princeton University, 8 December 1989, Princeton: Princeton University Press.
Wilson, D. M. (1984). *Anglo-Saxon art: From the seventh century to the Norman Conquest.* London: Thames and Hudson.

Southampton Town
Brisbane, M. (1988). "Hamwic (Saxon Southampton): An eighth century port and production centre." In R. Hodges and B. Hobley (eds.), *The rebirth of towns in the west AD 700–1050.* CBA Research Report 68: 101–108. York: Council for British Archaeology.
Hamerow, H. (2002). "Great sites: Hamwic." *British Archaeology* 66 [available at http://www.archaeologyuk.org/ba/ba66/feat3.shtml, accessed 19 March 2014].
Morton, A. D. (1992). *Excavations at Hamwic: Volume 1.* CBA Research Report 84. London: Council for British Archaeology.
Morton, A. D. (1999). "Hamwic in its context." In M. Anderton (ed.) *Anglo-Saxon trading centres: Beyond the emporia* (pp. 48–62). Glasgow: Cruithne Press.
Pay, S. (1987). *Hamwic: A Saxon town.* Southampton City Museums archaeology series, Horndean: Milestone Publications.

Spong Hill Cemetery
Higham, N. J. (2013). "The Anglo-Saxon cemetery at Spong Hill." In N. J. Higham and M. J. Ryan, *The Anglo-Saxon world* (pp. 112–119). Yale: Yale University Press.
Hills, C., & Lucy, S. (2013). *Spong Hill, part IX: Chronology and synthesis.* Cambridge: McDonald Institute for Archaeological Research.

Sutton Hoo Cemetery
Carver, M. O. H. (ed.) (1992). *The age of Sutton Hoo: The seventh century in northwestern Europe.* Woodbridge: Boydell Press.
Carver, M. O. H. (1998). *Sutton Hoo: Burial ground of kings?* London: British Museum.
Evans, A. C. (1986). *The Sutton Hoo ship burial.* London: British Museum.
Plunkett, S. J. (2002). *Sutton Hoo, Suffolk.* Site guidebook. London: The National Trust.

Tintagel Fort
Barrowman, R. C., Batey, C. E., & Morris, C. D. (2007). *Excavations at Tintagel Castle, Cornwall, 1990–1999.* London: Society of Antiquaries of London.
Thomas, C. (1993). *Tintagel: Arthur and archaeology.* London: Batsford and English Heritage.

Traprain Law Treasure
Armit, I. (2001). "Great sites: Traprain law." *British Archaeology* 57 [available at http://www.archaeologyuk.org/ba/ba57/feat1.html, accessed 28 February 2014].

Burley, E. (1956). "A catalogue and survey of the metal-work from Traprain Law." *Proceedings of the Society of Antiquaries of Scotland* 89: 118–226.

Curle, A. O. (1923). *The treasure of Traprain: A Scottish hoard of Roman silver plate.* Glasgow: MacLehose.

Wearmouth-Jarrow Monastery

Cramp, R. (2005). *Wearmouth and Jarrow monastic sites: Volume I.* Swindon: English Heritage.

Fisher, E. A. (1962). *The greater Anglo-Saxon churches: An architectural-historical study* (pp. 76–101). London: Faber and Faber.

West Heslerton Settlement and Cemetery

Montgomery, J., Evans, J. A., Powlesland, D., & Roberts, C. A. (2005). "Continuity or colonization in Anglo-Saxon England? Isotope evidence for mobility, subsistence practice, and status at West Heslerton." *American Journal of Physical Anthropology* 126 (2): 123–138.

Powlesland, D., et al. (1998). "The West Heslerton assessment." *Internet Archaeology* 5 [available at http://intarch.ac.uk/journal/issue5/westhes_index.html, accessed 19 March 2014].

Powlesland, D. (1999). "The Anglo-Saxon settlement at West Heslerton, North Yorkshire." In J. Hawkes and S. Mills (eds.) *Northumbria's golden age* (pp. 55–65). Stroud: Sutton.

Wroxeter Town

Barker, P., & White, R. (1999). *Wroxeter Roman city.* Swindon: English Heritage.

Ellis, P. (2000). *The Roman baths and macellum at Wroxeter,* Swindon: English Heritage.

Webster, G. (2002). *The legionary fortress at Wroxeter: Excavations by Graham Webster, 1955–1985.* Swindon. English Heritage.

White, R., & Barker, P. (1998). *Wroxeter: Life & death of a Roman city.* Stroud: Tempus.

Yeavering

Frodsham, P., & O Brien, C. (eds.) (2005). *Yeavering: People, power, place.* Stroud. Tempus.

Hinton, D. (2001). "Great sites: Yeavering." *British Archaeology* 58 [available at http://www.archaeologyuk.org/ba/ba58/feat3.shtml, accessed 19 March 2014].

Hope-Taylor, B. (1977). *Yeavering, an Anglo-British centre of early Northumbria.* London: Her Majesty's Stationery Office.

Pearson, S. (1998). *Yeavering Bell hillfort, Northumberland.* London: English Heritage.

MEDIEVAL MONARCHIES

Æthelwold's Benedictional

Backhouse, J., Turner, D. H., & Webster, L. (eds.) (1984). *The golden age of Anglo-Saxon art, 966–1066.* London: British Museum.

Prescott, A. (2002). *The Benedictional of St. Æthelwold: A masterpiece of Anglo-Saxon art—a facsimilie*. London: British Library.

Wilson, D. M. (1984). *Anglo-Saxon art from the seventh century to the Norman Conquest*. London: Thames and Hudson.

Alfred Jewel

Hinton, D. A. (2008). *The Alfred Jewel: And other late Anglo-Saxon decorated metalwork*. Oxford: Ashmolean Museum.

Wilson, D. M. (1984). *Anglo-Saxon art from the seventh century to the Norman Conquest*. London: Thames and Hudson.

Barton-upon-Humber Church

Fisher, E. A. (1962). *The greater Anglo-Saxon churches: An architectural-historical study* (pp. 264–260). London: Faber and Faber.

Rodwell, W. (1983). *St. Peter's church, Barton-upon-Humber*. London: Her Majesty's Stationery Office.

Rodwell, W., & Atkins, C. (2011). *St. Peter's, Barton-upon-Humber, Lincolnshire: Volume 1, history, archaeology and architecture*. Oxford: Oxbow Books.

Canterbury Cathedral

Blockley, K. (1993). "Canterbury Cathedral." *Current Archaeology* 12 (4): 124–130.

Blockley, K., Sparks, M., & Tatton-Brown, T. (1997). *Canterbury cathedral nave: Archaeology, history and architecture*. Canterbury: Canterbury Archaeological Trust.

Collinson, P., Ramsay, N., & Sparks, M. (1995). *A history of Canterbury Cathedral*. Oxford: Oxford University Press.

Woodman, F. (1981). *The architectural history of Canterbury Cathedral*. London: Routledge & Kegan Paul.

Canterbury St. Augustine's Abbey (Kent)

Gem, R. (1997). *St. Augustine's Abbey, Canterbury*. London: Batsford and English Heritage.

Chester Rows

Alcock, N. W. (2001). "The origins of the Chester Rows: A model." *Medieval Archaeology* 45: 226–228.

Carrington, P. (1994). *Chester*. London: Batsford and English Heritage.

Grenville, J., Figueiredo, P. de, & Brown, A. (1999). *The Rows of Chester: The Chester Rows Research Project*. London: English Heritage.

Durham Castle and Cathedral

Roberts, M. (1994). *Durham*. London: Batsford and English Heritage.

Roberts, M. (2003). *Durham: 1,000 years of history*. Stroud: History Press.

Fountains Abbey

Coppack, G. (1993). *Fountains Abbey*. London: Batsford and English Heritage.

Coppack, G. (2003). *Fountains Abbey. The Cistercians in Northern England*. Stroud: Tempus.

Mauchline, M., & Greeves, L. (2005). *Fountains Abbey and Studley Royal, North Yorkshire*. London: National Trust.

Goltho Aristocratic Residence

Beresford, G. (1987). *Goltho: The development of an early Medieval manor c. 850–1150*. London: English Heritage.

Gosforth Cross

Berg, K. (1958). "The Gosforth Cross." *Journal of the Warburg and Courtauld Institutes* 21 (1–2): 27–43.

Lewis Chessmen

Robinson, J. (2004). *The Lewis chessmen*. London: British Museum Press.

London Medieval Waterfront

Milne, G. (2002). "Great sites: London's Medieval waterfront." *British Archaeology* 68 BA [available at http://www.archaeologyuk.org/ba/ba68/feat3.shtml, accessed 19 March 2014].

Tower of London

Impey, E., & Parnell, G. (2000). *The Tower of London: The official illustrated history*. London: Merrell Publishers.

Parnell, G. (1993). *The Tower of London*. London: Batsford and English Heritage.

Parnell, G. (2009). *The Tower of London: Past and present*. Stroud: History Press.

Luttrell Psalter

Backhouse, J. (2000). *Medieval rural life in the Luttrell Psalter*. Toronto: University of Toronto Press.

Brown, M. P. (2006). *The world of the Luttrell Psalter*. London: British Library.

Repton Church and Viking Burials

Biddle, M., & Kjolbye-Biddle, B. (1992). "Repton and the Vikings." *Antiquity* 66 (250): 36–51.

Richards, J. D., Beswick, P., Bond, J., Jecock, M., McKinley, J., Rowland, S., & Worley, F. (2004). "Excavations at the Viking barrow cemetery at Heath Wood, Ingleby, Derbyshire." *Antiquaries Journal* 84: 23–116.

Taylor, H. M. (1987). "St. Wystan's Church, Repton, Derbyshire. A reconstruction essay." *The Archaeological Journal* 144: 205–45.

St. Cuthbert's Vestments

Miller, M. (2011). "The significance of St. Cuthbert's vestments." In P. Clarke & T. Claydon (eds.), *Saints and sanctity* (pp. 90–102). Studies in Church History 47, Woodbridge: Boydell & Brewer.

Wilson, D. M. (1984). *Anglo-Saxon art from the seventh century to the Norman Conquest*. London: Thames and Hudson.

Sandal Castle

Butler, L. (1991). *Sandal Castle*. Wakefield: Wakefield Historical Publications.

Mayes, P., & Butler, L. A. S. (1983). *Sandal Castle excavations 1964–1973*. Wakefield: Wakefield Historical Publications.

Towton Battlefield

Fiorato, V., Boylston, A., & Knüsel, C. (2007). (2nd ed.) *Blood red roses: The archaeology of a mass grave from the Battle of Towton AD 1461*. Oxford: Oxbow Books.

Gravett, C. (2003). *Towton 1461. England's bloodiest battle*. Campaign 120, Oxford: Osprey Publishing.

Vale of York Hoard

Williams, G., & Ager, B. (2010). *The Vale of York hoard*. London: British Museum.

Welsh Castles and Towns of Edward I

Ashbee, J. (2007). *Conwy Castle*. Cardiff: Cadw.

Gravett, C. (2007). *The castles of Edward I in Wales 1277–1307*. Oxford: Osprey Publishing.

Taylor, A. (2004). *Beaumaris Castle*. (5th ed.) Cardiff: Cadw.

Taylor, A. (2007). *Harlech Castle*. (4th ed.) Cardiff: Cadw.

Taylor, A. (2008). *Caernarfon Castle*. (6th ed.) Cardiff: Cadw.

Williams, D., & Kenyon, J. (eds.) (2010). *The impact of Edwardian castles in Wales*. Oxford: Oxbow Books.

Westminster Abbey

Jenkyns, R. (2011). *Westminster Abbey: A thousand years of national pageantry*. London: Profile Books.

Wilkinson, J., & Knighton, C. S. (2010). *Crown and cloister: The royal story of Westminster Abbey*. London: Scala.

Westminster Palace

Cooke, Sir R. (1987). *The Palace of Westminster*. London: Burton Skira.

Field, J. (2002). *The story of Parliament in the Palace of Westminster*. London: James & James Publishers.

Riding, C., & Riding, J. (eds.) (2000). *The Houses of Parliament: History, art, architecture*. London: Merrell Publishers.

Wharram Percy Deserted Medieval Village

Beresford, M., & Hurst, J. (1990). *Wharram Percy deserted Medieval village*. London: Batsford and English Heritage.

Bond, J. (2000). "Great sites: Wharram Percy." *British Archaeology* 52 [available at http://www.archaeologyuk.org/ba/ba52/ba52feat.html, accessed 19 March 2014].

Oswald, A. (2004). *Wharram Percy deserted Medieval village, North Yorkshire: Archaeological investigation and survey*. York: English Heritage.

Wrathmell, S. (1996). *Wharram Percy: Deserted Medieval village*. London: English Heritage.

Wrathmell, S. (2012). *Wharram: A study of settlement on the Yorkshire Wolds, XIII. A history of Wharram Percy and its neighbours*. York: University of York Department of Archaeology.

York City

Hall, R. (1994). *Viking Age York*. London: Batsford and English Heritage.

Hall, R. (1996). *York*. London: Batsford and English Heritage.

Ottaway, P. (1993). *Roman York*. London: Batsford and English Heritage.

REFORMATION AND REVOLUTION

Berwick-upon-Tweed Fortifications

Green, D. (1982). *Blenheim Palace.* Oxford: Alden Press.

Grove, D. (1999). *Berwick barracks and fortifications.* London: English Heritage.

MacIvor, I. (1990). *The fortifications of Berwick-upon-Tweed.* London: English Heritage. *Blenheim Palace.*

Cornish and West Devon Mines

Hancock, P. (2008). *The mining heritage of Cornwall and West Devon.* Wellington: Halsgrove.

Crossbones Graveyard

Brickley, M., Miles, A., & Stainer, H. (1999). *The Crossbones burial ground, Redcross Way, Southwark.* London: Museum of London Archaeology Service

Constable, J. (1999). *The Southwark mysteries.* London: Oberon Books.

Crossbones. (n.d.) *Crossbones graveyard—the living herstory,* http://www.crossbones.org.uk/ [accessed 16 January 2012].

International Union of Sex Workers. (2009). *Crossbones graveyard,* http://www.iusw.org/campaigns/cross-bones-graveyard/ [accessed 16 January 2012].

Culloden Battlefield

Reid, S. (2002). *Culloden Moor 1746: The death of the Jacobite cause.* Campaign series 106, Oxford: Osprey Publishing.

Reid, S. (2005). (2nd ed.) *Culloden 1746.* Barnsley: Pen and Sword Books.

Edinburgh Old Town

Edinburgh Old Town Association. (n.d.). Available at http://www.eota.org.uk/ [accessed 19 March 2014].

MacIvor, I. (1993). *Edinburgh Castle.* London: Batsford.

Tabraham, C. (2008). *Edinburgh Castle: Official guide.* Edinburgh: Historic Scotland.

Greenwich Hospital

Bold, J., Guillery, P., & Kendall, D. (2001). *Greenwich: An architectural history of the Royal Hospital for Seamen and the Queen's House.* Yale: Yale University Press.

Mary Rose Warship

Childs, D. (2007). *The warship Mary Rose: The life and times of King Henry VIII's flagship.* London: Chatham Publishing.

Gardiner, J. (ed.) (2005). *Before the mast: Life and death aboard the Mary Rose.* The Archaeology of the Mary Rose 4, Portsmouth: The Mary Rose Trust.

Hildred, A. (ed.) (2011). *Weapons of warre: The armaments of the Mary Rose.* The Archaeology of the Mary Rose 3, Portsmouth: The Mary Rose Trust.

Jones, M. (ed.) (2003). *For future generations: Conservation of a Tudor maritime collection.* The Archaeology of the Mary Rose 5, Portsmouth: The Mary Rose Trust.

Marsden, P. (2003). *Sealed by time: The loss and recovery of the Mary Rose.* The Archaeology of the Mary Rose 1, Portsmouth: The Mary Rose Trust.

Marsden, P. (ed.) (2009). *Your noblest shippe: Anatomy of a Tudor warship*. The Archaeology of the Mary Rose 2, Portsmouth: The Mary Rose Trust.

Rule, M. (1983). (2nd ed.) *The Mary Rose: The excavation and raising of Henry VIII's flagship*. London: Conway Maritime Press.

Stirland, A. J. (2000). *Raising the dead: The skeleton crew of Henry VIII's great ship, the Mary Rose*. Chichester: John Wiley & Sons.

Newark Fortifications

Hopkins, G. (2012). *The third & final siege of Newark, 26th November 1645–8th May 1646*, http://eventplan.co.uk/page74.html [accessed 19 March 2014].

Warner, T. (2003). *Newark Civil War and siegeworks*. Nottingham: Nottingham-shire County Council.

Nonsuch Palace

Biddle, M. (2005). *Nonsuch Palace: The material culture of a noble restoration household*. Oxford: Oxbow Books.

Biddle, M. (2012). "Nonsuch, Henry VIII's mirror for a prince: Sources and interpretation." In C. M. Sicca and L. A. Waldman (eds.), *The Anglo-Florentine Renaissance: Art for the early Tudors* (pp. 307–350). Yale: Yale University Press.

Gaimster, D. (2001). "Great sites: Nonsuch Palace." *British Archaeology* 60 [available at http://www.archaeologyuk.org/ba/ba60/feat1.shtml, accessed 19 March 2014].

Rose and Globe Theatres

Bowsher, J. (1998). *The Rose Theatre: An archaeological discovery*. London: Museum of London.

Bowsher, J., & Miller, P. (2009). *The Rose and the Globe— playhouses of Shakespeare's Bankside, Southwark*. London: Museum of London.

Mulryne, J. R., & Shewring, M. (1997). *Shakespeare's Globe rebuilt*. London: Cambridge University Press.

Studley Royal Park

Mauchline, M., & Greeves, L. (2005). *Fountains Abbey and Studley Royal, North Yorkshire*. London: National Trust.

Newman, M. A. (1996). *Fountains Abbey and Studley Royal estate: An archaeological survey*. London: National Trust.

Newman, M. A. (1993). *Medieval village of Studley Magna: Excavations at Studley Royal stables 1989–91*. London: National Trust.

INDUSTRIAL ADVANCE AND THE MODERN WORLD

Arthur's Seat Coffins

Dash, M. (2013). "Edinburgh's mysterious miniature coffins." *Smithsonian Magazine*, http://www.smithsonianmag.com/history/edinburghs-mysterious-miniature-coffins-22371426/?no-ist [accessed 19 march 2014].

Dash, M. (2010). "The miniature coffins found on Arthur's Seat." *A Fortean in the Archives*, http://aforteantinthearchives.wordpress.com/2010/01/10/the-miniature-coffins-found-on-arthurs-seat/ [accessed 19 March 2014].

Bath
Borsay, P. (2000). *The image of Georgian Bath, 1700–2000: Towns, heritage, and history*. Oxford: Oxford University Press.
Cunliffe, B. (1986). *The City of Bath*. Gloucester: Alan Sutton Publishing.
Blaenavon Industrial Landscape
Barber, C. (2002). *Exploring Blaenavon industrial landscape World Heritage Site*. Llanfoist: Blorenge Books.
Thomas, W. G. (1981). *Big Pit, Blaenavon*. Cardiff: National Museum of Wales.
Wakelin, P. (2006). *Blaenavon ironworks and World Heritage landscape*. Cardiff: Cadw.
Chatham Dockyard
MacDougall, P. (2012). *Chatham Dockyard: The rise and fall of a military industrial complex*. Stroud: The History Press.
Symonds, M. (2012). "Finding HMS Namur." *Current Archaeology* 273 [available at http://www.archaeology.co.uk/articles/features/finding-hms-namur.htm, accessed 19 February 2014].
Derwent Valley Mills
Cooper, B. (1983). *Transformation of a valley: The Derbyshire Derwent*. London: Heinemann.
Menuge, A. (1993). "The cotton mills of the Derbyshire Derwent and its tributaries." *Industrial Archaeology Review* XVI (1): 38–61.
Edinburgh New Town
Nimmo, I. (1991). *Edinburgh: The new town*. Edinburgh: John Donald Books.
Forth Bridge
Glen, A., Craig Bowman, C., Andrew, J., Donaldson, S-J., & Dodds, K. (2012). *Forth Bridge: Restoring an icon*. Ramsey: Lily Publications.
Paxton, R. (1990). *100 years of the Forth Bridge*. London: Thomas Telford.
SS Great Britain
Ball, A., & Wright, D. (1981). *SS Great Britain*. London: David & Charles.
Corlett, E. (1990). *The iron ship: The story of Brunel's SS Great Britain*. London: Conway Maritime Press.
Greenham Common Protest Site
Schofield, J. (2009). "An archaeology of protest at Greenham Common Air Base." *British Archaeology* 104 [available at: http://www.britarch.ac.uk/ba/ba104/feat3.shtml].
Ironbridge Gorge
Alfrey, J., & Clark, C. (1993). *The landscape of industry: Patterns of change in the Ironbridge Gorge*. London: Routledge.
Clark, C. M. (1993). *Ironbridge Gorge*. London: Batsford and English Heritage.
Jodrell Bank Observatory
Edmonds, M. (2010). "When they come to model Heaven: Big science and the monumental in post-war Britain." *Antiquity* 84 (325): 774–795.
Kew Royal Botanic Gardens
Desmond, R. (2007). (2nd ed.) *The history of the Royal Botanic Gardens Kew*. London: Harvill Press.

Liverpool
Belchem, J. (2006). *Liverpool 800: Culture, character & history*. Liverpool: Liverpool University Press.

New Lanark
Donnachie, I., & Hewitt, G. (1993). *Historic New Lanark: The Dale and Owen industrial community since 1785*. Edinburgh: Edinburgh University Press.

Pontcysyllte Aqueduct and Canal
Beard, C. (2010). *Pontcysyllte*. Llandysul: Gomer Press.

St. Kilda
Fleming, A. (2005). *St. Kilda and the wider world: Tales of an iconic island*. Oxford: Windgather Press.

Maclean, C. (1977). *Island on the edge of the world: The story of St. Kilda*. Edinburgh: Canongate.

Quine, D. (2000). *St. Kilda*. Grantown-on-Spey: Colin Baxter Island Guides.

Steel, T. (1988). *The life and death of St. Kilda*. London: Fontana.

St. Pancras Railway Station
Allington-Jones, L. (2013). "The phoenix: The role of conservation ethics in the development of St. Pancras Railway Station (London, UK)." *Journal of Conservation and Museum Studies* 11 (1): 1–21 [available at http://www.jcms-journal.com/article/download/jcms.1021205/72, accessed 8 December 2013].

Bradley, S. (2007). *St. Pancras station*. London: Profile Books.

Emery, P. A. (2006). "End of the line." *British Archaeology* 88 [available at http://www.archaeologyuk.org/ba/ba88/feat1.shtml, accessed 8 December 2013].

Emery, P. A., & Wooldridge, K. (2011). *St. Pancras burial ground: Excavations for St. Pancras International, the London terminus of High Speed 1, 2002–3*. London: Gifford.

Saltaire
Binns, S. (2013). *The aesthetics of utopia: Saltaire, Akroydon and Bedford Park*. Reading: Spire Books.

Firth, G., & Hitt, M. (2010). *Saltaire through time*. Stroud: Amberley Publishing.

Jackson, N., Lintonbon, J., & Staples, B. (2009). *Saltaire: The making of a model town*. Reading: Spire Books.

HMS Victory
Christopher, J. (2010). *The HMS Victory story*. Stroud: The History Press.

Eastland, J., & Ballantyne, I. (2011). *HMS Victory: First rate 1765*. Barnsley: Pen and Sword Books.

McGowan, A. (1999). *HMS Victory: Her construction, career and restoration*. Barnsley: Pen and Sword Books.

Welsh Slate Industry
Gwyn, D. (2005). "The landscape archaeology of the Vale of Ffestiniog." *Industrial Archaeology Review* 27 (1): 129–136.

Jones, R. C. (2006). *Dinorwic: The Llanberis slate quarry, 1780–1969*. Wrexham: Bridge Books.

Richards, A. J. (2001). *The slate railways of Wales*. Llanrwst: Gwasg Carreg Gwalch.
Williams, N. (2002). *The slate industry*. Princes Risborough: Shire Books.
Whitefield, Nelson Housing Estate
Walker, L. (2004). "Home and heritage." *British Archaeology* 75 [available at http://www.archaeologyuk.org/ba/ba75/feat4.shtml, accessed December 2013].
Wray, N. (2001). *By industry and integrity: Nelson a late 19th century industrial town*. London: English Heritage.

CHAPTER 6. MAJOR PERSONALITIES IN ARCHAEOLOGY

Fagan, B. (2003). *Archaeologists: Explorers of the human past*. Oxford: Oxford University Press.

THE PIONEERS

Sir William Dugdale
Broadway, J. (2011). *William Dugdale: A life of the Warwickshire historian and herald*. Gloucester: Xmera.
Dyer, C., & Richardson, C. (eds.) (2009). *William Dugdale, historian, 1605–1686: His life, his writings and his county*. Woodbridge: Boydell Press.
Lancaster, C. (2008). *Seeing England: Antiquaries, travellers and naturalists*. Stroud: Nonsuch.
Parry, G. (1995). *The trophies of time: English antiquarians of the seventeenth century*. Oxford: Oxford University Press
John Aubrey
Burl, A. (2010). *John Aubrey and stone circles: Britain's first archaeologist, from Avebury to Stonehenge*. Stroud: Amberley.
Lancaster, C. (2008). *Seeing England: Antiquaries, travellers and naturalists*. Stroud: Nonsuch.
Parry, G. (1995). *The trophies of time: English antiquarians of the seventeenth century*. Oxford: Oxford University Press.
Poole, W. (2010). *John Aubrey and the advancement of learning*. Oxford: Bodleian Library.
Tylden-Wright, D. (1991). *John Aubrey: A life*, London: HarperCollins.
William Stukeley
Haycock, D. B. (2002). *William Stukeley: Science, religion and archaeology in eighteenth-century England*. Woodbridge: Boydell Press.
Piggot, S. (1985). *William Stukeley: An eighteenth-century antiquary*. New York: Thames and Hudson.

THE FOUNDERS

Sir John Evans
MacGregor, A. (2008). *Sir John Evans 1823–1908: Antiquity, commerce and natural science in the age of Darwin*. Oxford: Ashmolean Museum.

Lord Avebury (Sir John Lubbock)
Owen, J. (2013). *Darwin's Apprentice: An archaeological biography of John Lubbock*. Barnsley: Pen and Sword.

Patton, M. (1997). *Science, politics & business in the work of Sir John Lubbock—a man of universal mind*. London: Ashgate.

Thompson, M. (2009). *Darwin's pupil: The place of Sir John Lubbock, Lord Avebury, 1834–1913, in late Victorian and Edwardian England*. Ely: Melrose Books.

Augustus Pitt-Rivers
Bowden, M. (1991). *Pitt Rivers: The life and archaeological work of Lieutenant-General Augustus Henry Lane Fox Pitt Rivers, DCL, FRS, FSA*. Cambridge: Cambridge University Press.

Thompson, M. W. (1977). *General Pitt-Rivers: Evolution and archaeology in the nineteenth century*. Bradford-on-Avon: Moonraker Press.

Sir Flinders Petrie
Drower, M. S. (1995). (rev. ed.) *Flinders Petrie: A life in archaeology*. Madison: University of Wisconsin Press.

Petrie, W. M. F. (1931). *Seventy years in archaeology*. London: Sampson, Low and Marston.

John Mortimer
Harrison, S. (2011). *John Robert Mortimer: The life of a nineteenth century East Yorkshire archaeologist*. Pickering: Blackthorn Press.

Hicks, D. (ed.) (1978). *A Victorian boyhood on the Wolds: The recollections of J. R. Mortimer*. East Yorkshire Local History Series 34, Beverley: East Yorkshire Local History Society.

Margaret Murray
Cohen, G. M., & Joukowsky, M. S. (2004). *Breaking ground: Pioneering women archaeologists*. Ann Arbor: University of Michigan.

Murray, M. A. (1963). *My first hundred years*. London: William Kimber.

Sheppard, L. K. (2013). *The life of Margaret Alice Murray: A woman's work in archaeology*. New York: Lexington Books.

Whitehouse, R. (2013). "Margaret Murray (1863–1963): Pioneer Egyptologist, feminist and first female archaeology lecturer." *Archaeology International* 16: 120–127.

THE HEROIC AGE

Sir Leonard Woolley
Winstone, H. V. F. (1990). *Woolley of Ur*. London: Secker and Warburg.

Gertrude Caton-Thompson

Caton-Thompson, G. (1983). *Mixed memories.* Gateshead: Paradigm Press.

Cohen, G. M., & Joukowsky, M. S. (2004). *Breaking ground: Pioneering women archaeologists.* Ann Arbor: University of Michigan.

Hamlin, A. (2001). *Pioneers of the past.* Cambridge: Newnham College.

Sir Mortimer Wheeler

Clark, R. W. (1960). *Sir Mortimer Wheeler.* New York: Roy Publishers.

Hawkes, J. (1982). *Mortimer Wheeler: Adventurer in archaeology.* London: Weidenfeld & Nicholson.

Wheeler, Sir R. E. M. (1956). *Still digging: Interleaves from the antiquary's notebook.* London: Michael Joseph.

Gordon Childe

Green, S. (1981). *Prehistorian: A biography of V. Gordon Childe.* Bradford-on-Avon: Moonraker Press.

Savile, A. (2009). "Special issue: Vere Gordon Childe—50 years after." *European Journal of Archaeology* 12 (1–3).

Sherratt, A. (1989). "V. Gordon Childe: Archaeology and intellectual history." *Past and Present* 125 (1): 151–185.

Trigger, B. G. (1980). *Gordon Childe: Revolutions in archaeology.* London: Thames and Hudson.

Dorothy Garrod

Adams, A. (2010). *Ladies of the field: Early women archaeologists and their search for adventure.* Vancouver: Greystone Books.

Cohen, G. M., & Joukowsky, M. S. (eds.) (2004). *Breaking ground: Pioneering women archaeologists.* Ann Arbor: University of Michigan.

Davies, W., & Charles, R. (eds.) (1990). *Dorothy Garrod and the progress of the Palaeolithic.* Oxford: Oxbow Books.

Dame Kathleen Kenyon

Cohen, G. M., & Joukowsky, M. S. (2004). *Breaking ground: Pioneering women archaeologists.* Ann Arbor: University of Michigan.

Davis, M. (2008). *Dame Kathleen Kenyon: Digging up the Holy Land.* Walnut Creek: Left Coast Press.

Sir Grahame Clark

Arkadiusz, M., & Coles, J. (eds.) (2010). *Grahame Clark and his legacy.* Cambridge: Cambridge Scholars Publishing.

Fagan, B. (2001). *Grahame Clark: An intellectual biography of an archaeologist.* Boulder: Westview Press.

THE NEW GENERATION

David Clarke

Hammond, N. (1979). "David Clarke: A biographical sketch." In D. L. Clarke, *Analytical archaeologist: Collected papers of David L. Clarke* (pp. 1–10). London: Academic Press.

Lord (Colin) Renfrew

Cambridge University, Division of Archaeology. *Professor Colin Renfrew (Lord Renfrew of Kaimsthorn)*, http://www.arch.cam.ac.uk/directory/acr10 [accessed 19 March 2014].

Curtis Brown, *Lord Colin Renfrew*, http://www.curtisbrown.co.uk/colin-renfrew/ [accessed 19 March 2014].

Peter Ucko

Wengrow, D. (2007). "Peter Ucko, 27th July 1938–14th June 2007." *Antiquity*, http://antiquity.ac.uk/tributes/ucko.html [accessed 20 February 2014].

Ian Hodder

Schaffer, J., Yazicioglu, G. B., & Marshall, M. E. (n.d.). "To the trowel's edge: An interview with Ian Hodder," *Exchange* [available at http://ucexchange.uchicago. edu/interviews/hodder.html, accessed 5 February 2014].

Stanford University, Department of Anthropology, *Hodder, Ian*, https://www. stanford.edu/dept/anthropology/cgi-bin/web/?q=node/109, [accessed 19 March 2014].

CHAPTER 7. CONTROVERSIES AND SCANDALS DISAGREEMENTS AMONGST ARCHAEOLOGISTS

The Antiquity of Early Man

Buckland, W. (1823). *Reliquiae diluvianae*. London: J. Murray.

Lyell, C. (1863). *Geological evidences of the antiquity of man*. London: J. M. Dent and Sons.

Grayson, D. K. (1983). *The establishment of human antiquity*. Waltham: Academic Press.

Riper, A. B. van (1983). *Men among the mammoths: Victorian science and the discovery of human prehistory*. Chicago, University of Chicago Press.

Beginnings of the Neolithic: Adoption or Migration?

Bradley, R. (2007). *The prehistory of Britain and Ireland*. Cambridge: Cambridge University Press.

Catling, C. (2011). "Gathering time: The second radiocarbon revolution." *Current Archaeology* 259: 12–19.

Thomas, J. (1988). "Neolithic explanations revisited: The Mesolithic-Neolithic transition in Britain and south Scandinavia." *Proceedings of the Prehistoric Society* 54: 59–66.

Whittle, A., Healy, F., & Bayliss, A. (2011). *Gathering time: Dating the Early Neolithic enclosures of southern Britain and Ireland.* Oxford: Oxbow Books.

Arthur: Fact or Fiction?

Alcock, L. (1971). *Arthur's Britain: History and archaeology AD 367–634*. Harmondsworth: Penguin Press.

Crawford, O. G. S. (1935). "Arthur and his battles." *Antiquity* 9: 277–91.

Dumville, D. (1977). "Sub-Roman Britain: History and legend." *History* 62: 173–92.

Higham, N. J. (2002). *King Arthur: Myth-making and history*. London: Routledge.

Mersey, D. (2004). *Arthur: King of the Britons, from Celtic hero to cinema icon*. Chichester: Summersdale.

Morris, J. (1973). *The age of Arthur: A history of the British Isles from 350 to 650*. Chichester: Phillimore.

Thomas, C. (1993). *Tintagel: Arthur and archaeology*. London: English Heritage.

Anglo-Saxon Origins

Arnold, C. (1988). *An archaeology of the early Anglo-Saxon kingdoms*. London: Routledge.

Henson, D. (2006). *The origins of the Anglo-Saxons*. Hockwold-cum-Wilton: Anglo-Saxon Books.

Hill, C. (2003). *Origins of the English*. Duckworth Debates in Archaeology, London: Gerald Duckworth.

Hines, J. (ed.) (1997). *The Anglo-Saxons from the migration period to the eighth century: An ethnographic perspective*. Woodbridge: Boydell Press.

Pryor, F. (2004). *Britain AD*. London: Harper Collins.

Wiseman, H. W. (2007). "Review of Pryor, Francis. 2004. Britain AD: A Quest for Arthur, England and the Anglo-Saxons. Great Britain: Harper Collins. 268 pages. 0007181868," *The Heroic Age* 10 [available at http://www.heroicage.org/issues/10/reviews.html].

The Archaeology of Now

Chapple, R. M. (2012). "The archaeology of an archaeologist: A reassessment of the Transit Van excavation." Robert M. Chapple, archaeologist (blog) [available at http://rmchapple.blogspot.co.uk/2012/07/archaeology-of-archaeologist.html?goback=%2Egde_3938335_member_200539499#!, accessed 1 March 2014].

Defence of Britain, http://www.archaeologyuk.org/cba/projects/dob [accessed 1 March 2014].

Home Front Legacy, http://new.archaeologyuk.org/first-world-war/ [accessed 1 March 2014].

Kiddey, R., & Schofield, J. (2010). "Digging for (invisible) people." *British Archaeology* 113 [available at http://www.archaeologyuk.org/ba/ba113/feat2.shtml, accessed 1 March 2014].

Newland, C., Bailey, G., Schofield, J., & Nilsson, A. (2007). "Sic transit gloria mundi." *British Archaeology* 92 [available at http://www.archaeologyuk.org/ba/ba92/feat2.shtml, accessed 1 March 2014].

Theoretical Battles

Chippindale, C. (1993). "Ambition, deference, discrepancy, consumption: The intellectual background to a post-processual archaeology." In N. Yoffee & A. Sherratt, *Archaeological theory: Who sets the agenda?* (p. 35).

Hawkes, J. (1968). "The proper study of mankind." *Antiquity* 42: 255–262.

Displays of Human Remains

Alberti, S. J. M. M., Bienkowski, P., Chapman, M. J., & Drew, R. (2009). "Should we display the dead?" *Museum & Society* 7(3) [available at http://www2.le.ac.uk/

departments/museumstudies/museumsociety/documents/volumes/alberti2.pdf, accessed 3 March 2014].

Broughton, J. (n.d.). *The display of human remains*. London: British Museum (Powerpoint presentation) [available at http://visitors.org.uk/files/human_remains.pdf, accessed 3 March 2014].

Roberts, C. (2012). (revised ed.) *Human remains in archaeology: A handbook*. York: Council for British Archaeology.

DISPUTES BETWEEN ARCHAEOLOGY AND SOCIETY

The Elgin Marbles or the Parthenon Frieze?

Beard, M. (2004). *The Parthenon*. London: Profile Books.

Greenfield, J. (2007). *The return of cultural treasures*. Cambridge: Cambridge University Press.

Hitchens, C. (1998). *Imperial spoils: The curious case of the Elgin marbles*. London: Verso Books.

Jenkins, I. (2002). *The Parthenon frieze*. London: British Museum Press.

King, D. (2006). *The Elgin marbles*. London: Hutchinson.

St. Clair, W. (1998). *Lord Elgin and the marbles*. Oxford: Oxford University Press.

Archaeology and Developer Funding

Biddle, M. (1989). "The Rose reviewed: A comedy (?) of errors." *Antiquity* 63: 763–760.

Thomas, R. (2013). "Making the most of development-led archaeology." *The Archaeologist* 89: 12–16.

Access to Stonehenge

Chippindale, C. (1986). "Stoned Henge: Events and issues at the summer solstice, 1985." *World Archaeology* 18 (1): 35–58.

Worthington, A. (ed.) (2005). *The battle of the beanfield*. Eyemouth: Enabler Publications.

The Battle over Seahenge

Brennand, M., & Taylor, M. (2003). "The survey and excavation of a Bronze Age timber circle at Holme-next-the-Sea, Norfolk, 1998–9." *Proceedings of the Prehistoric Society* 69: 1–84.

Brennand, M. (2004). "This is why we dug Seahenge." *British Archaeology* 78 [available at http://www.archaeologyuk.org/ba/ba78/feat5.shtml].

Pitts, M. (2001). "Seahenge timber circle heading for reburial." *British Archaeology* 57 [available at http://www.archaeologyuk.org/ba/ba57/news.html].

Pryor, F. (2012). *Seahenge: A quest for life and death in Bronze Age Britain*. London: Harper Collins.

Watson, C. (2005). *Seahenge: An archaeological conundrum*. Swindon: English Heritage.

FAKES AND FORGERY: THE PILTDOWN FORGERY

Miller, R. (1972). *The Piltdown men: A case of archaeological fraud*. New York: St. Martin's Press.

Natural History Museum. *Piltdown Man—the greatest hoax in the history of science?* http://www.nhm.ac.uk/nature-online/science-of-natural-history/the-scientific-process/piltdown-man-hoax/ [accessed 19 March 2014].

Russell, M. (2012). *The Piltdown man hoax: Case closed*. Stroud: History Press.

Spencer, F. (1990). *Piltdown: A scientific forgery*. Oxford: Oxford University Press.

Weiner, J. S. (2003). *The Piltdown forgery: The classic account of the most famous and successful hoax in science*. (new ed.) Oxford: Oxford University Press.

ARCHAEOLOGY VERSUS COMMERCE

Maritime Treasure Hunting

anon. (2009). "Spoilheap. Pension advice from an archaeologist—theory you can trust." *British Archaeology* 105 [available at http://www.archaeologyuk.org/ba/ba105/spoilheap.shtml, accessed 10 March 2014].

Connolly, D. (2003). "Giffords to dig 'billion dollar' site." *The Digger* 30 [available at http://www.bajr.org/diggermagazine/TheDigger30/article3.html, accessed 10 March 2014].

Council for British Archaeology. (2002). "HMS Warship Sussex: Treasure hunt." *CBA Conservation* [available at http://www.archaeologyuk.org/conservation/portant/warshipsussex, accessed 10 March 2014].

Council for British Archaeology. (2009). "Letters." *British Archaeology* 106 [available at http://www.archaeologyuk.org/ba/ba106/letters.shtml, accessed 10 March 2014].

Dromgoole, S. (2004). "Murky waters for government policy: The case of a 17th century British warship and 10 tonnes of gold coins." *Marine Policy* 28 (3): 189–198.

Giles, J. (2007). "Interview: Modern-day treasure hunter." *New Scientist* 196 (2629): 74–75.

Odyssey Marine Exploration. (n.d.). *HMS Sussex project overview*, http://www.shipwreck.net/hmssussex.php, accessed 10 March 2014].

Odyssey Marine Exploration. (n.d.). *SS Gairsoppa project overview*, http://www.shipwreck.net/ssgairsoppa.php, accessed 10 March 2014].

Rescue. (2003). "HMS Sussex." *Rescue News* [available at http://www.rescue-archaeology.freeserve.co.uk/news/hms-sussex.html, accessed 10 March 2014].

Metal Detecting and Archaeology

Bland, R. (2004). "The Treasure Act and the Portable Antiquities scheme: A case study in developing public archaeology." In N. Merriman (ed.), *Public archaeology* (pp. 272–291).

Chester-Kadwell, M. E. (2004). "Metallic taste: Archaeologists and treasure hunters." In D. A. Barrowclough (ed.), *Our precious past* (pp. 49–68).

Crowther, D. R. (1983). "Swords to ploughshares: A nationwide survey of archaeologists and treasure hunting clubs." *Cambridge Archaeological Review* 2 (1): 9–20.

Dobinson, C., & Denison, S. (1995). *Metal detecting and archaeology in England*. York: Council for British Archaeology.

Gregory, A. (1983). "The impact of metal detecting on archaeology and the public." *Cambridge Archaeological Review* 2 (1): 5–8.

Gregory, A. (1986). "Whose fault is treasure hunting?" In C. Dobinson & R. Gilchrist (eds.), *Archaeology, politics and the public* (pp. 25–27). York: York University Archaeological Publications, No. 5.

O'Connell, M. G., & Bird, J., with Cheesman, C. (1994). "The Roman temple at Wanborough, excavation 1985–86." *Surrey Archaeological Collections* 82: 1–168.

Oxford Archaeology. (2009). *The nighthawking survey*. Oxford: Oxford Archaeology.

Thomas, S. (2009). "Wanborough revisited: The rights and wrongs of Treasure Trove law in England and Wales." In S. Thomas & P. G. Stone (eds.), *Metal detecting and archaeology*. Woodbridge: Boydell Press.

Thomas, S. (2013). "Editorial: Portable antiquities: Archaeology, collecting, metal detecting." *Internet Archaeology* 33 [available at http://dx.doi.org/10.11141/ia.33.12, accessed 10 March 2014].

The Antiquities Trade

Brodie, N., Kersel, M. M., Luke, C., & Tubb, K. W. (2006). *Archaeology, cultural heritage, and the antiquities trade*. Gainesville: University of Florida.

Johnson, A . (2007). "British university forced to return 'looted' Iraq treasure." *The Independent* [available at http://www.independent.co.uk/news/uk/this-britain/british-university-forced-to-return-looted-iraq-treasure-396230.html, accessed 24 February 2014].

Mackenzie, S. R. M. (2005). *Going, going, gone: Regulating the market in illicit antiquities*. Leicester: Institute of Art and Law.

Renfrew, C. (2000). *Loot, legitimacy and ownership: The ethical crisis in archaeology*. London: Gerald Duckworth.

Rothfield, L. (2009). *The rape of Mesopotamia: Behind the looting of the Iraq museum*. Chicago: University of Chicago Press.

Worrell, S., Jackson, R., Mackay, A., Bland, R., & Pitts, M. (2011). "The Crosby Garrett Roman helmet." *British Archaeology* 116 [available at http://www.archaeologyuk.org/ba/ba116/feat1.shtml, accessed 24 February 2014].

CHAPTER 8. CURRENT AND RECENT RESEARCH PREHISTORIC BRITAIN

Early Hominins Reach the Far North-west of Europe (Happisburgh)

Ashton, N., Lewis, S. G., De Groote, I., Duffy, S. M., Bates, M., Bates, R., Hoare, P., Lewis, M., Parfitt, S. A., Peglar, S., & Williams, C. (2014). "Hominin footprints from Early Pleistocene deposits at Happisburgh, UK." *PLoS ONE* 9 (2), e88329. doi:10.1371/journal.pone.0088329 [accessed 12 March 2014].

British Museum. (n.d.). *Happisburgh: The earliest humans in northern Europe*, http://www.britishmuseum.org/research/research_projects/all_current_projects/featured_project_happisburgh.aspx, [accessed 12 March 2014].

Parfitt, S., Ashton, N., & Lewis, S. (2010). "Happisburgh." *British Archaeology* 114 [available at http://www.archaeologyuk.org/ba/ba114/feat1.shtml].

Wymer, J., & Robins, P. (2005). "Happisburgh and Pakefield: The earliest Britons." *Current Archaeology* 201: 458–467.

Climate Change Is Not New (Doggerland)

Gaffney, V., Fitch, S., & Smith, D. (2009). *Europe's lost world: The rediscovery of Doggerland*. York: Council for British Archaeology.

Landscapes of the Living and the Dead (Stonehenge)

Atkinson, R. (1979). (3rd ed.) *Stonehenge*. Harmondsworth: Penguin.

Burl, A. (2006). *Stonehenge: A new history of the world's greatest stone circle*. London: Constable.

Chippindale, C. (2004). (3rd ed.) *Stonehenge complete*. London: Thames and Hudson.

Darvill, T. C. (2006). *Stonehenge: The biography of a landscape*. Stroud: Tempus.

Fitzpatrick, A. P. (2011). *The Amesbury Archer and the Boscombe Bowmen—Bell Beaker burials at Boscombe Down, Amesbury, Wiltshire*. Salisbury: Wessex Archaeology.

Grinsell, L. V. (1978). *The Stonehenge barrow groups*. Salisbury: Salisbury and South Wiltshire Museum.

Needham, S., Lawson, A. J., & Woodward, A. (2010). "'A noble group of barrows': Bush Barrow and the Normanton Down Early Bronze Age cemetery two centuries on." *Antiquaries Journal* 90: 1–39.

Parker Pearson, M (2007). "The Stonehenge Riverside Project: Excavations at the east entrance of Durrington Walls." In M. Larsson and M. Parker Pearson (eds.), *From Stonehenge to the Baltic* (pp. 125–44). British Archaeological Reports Series 1692.

Parker Pearson, M. (2012). *Stonehenge: Exploring the greatest stone age mystery*. London: Simon & Schuster.

Pitts, M. (2001). (2nd ed.) *Hengeworld*. London: Arrow Books.

Richards, J. (1991). *Stonehenge*. London: Batsford and English Heritage.

Richards, J. (2007). *Stonehenge: The story so far*. London: English Heritage.

Thomas, J. S. (2007). "The internal features at Durrington Walls: Investigations in the Southern Circle and Western Enclosures, 2005–6." In M. Larsson and M. Parker Pearson (eds.), *From Stonehenge to the Baltic* (pp. 144–158). British Archaeological Reports Series 1692.

Wainwright, G. J., & Longworth, I. H. (1971). *Durrington Walls: Excavations 1966–1968*. London: Society of Antiquaries.

Religion and Power in the Far North (Ness of Brodgar)

Orkneyjar. (2014). "The Ness of Brodgar excavations," http://www.orkneyjar.com/archaeology/nessofbrodgar/ [accessed 12 March 2014].

Wickham-Jones, C. (2007). *Orkney: A historical guide*. Edinburgh: Birlinn.

Bronze Age Life Revealed (Must Farm)

Knight, M. (2009). "Excavating a Bronze Age timber platform at Must Farm, Whittlesey, near Peterborough." *Past* 63: 1–4.

Knight, M. (2012). *Must Farm, must read*. Cambridge: Cambridge Archaeological Unit.

HISTORIC BRITAIN

Life and Death of a Roman Town (Silchester)

Boon, G. C. (1974). *Silchester: The Roman town of Calleva*. Newton Abbot: David & Charles.

Clarke, A., & Fulford, M. (2002). "Silchester, a crowded late Roman city." *Current Archaeology* 177: 364–371.

Clarke, A., Fulford, M. G., Rains, M., & Tootell, K. (2007). "Silchester Roman Town Insula IX: The development of an urban property c. AD 40–50—c. AD 250." *Internet Archaeology* 21 [available at http://intarch.ac.uk/journal/issue21/silchester_toc.html, accessed 5 March 2014].

Fulford, M. (1989). *The Silchester amphitheatre: Excavations of 1979–85*. London: Society for the Promotion of Roman Studies.

Kennedy, M. (2012). "Silchester Iron Age finds reveal secrets of pre-Roman Britain." *The Guardian* 31 July 2012 [available at http://www.theguardian.com/uk/2012/jul/31/silchester-iron-age-roman-britain, accessed 5 March 2014].

University of Reading. *Silchester Roman town*, http://www.reading.ac.uk/silchester/ [accessed 5 March 2014].

Lives and Letters on the Edge of Empire (Vindolanda)

Birley, R. (2005). *Vindolanda: Extraordinary records of daily life on the northern frontier*. Greenhead: Roman Army Museum Publications.

Bowman, A. K. (1994). *Life and letters on the Roman frontier: Vindolanda and its people*. London: British Museum Press.

Vindolanda Tablets Online, http://vindolanda.csad.ox.ac.uk/ [accessed 5 March 2014].

Searching for the Origins of England (Bamburgh)

Bamburgh Research Project, http://bamburghresearchproject.co.uk/ [accessed 6 March 2014].

Young, G. L. (2009). "Bamburgh Castle: Digging the home of Northumbria's kings." *Current Archaeology* 237: 36–41.

Young, G. L. (2011). "At the heart of Bamburgh Castle." *British Archaeology* 118: 44–47.

Ziegler, M. (2001). "The Anglo-British cemetery at Bamburgh: An e-interview with Graeme Young of the Bamburgh Castle Research Project." *The Heroic Age* 4 [available at http://www.mun.ca/mst/heroicage/issues/4/Bamburgh.html, accessed 6 March 2014].

All that Glitters Is Often Gold (Staffordshire Hoard and Prittlewell Burial)

Blari, I., Barham, E., & Blackmore, L. (2004). "My lord Essex." *British Archaeology* 76: 10–17.

Museum of London Archaeology Service. (2004). *The Prittlewell prince: The discovery of a rich Anglo-Saxon burial in Essex*. London: Museum of London.

Portable Antiquities Scheme. *Papers from the Staffordshire Hoard Symposium*, http://finds.org.uk/staffshoardsymposium [accessed 26 February 2014].

Staffordshire Hoard, http://www.staffordshirehoard.org.uk/ [accessed 26 February 2014].

Rethinking Richard (Richard III and Bosworth battlefield)

Bennett, M. (2000). (2nd ed.) *The Battle of Bosworth*. London: Sutton.

Buckley, R., Morris, M., Appleby, J., Cooper, N., King, T., & Foxhall, L. (2013). "Richard III: King of England. Man of Leicester." *British Archaeology* 130: 14–19.

Foard, G. (2004). *Bosworth battlefield: A reassessment*. Leicester: Leicestershire County Council.

Foard, G., & Curry, A. (2013). *Bosworth 1485: A battlefield rediscovered*. Oxford: Oxbow Books.

Foard, G., & Morris, R. K. (2012). *The archaeology of English battlefields*. CBA Research Report 168. York: Council for British Archaeology.

Foss, P. J. (1998). *The Field of Redemore: The Battle of Bosworth, 1485*. Newtown Linford: Kairos Press.

Gravett, C. (2000). *The Battle of Bosworth*. Botley: Osprey.

Langley, P., & Jones, M. (2013). *The King's grave: The search for Richard III*. London: John Murray.

PRACTICING ARCHAEOLOGY

Televising Archaeology

Clack, T., & Brittain, M. (2007). *Archaeology and the media*. Walnut Creek: Left Coast Press.

Daniel, G. (1954). "Archaeology and television." *Antiquity* 28 (112): 201–205.

Henson, D. (2010). "Chronicle: A glimpse of TV heaven." *Viewfinder* 79: 14–15.

Hills, C. (2003). "What is television archaeology doing for us? Reflections on some recent British programmes." *Antiquity* 77 (295): 206–211.

Johnstone, P. (1957). *Buried treasure*. London: Phoenix House.

Jordan, P. (1981). "Archaeology and television." In J. Evans, B. Cunliffe, & C. Renfrew (eds.), *Antiquity and man: Essays in honour of Glyn Daniel*. London: Thames and Hudson.

Kulik, K. (2006). "Archaeology and British television." *Public Archaeology* 2: 75–90.

Light, N. (1999). "Tabloid archaeology: Is television trivializing science?" *Discovering Archaeology* (March–April 1999): 98–101.

Norman, B. (1983). "Archaeology and television." *Archaeological Review from Cambridge* 2 (1): 27–32.

Paynton, C. (2002). "Public perception and 'pop archaeology': A survey of current attitudes toward televised archaeology in Britain." *The SAA Archaeological Record* 2 (2): 33–36.

Piccini, A. & Henson, D. (2006). *Survey of heritage television viewing 2005–06.* York: Council for British Archaeology [available at http://hc.english-heritage.org. uk/content/pub/eh_tvcounts_report_final.pdf, accessed 23 March 2014].

Piccini, A., & Kulik, K. (2007). "Archaeology viewers count." *British Archaeology* 94: 56–57.

Richards, J. (2004). "Archaeology as a media experience." *Treballs d'Arqueologia* 10: 47–54.

Sutcliffe, R. (ed.) (1978). *Chronicle: Essays form ten years of television archaeology.* London: BBC.

Taylor, T. (1998). *Behind the scenes at Time Team.* London: Channel 4 Books.

Community Archaeology

Dawson, T., Oliver, I. A., Miller, A. H. D., Vermehren, A., & Kennedy, S. E. (2013). "Digitally enhanced community rescue archaeology." In S. E. Kennedy, R. Fawcett, A. H. D. Miller, R. J. Sweetman, L. Dow, A. Campbell, I. A. Oliver, J. McCaffery, & C. Allison, *Proceedings of UNESCO Congress on Digital Heritage.* IEEE, Digital Heritage International Congress 2013, Marseille, France, 28–1 November [available at http://research-repository.st-andrews.ac.uk/handle/10023/4189, accessed 5 March 2014].

Dyfed Archaeological Trust. Arfordir Coastal Heritage, http://www.dyfedarchaeology.org.uk/arfordir/arfordir1.htm [accessed 5 March 2014].

Nevell, M. (2013). "Archaeology for all: Managing expectations and learning from the past for the future—the Dig Manchester community archaeology experience." In C. Dalglish (ed.), *Archaeology, the public and the recent past* (pp. 65–76). Woodbridge: Boydell Press.

Shorewatch, http://www.shorewatch.co.uk/index.htm [accessed 5 March 2014].

Accessing Archaeology Online

Archwilio, http://www.archwilio.org.uk/ [accessed 5 March 2014].

Insole, P., & Piccini, A. (2013). "Your place or mine? Crowdsourced planning, moving image archives and community archaeology." *Archäologische Informationen.* Early View, published online 14 October 2013 [available at http://www.dguf.de/index.php?id=9, accessed 5 March 2014].

Helping People through Archaeology

Defence Archaeology Group, http://www.dmasuk.org/ [accessed 5 March 2014].

Walshe, D. (2013). "Time heals: Digging Caerwent with Operation Nightingale." *Current Archaeology* 282 [available at http://www.archaeology.co.uk/articles/time-heals-digging-caerwent-with-operation-nightingale.htm, accessed 5 March 2014].

Walshe, D., Osgood, R., & Brown, M. (2012). "Archaeology as rehabilitation." *British Archaeology* 122 [available at http://www.archaeologyuk.org/ba/ba122/feat5.shtml, accessed 5 March 2014].

LEARNING LESSONS?

Collins, D., Whitehouse, R,. Henig, M., & Whitehouse, D. (1973). *Background to archaeology: Britain in its European setting.* Cambridge: Cambridge University Press.

Evans, J. G. (1999). *Land and archaeology: Histories of human environment in the British Isles.* Stroud: History Press.

Lamb, H. H. (1995). (2nd ed.) *Climate, history and the modern world.* London: Routledge.

Simmons, I. G. (2001). *An environmental history of Great Britain: From 10,000 years ago to the present.* Edinburgh: Edinburgh University Press.

Woodell, S. R. J. (ed.) (1985). *The English landscape, past, present and future.* Oxford: Oxford University Press.

INDEX